# WE BORROW THE EARTH

'2

'02

Please contact the address below for further information and courses on Romani Gypsy shamanism:

The Romani Life Foundation
P.O. Box 103
Hailsham
BN27 4HP
UK

# WE BORROW THE EARTH

## AN INTIMATE PORTRAIT OF THE GYPSY SHAMANIC TRADITION AND CULTURE

Patrick 'Jasper' Lee of the *Purrum* clan

Thorsons

Thorsons
An Imprint of HarperCollins*Publishers*
77–85 Fulham Palace Road
Hammersmith, London W6 8JB

The Thorsons website address is: www.thorsons.com

Published by Thorsons 2000

10 9 8 7 6 5 4 3 2

A catalogue record for this book
is available from the British Library

ISBN 0 7225 3994 0

Printed and bound in Great Britain by
Creative Print and Design Wales, Ebbw Vale

To my great-grandfather,
*Jack Lee*,

—

indigenous *Chovihano*
of the *Purrum* CLAN

—

# Contents

# Acknowledgements

—

Of the many who have helped and supported me during the writing of the book, the following have made a particularly significant contribution:

Agatha, Lady Rodgers, for all the stimulating conversations and for her help when it was most needed; the spirit of 'Baby' (Agatha's computer), whose services made this book possible; Liz Puttick, my literary *Puri Dai*, for her tireless energy and for simply believing in me; 'Mike' Birkett, for her encouragement, constant enthusiasm, and for 'standing in front of tanks'; Roger Moreau, for his insight, inspiration and understanding of the Gypsy race; Dot, for presenting me with heather always at the right time; the *lovo chiriklos* (wagtails) for being a sign of hope and comfort when the going got tough; my shamanic pupils who are continuously showing me what the *Chovihano* is all about; and lastly, Lizzie May, my partner, for her tremendous patience, dedication and love, given freely throughout the preparation of this work.

# Introduction

The fire crackled in the hearth of the darkening room of a small terraced house in Erith in Kent. The old white-haired Gypsy sat in the armchair with the sleeping child in his arms, gazing into the flames of the fire as he had done many times before beside his camp-fire in the open air. Deep inside him there stirred a familiar feeling, which disturbed him, for he knew that he was losing something precious, something he and his people would call the *tacho Romano drom* - the true Gypsy path or way.

The house and all the 'perks' of mid twentieth-century England were said to be beneficial, but he wasn't so sure. He had, however, been temporarily blinded by them, together with the pressures imposed by modern civilization.

In the earlier part of the twentieth century his people had wandered more freely in Britain. There had even been a time when it was fashionable to be a Gypsy, for intellectuals and the upper classes had wanted to live with the nomads and adopt their 'Bohemian' lifestyle - they obviously felt the pressures of civilization too. But some of his kinsfolk were never quite in agreement with this, for it meant that after long years of persecution and victimization Gypsies had suddenly been romanticized and become merely a novelty. The *gaujo*, the non-Gypsy, was strange like that, a victim to whims dictated by whatever was in vogue.

In the old days this old man had felt so special. He had inherited his own shamanic sacred way, a healing ability together with the old Romani sorcerer's art, from an ancient past. He didn't really know what this ancient past was, but he treasured it. So he could only sigh now. 'What have I done?' was all he could say to himself, quietly, as he looked up to the window, where a small sprig of rosemary hung, twirling in the draught. The herb was hanging there for protection, but he never really felt quite safe in this house, for it was dark and enclosed and airless, and he sometimes felt as if he needed to run outside to breathe properly. Becoming a house-dweller was akin to being imprisoned, for your home did not move any more and you just stayed in one place within it - and within yourself.

The old Gypsy looked down once more at the sleeping child, who was no more than two years old. He instinctively felt that this child was destined to develop as a healer and a sorcerer in the old way, destined to travel regularly to and from the Otherworld and to learn the ancient shamanic craft of the race, which also meant meeting with the darker forces of life in their many different and dramatic forms. In truth, this child would be inheriting something rare in these times, an indescribable power that was as old as the Earth herself.

As he looked back into the flames of the fire, my great-grandfather shed a quiet tear for the power he felt he had misused and for the life he felt he had lost. That tear probably fell on me as I lay sleeping in his arms. He had tried to buy the Earth, he said to my father, his grandson, who was sitting nearby, observing all this, and you could never buy the Earth, no matter how much you paid for her; you could only borrow the Earth, as you could only ever really borrow all the things you came across in your life.

I have my father to thank for that account, but I remember Jack Lee, my great-grandfather, extremely well, as he lived far into his eighties. He was a quite slender man of medium height with a shock of white hair, a dark weathered face, equally dark mischievous eyes and a tobacco-stained moustache. Whenever I saw him he was dressed in a collarless shirt and dark waistcoat, with a muffler, which we call a *diklo*, at his neck, often sitting gazing thoughtfully at the fire. He was, like many Romani Gypsies, non-literate, and something of a mystery, for even after he became a house-dweller he travelled far and no one ever knew exactly where he went. He always returned quite casually after each sojourn - which would sometimes amount to weeks at a time - as if he might only have popped out for some tobacco!

This man was my role model and was instrumental in helping me take my first steps along the Romani shamanic path. He taught me that to be a *Chovihano*, or shaman, you had not only to be in contact with nature, but also needed to be a true spokesperson for her in her many forms, telling her story for her since humans had severed their ancient spiritual connections with her. For the *Chovihano* had long spoken with her voice.

I learned from Jack Lee to tread where others fear to tread, and to spread my wings and fly, not in imitation of a bird, but *as* a bird. I learned that to be as small as a ladybird and as large as an ocean, with all the accompanying thoughts and feelings, calls for an imaginative sensitivity and identification which transcends the boundaries of human understanding. I had to learn that to practise as a shaman of the highest order you had to be, more than anything else, emotionally free and also emotionally courageous, for there were times when you would feel vulnerable and subject to feelings and sensations which were not within the obvious realms of human understanding. Jack Lee, in his own sensitive way, introduced all this and more to me.

I still remember the loud infectious laughter of this old man; his sense of humour, rather childlike in essence, was in fact just one of the rare and treasured gifts he passed down to his family, and it also helped to balance the more serious side of the craft I was learning.

But there was also the curse! Like a gaping wound, we all seemed to carry the burden of the mistake Jack Lee had made in leaving his native past behind. It was as if something had stepped out of time with its well-established dependable rhythm. A curse can hang over your head with the heaviest of weights. It would have been something of a disturbing thought for Great-grandfather himself, because for hundreds of years, if not thousands, his ancestors had walked the nomadic path and the realization that he might just have been the first person in his immediate line to step off that path must have been devastating indeed.

He was not, of course, to blame for becoming a house-dweller, for he, together with his wife and many other Romani Gypsies, was very much a victim of modern progress, as many tribal people still are today. The nomadic Gypsies with their *vardos*, or wagons, and their shaggy piebald *grais* walking freely along leafy lanes were destined to meet with opposition and restriction in a society bent on land ownership and living apart from nature. There was no more room for these tribespeople, who had been living in this country for at least 500 years.

For Jack, and Amy, his wife, as well as the rest of my family, there was no longer a tribal/Earth relationship upon which to depend, a partnership steeped in ancient and sacred tradition. The Lee, or *Purrum*, clan, a clan long associated with seership and sorcery, all with a view to healing, was bequeathed a legacy from tribes past: befriend and borrow the Earth, and the Earth will befriend and borrow you, and she will freely give all her natural wealth to you, all her fruits and spiritual insights. But try to own her and you could find your relationship with her breaking down. That is how it was always put over to me as a child.

When the idea for this book was first suggested to me it was rather daunting to think of writing openly about something which had lived for a long time, and quite deliberately so, in the shadows. It is true that in my healing work I have, about 90 per cent of the time, used Romani Gypsy shamanic methods, but I have never talked about them so freely before. Few Gypsies will talk of their Romani blood - unless of course they happen to be talking to other Romanies! Fewer still will talk about the old shamanic arts. Though I had grown up playing a central role in the shamanic life of my community, I was not expected to talk about it openly, so I didn't - until now!

There is, however, every reason to speak freely now, for our world is quite plainly in a desperate mess and tribes of all peoples everywhere are threatened with extinction. My great-grandfather must have known that this mess would worsen when he said that the curse would extend to all mankind if it insisted on owning rather than borrowing, which indeed it has done, in a big way.

The Gypsy spirit is undeniably strong, however. One thousand years ago Romanies were practising their old magic and tribal way of life; barely 50 years ago, there were still many doing exactly the same. There cannot be many tribal people in the world who have lived alongside the iron-hard fist of progress whilst remaining unaffected by that progress - and who have lived to tell the tale!

I am perhaps living proof of that. In my mind I sometimes watch bands of ancestors moving across old Asia, or across sixteenth-century Europe, meeting all the misfortunes that came their way in those times, but always I see the remarkable resilience that always accompanied them, the natural desire for freedom, the courage and humour and discipline, and the instinctive devotion to the Earth. Perhaps no race could have been more unwelcome on the Earth, but no race could have loved and respected the Earth more.

A great comforter to me in these more lonely times is a spirit guardian in the form of a Romani ancestor who accompanied Jack Lee through his life and who now accompanies me through mine. We do not know where he came from, or his name, or how ancient he is. He will long remain a mystery, for it is not appropriate for Gypsy *Chovihanos* to ask questions of ancestors. That would bring *wafdo bok* - bad luck. But as teacher and guide, a Romani ancestor is a vital thread who has the power to weave countless generations of Gypsies together.

There is no doubt that preserving and practising this culture's shamanism has presented a difficult road for me and if my great-grandfather were here today I know that he would undoubtedly shake his head as he looked on at our muddled modern world, with the words, '*Dordi, dordi!* Oh dear, oh dear!'

But in spirit I now rock him in my arms to console him, just as he rocked me that day when I was just two years old.

It is time, Jack, for the curse to be lifted.

# 1

## A CHILD OF THE WIND
## A ROMANI GYPSY CHILDHOOD

I had a most unusual childhood, in some ways perhaps a childhood straight out of the past. I grew up in a world of fairy-tale castles, dreams and omens, a world in which life and death were sometimes somehow intertwined, and where the Otherworld was not at all a secondary world, but a place that was every bit as real as the physical world, and where I myself was expected to spend much of my time.

My own family was sandwiched between the Gypsy world and the *gaujo* world, and I laughed and cried and fought and dreamed like every other youngster, except I was not entirely like every other youngster, a reality which perhaps first came home to me in my early days at school.

I proved to be a formidable pupil in my junior school whenever I stood up in class insisting that a Romani word was a word commonly used in the English language - which of course it wasn't, because no one else had heard of it, except other Romanies!
'And so this is a - a what?' my teacher asked one day in embarrassment and confusion as she held up a picture of a hedgehog.
'A *hotchiwitchi*, Miss.'
'A hot - a what?'
'A *hotchiwitchi*.'
She smiled, and the children were all laughing, as if I had just made up a fancy word.

The hedgehog was an important and respected animal to the Romani Gypsy, a *pal* of the *bor*, or 'brother of the hedge'. He was not only a delicacy at Gypsy meal-times but was also considered to be, in spirit, a Gypsy too. I had been told stories by my great-grandfather of how our guardian Ancestor could change into animals, a *hotchiwitchi* being one of them. I had also been told by my great-grandfather that I too could change into a *hotchiwitchi*. He spoke very seriously about it, so I considered it to be normal. I did not, however, tell my teacher any of this, for you didn't brag about having Gypsy roots, and you certainly didn't talk about the shamanic aspects of your culture. But I did continue presenting my teachers with many different words, some of which were indeed made up, and I ended up not knowing which word was Romani, which was English and which was made up. And when I was at home it didn't matter anyway, because a word was a word, unless it was used in magic and rituals, and then it carried greater emphasis. Otherwise, words did not have to meet any recognized standards.

I spent very little time at school. While other children played truant to avoid specific lessons, I could simply go home, as my parents did not consider truancy to be a problem. The old Gypsy attitude towards education is that you can do it if you want to, but don't necessarily have to if you don't feel you need to! It is a good philosophy because it cuts out unnecessary pressure. It took a long time for Gypsies to accept the education system and in the past many deliberately kept their children away from school. The Gypsies in North Wales referred to it as 'weekday church', as for them school was always connected with religion and was therefore a means of indoctrination.

Jack Lee had not been formally educated and my father received very little schooling, because, in his own words, 'I was never long enough in the same place to attend school!' Some people have found it difficult to believe that I have not been educated through the normal channels either. But true Romani Gypsies are not unintelligent and, like children of many native peoples all over the world, Gypsy *chavvies* are encouraged to have fun and gain experience by experimentation, which is always put before education, and which involves free and open emotional expression and use of the senses, something other children rarely know because *gaujo* discipline is usually too full of restrictions. This doesn't mean that Romani children are spoilt, however. Within the Gypsy home environment there is a very fine set of rules, or more correctly, a respect for others that is instinctive, because it is demonstrated by the adults and not imposed by them.

My own family's attitude towards *gaujo* discipline was that it was simply best to keep a sense of humour about it! Thus, following in Great-grandfather's footsteps, we all laughed a good deal at the way people - both Gypsy and *gaujo* - tended to behave. This very valuable philosophy has helped me through many difficult phases in my life and enabled me to laugh at both good and bad situations.

Learning that I was - and still am - part of a large network came quickly to me, when we *chavvies* became true children of the wind, riding some of the horses belonging to some sedentary Gypsies who lived on marshland. We rode bare-back, which is a wonderful experience to have with a horse and is the way many Gypsies ride. Maintaining contact, you became part of the horse, just as the horse became part of you. If you fell off, or encountered a problem with your horse, it was more than likely your fault and not the fault of the horse, for you built a special bond with your animal, which spoke volumes about who you were. 'He wants you to do something in a different way,' another child might say when a horse was suddenly giving you a hard time. What this really meant was that the child was interpreting the

signals your horse was giving you, signals which you
were probably unable to interpret for yourself.

At this time in my life I was learning to hear many
animals speak, learning to delve deep down into what
they were and to know not just what they were
thinking but what was going on in their very souls, a
necessary education in any shamanic training.

This education also extended to trees. I spent a lot of
time in my earlier years alone in the garden talking
to an apple tree. I was encouraged to do this by my
elders. In fact, I was encouraged to communicate
with all spirits, from the spirits within people to the
spirits within my colouring pencils! Everything could
talk to you, and everything lived, so much so that I
still find myself talking to inanimate objects a good
deal of the time today, with no embarrassment whatsoever. They can reply to you in a very simple childlike way, providing you are that way yourself, and
like to see it all as fun.

When I reached puberty, I spent hours sitting alone
in a darkened room thinking, and often rocking and
singing and travelling about in my imagination, which
today most people would know as shamanic journeying. Again encouraged by my elders, I sometimes sat
with my fingers in my ears in that very dark room,
rocking backwards and forwards and working myself
into a kind of frenzied dream state, through which I
went to all kinds of wonderful places, from fairy-tale
castles to 'real' places that were near to my home. I
often visited the nearby park in these dreams, and
also flew and walked about at the bottom of our

5

garden where I normally went to play ball during the daytime. The journeys were always vivid and I felt as if I was physically in these places, even though I knew it was also a dream. But this became an important lesson: learning about the strength of the dream and the imagination, and the part this kind of understanding played within what we call reality.

We adults are sometimes very confused about and afraid of our fantasy worlds, so much so that we prefer to dismiss just about everything if it cannot be explained in a rational way. But part of life's challenge, particularly today, is learning where thoughts of various kinds fit into our personal quests, and this begins in early childhood. By shutting the imagination out in our childhood years, which most of us are invariably taught to do, we shut out a vital part of ourselves. This does not happen when a child is taught in the old Romani Gypsy way. Self-belief is of prime importance and involves believing in the whole of yourself - including your own imagination - so the dream does not die but becomes a very valuable and real learning tool. Thus, a fairy-tale castle is as real as the house next door, because when you visit it you can learn just as many things.

The habit of rocking during these early journeying exercises developed when I was about four years old, when I frequently asked questions - and sometimes also provided the answers - regarding the structure of the universe. I remember pedalling up and down the garden on my small tricycle wondering what was at the end of the sky. My mother told me that I constantly drew a circle with a dot at its centre and attempted to instruct her on the nature of life. Then one day I rolled off a sofa whilst rocking and broke my arm, which was a sign to my great-grandfather that I was moving a little too fast.

Today, most people would find it strange that a young teenager should be left alone in a darkened room – for up to four hours at a time on the odd occasion. But I was not disturbed and my elders were not being cruel. My mother, who was extremely psychic, always monitored my progress. She would enter the room to ask me if I were all right. I would reply, 'Yes, Mum, I can see quite well in the dark,' and I can remember her nod of approval before she left the room again. Along with all the other adults in the house, she knew that I was following in the footsteps of Great-grandfather Lee, taking the path that all Romani Gypsy healers had taken before me down through the ages. My journeying eventually led me to have some interesting out-of-the-body experiences at a later date. But it is somewhat sad to think that just 100 years ago I might have been sitting out in the forest having this kind of experience and taking instruction from the birds, animals and trees.

I still journey in the same way today when I conduct my healing sessions and shamanic work, usually in a darkened room, rocking about. And those times I spent in the darkness also taught me much about the nature of darkness, something I have never been afraid of.

Puberty was a most powerful time for me, as it can be for many youngsters, and I was suddenly presented with a new kaleidoscopic dimension within, brimming over with pictures and sensations, colourful and dramatic experiences which, so I was told, were all considered to be a natural part of my development. I believe there is no harm in encouraging youngsters to deal with these inner changes alone, so long as adults are standing by in support, and so long as those adults are ready to listen and perhaps even interpret what that youngster is experiencing. But a natural-born *Chovihano*, or healer, will *need* to pay attention to the inner life at this delicate time.

While I was undergoing this vital transformation, sitting in my darkened room allowing my spirit to fly, other youngsters around me in the *gaujo* world were busy doing what all adolescents do in our modern society - listening to pop music, flirting or just hanging around on street corners, getting bored and frustrated with their lives.

I was not to know at that time that I was going through a quite ancient process, which had been practised in Europe for many thousands of years, but which is now extinct in Britain.

My elders considered this rite of passage - which to me seemed like a great internal explosion - quite normal. They had anticipated something rather dramatic taking place because of Great-grandfather's predictions, but also because another Gypsy had forecast it too. This was Marie, a woman who gave me the name Jasper, which began as 'Jazzie' because of the bright colours I used to wear at school. She had also foreseen the development of something

8

special - or 'something unusual in the future with the *gaujos*', to use her words.

At the time she gave my mother this message I was indeed unusual, because I was having something of a fight with the school authorities regarding my clothing. The school uniform was dark blue, but my mother sent me to school wearing a bright purple jumper, with the result that I was constantly being reminded to attire myself in the appropriate colour. 'Just tell 'em I'm still knitting you one,' my mother would say, laughing, whenever I brought home a complaint. She was still knitting that blue jumper four years later and I ended up being the only child in the whole school wearing a bright purple jumper for the whole of that time. This was amusing to the psychically gifted woman who called me 'Jazzie' and who, remarkably, so long ago told my mother what I would be doing today. It is thus in Marie's memory that I still use Jasper as my middle name. I consider it to be a lucky name.

A Romani Gypsy child is quite often given a private or secret name as well as a public or pet name, and this secret name is never uttered to outsiders and acts as magical protection against bad spells, or in today's language, negative influences. The theory is that if a harmful force is denied knowledge of all your names, it cannot possibly do you much harm. This has a very positive therapeutic effect, for by attaching a private name to an inner part of yourself that you love and respect, you keep that part untouched and sacred, and this helps to keep you strong. This is indeed old magic; it dates back many

9

thousands of years. My own private name is known to only a few. It is possible to create a name for yourself and to associate something good about yourself with that name. But take care never to tell anyone except those you truly trust what that name is.

My grandmother, Gladdy Lee, the *Puri Dai* (this literally means 'old mother'), was very much a guide to me throughout these dramatic and exciting years. She was one of the strongest women I have ever known. Only just over five feet tall, with thick dark hair and grey eyes, she had been a beauty in her youth and was formidable in her old age, for she not only cursed people in the old Gypsy way but could also deliver them a neat upper-cut - which some Gypsy women are not afraid of doing!

Gladdy Lee was something of a character. She had laid a curse on a woman's hairdressing shop when I was a child, after the hairdresser had verbally abused Amy Lee for no apparent reason. The business fell to ruin just two months later. And when the vicar at Jack Lee's graveside made the mistake of advising mourners to think of my great-grandfather's remains as little more than a bundle of rags - presumably to console them - he had cause to shiver when my grandmother silently threatened him with her dark powerful eyes. Few people can remain at ease when a Gypsy stares at them in such a way and the Reverend is said to have always avoided Gladdy Lee after that occasion.

The Romanies developed an ambiguous relationship with Christianity during the centuries that they travelled in Europe and this was certainly reflected in my own family. Romanies who remained loyal to their ancient traditions felt they would earn more respect from the *gaujo* community they were having to live with if they were married, baptized or buried in Christian churches. A highly persecuted people gained more credibility if they had the Christian seal of approval. Jack Lee, like many old Romanies, always taught his family to laugh at religion, or at least to take it lightly, and yet he, like many, was buried in a Christian graveyard. When I was young I was taught that you gave just enough to religious authority to procure respect. You could then be left alone. Fortunately, it is no longer necessary to do this. But it was considered by my elders to be better to conform half-heartedly rather than not conform at all, for that might bring you far too much attention. Romani Gypsies have never been rebels who go out to attract attention to themselves. Their way is to work quietly, unnoticed, in the background.

So when the vicar uttered those disrespectful words beside the grave that day, my grandmother's attitude was, 'I'll conform to your religion enough to keep our *Chovihano's* body safe and respected, but don't ask me to wear your Christian shoes.'

My grandmother set me many such examples. Her hardy character, robust health and wicked sense of humour reflected her unique spirit, which remained strong up until the day she died. She taught me a great deal on an everyday level. Strange as it may sound, some of the most important training for my shamanic work took place at the local supermarket check-out, where my grandmother advised me to *dik ta shoon* - watch and listen. This mostly involved reading the body language of others, for if you observed the way people behaved you could get to know more about their inner lives. Many times whilst queuing with our groceries my grandmother would nudge me, drawing my attention to the person in front of us. 'This one'll be an awkward bugger!' she would whisper softly. And usually it was true.

My brother and I sometimes camped outside in the garden at night and often shared our experience with the *Puri Dai*. This may not seem so unusual for Gypsies, but by that time my grandmother was 70 years old and most people in our neighbourhood didn't camp out in the garden at that age!

I have vivid memories of us all lying on the grass and looking up into a summery starlit sky, my mother and grandmother relating what they could see up there in the big wide dome of heaven. It was sometimes as if a stairway stretched up to the stars.

This was where I learned to see visions in the sky. You just lay there flat on the grass looking up into the velvety darkness in the same way that you might gaze into a crystal ball, staring until a milkiness blinded you and you saw pictures in the stars or around the moon. We regularly saw animals and faces and objects, reeling them off to each other and fitting them into our lives as guiding forces of change. This, I still believe, is a wonderful and most constructive exercise for children of all ages.

During these 'games', I was also told about the pictures Jack Lee would see when he practised this exercise and how he would read omens into just about everything he saw. Before he died he said that in civilized communities we spent too much time in artificial light, which prevented us from seeing our visions. Street lights and car lights now blur the screen where visions once played for Gypsies and all earlier peoples. Because of this, we all miss out on one of the most spectacular and natural playgrounds for our dreams, and actually increase our fears of darkness.

It was through this heavenly game that I was also introduced to the different worlds that exist: the Upperworld, the Middleworld and the Lowerworld. It was easy for me as a child to stitch all these together, for they made such sense, and I can remember comparing such a concept with the religious idea of Heaven and Hell, which I thought particularly confusing, for it seemed rather severe and unjust. It didn't allow you to go anywhere, either up or down, without being good or bad. When you travelled up or down in the Gypsy way, good and bad didn't come into it. You just went, if you were able to. The Upperworld, unlike Heaven, was a place of fairy-tale castles and fantastic daring adventures, and the Lowerworld was a place of mystery and great challenges.

At school when I started to learn about religion and about Jesus, I found this very powerful religious figure intensely frightening, because I was told he lived in the sky - or the Upperworld. One night, my cousin and I, who were sharing a bedroom, were looking up at the clouds through the window to see what shapes we could see and in the fading light a particular cloud took on the form of two large feet. These had to be Jesus's feet. He was such a big person in the *gaujo* world, my cousin said, that his feet were over our heads whilst his head was over Australia. Terrified, we giggled at this and dived under the bedclothes to hide from him, but that image remained with me as a child, and I lay sweating under the bedclothes for quite a few nights afterwards, whilst my cousin, who was a little older than me, slept soundly.

Fortunately, my family laughed at this - as they laughed at anything to do with religion. At that time I decided that I didn't like religion and I didn't like Jesus. My great-grandfather said that religion was full of traps, that it could 'trap' the spirit and hold it prisoner, and as I grew, I learned to understand what he meant by this. In truth, he also said, all life was a mirror, all things reflecting all things. This sounded far more sensible to me.

Whilst I was a child, many Gypsies around us were beginning to turn to the Christian religion to satisfy their spiritual needs as their old magic was beginning to fade, but fortunately for me this did not happen in my own community and we retained our unique Romani Gypsy spirit throughout. If the ancient flavour of that spirit hadn't been preserved, I know I would never have developed my shamanic healing abilities in the way that I have. Thus cocooned from the rest of society as a child, this ancient spirit was able to flourish within me, untarnished and unimpaired.

Under the influence of my elders, then, I learned to hear the robin sing and the raindrops patting the leaves outside the window, or a dog barking somewhere, no matter how distant it happened to be. And I learned to look beyond rainbows, to believe in fairy-tale castles, and to understand the language of bees and trees and buttercups and all manner of natural living things. As poetic as all this sounds, it is a Gypsy truth. Looking beyond the obvious is something *gaujos* do not teach their children. Watching people in cafés or in the street without even turning round, that is the kind of observation that all ancient people would have practised - to see without looking, to hear without listening. It is an art that might be dismissed as sheer nosiness today.

I learned all these things, and more, from my family. I remember my childhood as happy and fun, and much like a magical adventure. There was always music and laughter in the house, and we had many musical instruments scattered around, which my father boasted he could play, though of course he couldn't play all of them! But that did not mean that he or anyone else played badly. Some people are under the misapprehension that Romani Gypsies sit around their camp-fires playing any old how, but the truth is very different. Both I and my brother were trained to be good musicians simply by being teased and told the truth if we weren't playing well. It was good to be a child during these musical evenings, because every adult was a child as well, and I know of no other people who entertain themselves so openly and so humorously as the Romanies, because self-consciousness is rarely an issue for them. Yet their musical world is invariably also an artistically precise world, a world in which if you are doing anything you might as well do it well.

Because of the ancient shamanic skills I was developing, Jack and Gladdy Lee kept a close eye on me and soon observed that at times my behaviour was erratic, with strong mood swings. I was also highly creative, especially with music, and was soon also developing the desire to draw, paint and write. I was suffering from what was later to be described as a hormone imbalance. To the Gypsy mind this meant that I probably had access to a deeper level of consciousness or understanding; to the *gaujo* mind it meant that I was simply odd! These 'problems', to my elders, were omens, signs that I was treading a certain path and was destined to do something unusual.

I eventually emerged from my school years without a single certificate and was told by my teachers that I was a no-hoper. Clearly, though, I was destined for a different kind of path and I knew without doubt that that was more important. I was encouraged from the beginning to see the Earth as the best teacher and in addition was taught the old Gypsy arts of surviving the *gaujo* world, much of which involved surviving the world outside your door emotionally. And the first rule for any developing youngster in our modern society is to remember that the world outside is probably going to take you for a ride!

To become a man or a woman in Gypsy society you will be asked to face the horrors of the civilized world outside. This is equivalent to entering a large pool filled with hungry crocodiles. Are you courageous or are you afraid? You can avoid being the victim if you hold on to your true inner heritage. So you are encouraged to live in the modern world whilst at the same time not allowing yourself to be sucked into it, so that the Romani values are not forgotten. And to become a *Chovihano*, you will be expected to take on the workings of the Otherworld as well, and to understand the transition in life from birth to death and all the complex lessons held therein.

This 'initiation' has its roots in a much earlier period when the modern Western world was in its infancy and when humans began modifying Earth-based traditions in order to suit civilized needs. The test of endurance may or may not be an ancient one, but it has certainly developed as modern civilization has developed; it is the Romani shamanic way of constructively fighting what is considered to be an unlucky darker force which is opposing the natural order of things, so that it becomes possible to understand it and live with it more easily.

In this way, for many centuries, it was as if the Romanies were behaving as if the Western world was only just being created. They were constantly reminding themselves that the civilized way was not the natural ancient nomadic way. And so they encouraged their youngsters to walk out and face 'the civilized way', preparing them for its obvious perils.

Today, the perils of civilized living may be a test for all of us, even though we don't know it, but perhaps the Romani Gypsy is able to see these more clearly than most because of having lived, deliberately, on the fringes of society for so long.

I had one of my greatest lessons around this theme when I once watched my father in a courtroom, cleverly twisting a whole case around so that he was finally cleared, even though he was partially to blame within the eyes of the law for what had happened - a problem over some land - and the plaintiff was not a lover of Gypsies. But I will never forget my father's courage, his wit and the sparkle in his eye when he came out of that courtroom. A Gypsy still carries the fear that if a Gypsy and a *gaujo* are in a court of law together, the Gypsy will come off worse. But what I retained from that experience was not civilized law's attempts to demonstrate human beings' rights to land ownership, but my father's guts and honesty; in so many words he was trying to tell everyone that we might do better to borrow rather than own the Earth. He happened to be very clever with words, and amusingly expressive, so the court could only warm to him.

Sadly, as time passed, I saw my father slowly lose that spark, and echoing down the years I could hear my *boro dad*, my great-grandfather, speaking of the curse, how civilization would claim the soul of every Gypsy in the end. It had been a very real fear for him and I know it was something my grandmother also feared. But it was beyond our control. The Children of the Wind and the Earth were becoming the Children of Civilization, like other tribal people who were also, by degrees, losing their spark and becoming extinct.

At the beginning my father had had that strong Romani Gypsy fire burning within him. He had nearly been named 'Gus', after the artist and friend of the Gypsies, Augustus John, or 'Sir Gus', as they had called him. This had been Jack Lee's idea, as he often spoke highly of the man. But my father somehow ended up as Walter and slowly, as he grew older, his fire burned down. He contracted throat cancer at around the age of 55 and although he was cured, afterwards he was never the same. At this time, my mother and brother were still clinging on to the old ways, the old ideas, but I could see, perhaps more than they, that only the ashes remained of our once colourful and quite powerful culture.

It is a fact that indigenous peoples, or those who have lived within an ancient tribal-based community, will suffer more from being pushed too quickly into the modern world than perhaps those who have become acclimatized to such a world over a longer period of time. Suicides, mental problems, drink and drug abuse and depression can result as people are forced into sacrificing their ancient and dependable way of life.

Romani Gypsies may have suffered less in this way because of usually keeping themselves to themselves. They are in fact sometimes condemned for wishing to separate themselves from the rest of the world, but this happens because they think differently. This can, however, inevitably bring a great sense of isolation, particularly when families break down, for individuals who find themselves alone.

There was certainly an undeniable feeling of 'us and them' when I was a child and I was often encouraged by my elders not to get too close to outsiders. It was true that if other children knew too much about your roots they were quick to condemn you for it and more than once I was savagely attacked by another boy who bullied me. I would also find myself standing in front of a whole room full of children at school, being made to use counters by an unsympathetic mathematics teacher, an experience designed to be humiliating - for I was 14 years old at the time and my teacher should have known better. But perhaps this man was repaying me for making fun of his lesson. 'How many pips are there in an orange?' I once boldly asked him. He would grab me by the collar at times like these and shake me, and as he stared at me with frustration I could see in his eyes that he was thinking me simply not worth the time. On other occasions I would be happily playing with a group of *gaujo* children when suddenly a strange feeling would overwhelm me, a feeling of being somehow out of my depth, and I would become paralysed and stand very still with my eyes wide, staring hard at those about me, until I would suddenly bolt off at high speed, away from them. I naturally gained a reputation for being strange, but my brother fared even worse, finding that he could not mix with other children at all. These kinds of experience perhaps constituted the 'down' side of a Gypsy childhood.

But at the end of the day it was often the case that I had more confidence than other children, if only because I was convinced that this was not the real world, or the real life. I had always been taught that

the material *gaujo* world was the 'shadow' world and
that the world of the unseen, the world of the imagination and of fairy-tale castles, was the more real. In
fact, the older I grew, the more I believed this.

The greatest highlight of my early childhood, however, was the time I spent with my great-grandfather
and the occasions when I was honoured to witness
him practising the old ways. He was clever, observant,
funny and patient with children, and he was intuitive
to a high degree. One had the feeling that he constantly kept some kind of antenna waving around on
the top of his head, given the way he could perceive
what was going on within the minds and hearts, and
usually the very souls, of most individuals. He looked
*into* you with his dark eyes, rather than at you.

My most vivid memory of him will always be watching him at a ritual, which I was encouraged to observe
due to the fact that I might well be practising the
same thing one day. I remember the darkened room,
the atmosphere created by the warm candlelight and
the ecstatic feeling. I remember my great-grandfather
burning things in the flame of the candle – paper,
and sometimes pieces of material, which formed the
workings of a spell, while he muttered to himself in
the Romani language. These were activities I did not
always understand when I was young, but I remember giggling, which was allowed, not purely because
I was a child, but because most adults usually giggled too. Nothing was ever that serious; even Jack
Lee referred to himself as 'the old *Chovihano*' in a
light-hearted way, although everyone around him
treated him and his work with the greatest respect.

He obviously carried a much heavier weight inside himself, which I was not to fully appreciate or understand until a much later date.

During these sessions as a child I felt myself to be half in and half out of these strange but comforting scenes. We were cocooned in a timelessness difficult to understand unless you have experienced the closeness of a community which practises ancient traditions. The feeling of being woven into a reliable and harmonious tapestry that has existed for thousands of years, and being empowered by this, is hard for many to comprehend, but the best analogy I can give is that of a continuously flowing river, for none of the parts of a river can be separated, those parts that are ahead of you and those parts that are far behind you are inseparable, and all are very much a part of what you are yourself at this moment in time. It is the *essence* of the river that you are experiencing, like the spirit of water itself. It can run through and within and around, and there is nowhere where it cannot be. This is exactly what we were as a clan, or a tribe. The clan's essence seeped into all of us and bound us all together.

Part of this great essence was the Otherworld itself, a place where you could live, and where you found dragons and giants and fairy people and castles and great vast landscapes of extraordinary dimensions, things which you could never find in the so-called 'real' world. The Otherworld was a place where absolutely everything started and finished, whose essence was indeed creation and life-force at its most profound level.

All this strengthened me as a child. It might be said that if you subject a growing child to too much fantasy, that child may not be able to survive in the real world when it comes to living in it as an adult. But I do not believe that this is so. The world of the imagination is a world yet to be understood, for it has yet to be rescued from the slumbering depths of the harsh worlds we have created around material themes. The Romani Gypsies always worked very differently where the imagination was concerned, schooling their children in how to use it, so that by the time you were fully grown you were able to use it constructively, rather than ignoring and fearing it, and indeed growing out of it.

Perhaps my greatest challenge in childhood was in facing the changes which came upon my family as its bonds weakened with the passing of Jack and Gladdy Lee, who undoubtedly held the family together. But the memories always remained strong and there was much for me to do in the future since I had stepped on to that very special path which many before me had walked for thousands of years. It was quite a responsibility and had to be respected and protected if I was to preserve its power.

I never wanted to let Jack Lee down, so armed and ready, I took what I had learned in my Romani Gypsy childhood and walked out into the adult world.

23

# 2

## THE DARK PAST
## WHERE DID THE
## GYPSIES COME FROM?

**M**any Gypsies, even in more recent times, have not been able to say where they originally came from. In the past they have been inclined to reel off the kind of story they think a listener wishes to hear, however fantastic. Inevitably, this has frustrated those who have not taken the time to understand the workings of the Romani Gypsy mind, which may appear to be complex, but is in fact extremely imaginative and childlike in its psychological make-up.

This simplicity proved to be an asset in the past for a people who have so often needed to shrug off the negative labels which have been unfairly attached to them. There is a reason for the Gypsies' 'obsession' with stories and fantasy, though, and reasons why they have been shrouded in the mists of a particularly mysterious and dark past.

Gypsies earned many titles on their travels through different lands, including the Children of Ancient Egypt, Children of the Wind, or of the Earth, and were variously described as the survivors of Atlantis, or the descendants of a royal house in Asia Minor. It was in fact common for many of the old Lees to boast that they had royal blood. They often claimed to be the aristocrats of the Gypsy race, for they had 'breeding', and more class, or so they said. Jack and Gladdy Lee always echoed this, instilling in me a pride about myself and a quality about everything I do. Yet no documented history was ever written by the Romani Gypsies themselves, as everything was always passed down from generation to generation; indeed, the Romanies have no written language, which has of course only served to deepen their mystery.

The study of Romanes, the Gypsy tongue, has so far provided the most reliable clue to the Gypsies' origins, placing their homeland in north-west India. It has also been possible to trace the route they travelled through Asia to Europe through the many 'borrowed' words which have entered their language. In addition to this, the Gypsies' characteristics, style of dress and their affinity with the Hindu religion have brought gypsiologists and researchers to the same conclusion: Romanies are in essence Indian.

Opinions vary, however, as to why the Gypsies left their homeland. Some authorities claim they left during the ninth or tenth centuries AD during various periods of unrest; others claim they left later than this, or even earlier. What most tend to agree upon is that the Gypsies left India voluntarily, even though there is no evidence to support this. Personally, I have never believed that they came out of India of their own free will. Nomads, be they of human or animal origin, live by following, year in, year out, a seasonal circuit which takes them to places where food and water will be readily available. They do not deviate from this structured path, as life can hang in the balance if you do not have food or water. Only if these essentials are not available will nomadic wanderers veer off their familiar routes. Therefore, there seems to me no sound reason why a race as simple as the Romani people, people who are neither adventurous nor conquering, should suddenly want to embark upon one of the longest migrations ever undertaken by human beings, risking life and limb crossing vast deserts and unchartered terrain where food and water would be scarce. All this for a whim? And where exactly were they going anyway?

We may travel fairly easily today, with backpacks, by train, bus and plane, purely to see the sights, with modern amenities peppering our route. But these people were covering thousands of miles, mostly on foot, with the horse their most efficient, and fastest, means of transport - and a horse also had to be fed and watered whilst travelling such vast distances.

After studying various sources on the history of India and Asia, it seemed clear to me that the Gypsies must either have been taken out of India against their will, perhaps as slaves, or were so heavily persecuted that they simply had to leave.

Some might argue that the Gypsies may have needed to travel further afield in order to find customers for their ancient smithing skills and that sale of their craftwork would have been a dominant feature in their migration. However, in the past there would not always have been an economic structure to their lives, as in more modern times. Apart from this, if the Gypsies had been so fond of accumulating wealth, would they not have made use of their large numbers in early days either to defend their own territories in their homeland or to conquer the lands they passed through, as other, more warring nomads were doing? If this were so, they might have abandoned their old primitive ways of life and taken up a position in the civilized society developing all around them a lot earlier.

I finally came across a theory providing a more feasible solution to the puzzle of the Gypsies' early days. Roger Moreau, in *The Rom: Walking in the Paths of the Gypsies*, suggests that the Gypsies were taken from their homeland in vast numbers as slaves in the ninth century AD by the Afghan-Turks, who used them to ferry booty out of India into Afghanistan. Three tribes, the Lohar, the Banjara and the Kanjar, who bore a great resemblance to the Gypsies in Europe and who were also at the lower end of the caste system in India, proved easy pickings for these ruthless marauders in their greed for India's vast wealth.

The Afghan-Turks were by no means the first to set their sights on India, for the Greeks had arrived in the fourth century BC and then the Arabs in the seventh century AD and it is not unreasonable to assume that some of the resident nomadic tribes may have left India at these times if being repressed or forced to remain sedentary. Certainly there have been a great many accounts giving descriptions of nomads befitting Romani Gypsies in places as far away as Egypt and in the Balkans long before any officially documented accounts of them appeared in the fifteenth century. So this must always remain a possibility.

In these earlier centuries, however, the Eastern world was constantly in upheaval, ever changing as religious powers, namely Muslim and Christian, rose up to exert rights over many nations. For humble nomads, such as the Romani Gypsies, still pagan in essence, still practising their magic, still believing the Earth, moon, stars and spirits to hold the essential key to all life, and above all, still borrowing the Earth, this was a most bewildering and ill-fated time as a wilful new society began springing up all around them, a society which claimed to hold the key to everyone's destiny.

This was, understandably, a society which the Gypsies, from the earliest times, did not want to associate with, for it had developed an insatiable thirst for wealth, land and converts, and there were devastating consequences for those courageous enough to question or defy such a power. Such are the roots of what we call religion, and religion has saturated many primitive cultures the world over, killing the natural tribal-Earth relationships we all once had and replacing them with prophet-based relationships, thus shifting the emphasis from Earth to man.

The word 'religion' itself has its roots in domination. It comes from the Latin *religio*, which means 'obligation', or being bonded, and this itself stems from the verb *religare*, 'to tie back, tie tight'. For many tribespeople living in the ancient way, be they Romani, Native American, Australian aborigine, or any other, there was only one option: *conform* - if you don't you will indeed perish!

Roger Moreau put forward the new idea that the Gypsies were held for some 300 years or so in a place called Dasht i Nawar, which means 'Desert of the Gypsies', by Muslims, in a slave encampment near Ghazni, in Afghanistan, which he likens to a large concentration camp. This indeed answers many questions and makes a good deal of sense. The Gypsies have been victims of persecution and slavery throughout their long history; might they not also have been slaves in those earlier times?

It is also reasonable to assume that when the Gypsies were finally freed from this camp - the Afghan-Turks eventually conquered India proper, so had no more need of slaves to help them plunder it - they would have been prevented from returning to their homeland because of the unrest going on there. It is also likely that the three tribes involved would have merged and interbred, which was not permitted by the caste system back home, and which would only bring shame and bad luck on a return to the Motherland.

There was no option but to turn west.

Many authors will refer to this long migration west as some sort of adventure, but the reality would have been very different. A journey across Asia in the twelfth century was no holiday. The Gypsies would have risked being taken as slaves again by other warring peoples, they risked being attacked and killed, and their children and old folk would certainly have risked perishing. These very real dangers would have accompanied the Gypsies every step of the way.

One of the Gypsies' greatest gifts, however, is a strong spirit and this would have supported them as they migrated in steady droves along the Silk Road across Asia, moving west towards Turkey. Numbed by the pain of their ordeal, they would have continued to travel rather as nomadic animals might, instinctively looking for a new day, tired, nervous and alert, but nevertheless able to let go of all that was behind them, just as animals do. For they moved as nature moved, as the stars, moon and sun moved; they knew that nothing in nature ever stays still. And when they found a suitable resting-place they borrowed the facilities offered by the Earth, as they had always done. They would continue to do so for the next 1,000 years.

Yet by the time they entered Europe, some 200 years later, in the fifteenth century, they came with an almost regal air, with dukes and counts as their leaders, who said they were from a place called Little Egypt, announcing that they were all doing penance as pilgrims for infidelity to the Christian faith.

This may seem a little theatrical or fanciful, but the Romani Gypsies were no different from any other tribal people the world over who were busy aping 'civilized' superiority and aristocratic ways, especially when they saw the respect such behaviour brought from the masses. The Lees and Boswells in particular were extremely fond of claiming to be 'aristocratic', a claim which lasted right up until modern times. Gypsy kings in Scotland lived in hovels - which they called palaces - and were often photographed in their finery, particularly the clothes that had been discarded by the well-to-do. We must remember, of course, that these people were also excellent mimics and could adopt the air of an aristocrat very easily.

But the point is that the Gypsies had still not integrated with the masses of civilization. They were still living in their tribes, in their ancient way, still managing, indeed preferring, to keep themselves to themselves.

They had of course undergone quite a dramatic change from the degenerate rabble of ex-slaves in the twelfth century to the colourful and confident bands of 'Christian pilgrims' openly welcomed in Europe by the fourteenth century. Their passage through Constantinople in Turkey (now Istanbul) and Greece, I believe, strongly influenced this change, for both these centres of cultural excellence had served to equip them for the new political climate now stealing over a fast-developing Europe. In Europe the menaces of religious dominance and particularly land ownership were destined to become irreversible, and this gave the Gypsies a taste of things to come. As committed non-warring pagans, they were now socially and spiritually focused, armed and ready for these political changes.

They appeared to conform, but for the most part, Romani Gypsies have always maintained a pacifist attitude anyway. They may fight each other, but rarely will they fight the *gaujos* around them, for always wits are far more important, and, as my mother often used to tell me, 'You've nothing to gain by stirring up a rumpus if there's something you don't agree with.' Perhaps a typical Romani attitude if being confronted with a charging bull would be to simply step out of the way so that the bull could charge right past! A few Romanies have gone to war, but most prefer to avoid the political confrontations which develop in the *gaujo* world, as these are seen as not being their quarrel, and traditionally, anything out of harmony with the rest of nature is best avoided wherever possible.

Similarly, most Romanies will never vote, because they do not believe a central government can make decisions for the rest of the population and also for other living things. I have long understood this view myself. The chief of a tribe in a small intimate community is very involved with the tribe's politics and will make decisions based upon every individual's

needs, which a larger central government cannot do.
To sit down and talk to your chief, who knows a good
deal about you as a person, is a very different political
situation; you can rarely sit down and talk to the
Prime Minister!

For the larger percentage of old Romani Gypsies,
then, traditions have always been of great importance
in any political situation, because to practise your
traditions brings luck and luck will always protect you
far more than anything else.

Most have said that the place called Little Egypt in
Greece, where the Gypsies' traditions were probably
revived, was a fabrication of the highly imaginative
Gypsy mind, but this story does have a basis, because
the Gypsies earned the title of 'Egyptians' at this
time. It was when passing through Constantinople,
that I believe the 'Rom' were finally stamped with
the name 'Gypsy', a name that was to carry them
into their future.

The Byzantine Empire, once a major superpow-
er, was well into decline by the eleventh and
twelfth centuries when the Gypsies arrived in
Constantinople, its old capital. Spiritually at this time
people were sandwiched between the old world of
the magical arts and the new world of Christianity.
New man-made religion had already taken hold, but
just as a minority are nourished by the revival of the
magical and shamanic arts today, so a minority
would have been hanging on to them as they began
to diminish in those early times. Many individuals
would have been wrestling with themselves, still

troubled by having to bid farewell to the old Earth-based spirituality. It was far safer to follow the new man-made religions - they were, after all, approved of by officialdom.

Civilizations like that of ancient Egypt were already history. The ancient Egyptians, then as now, were people swathed in mystery, having been repeatedly conquered, not unlike the natives of India. Successive waves of Greeks, Romans, Persians and Arabs, and particularly Christians and Muslims, had left Egypt numbed to the magical power it had once enjoyed.

It is perhaps not too difficult to imagine how the people of Constantinople might have confused the Romanies with Egyptians, for there were great similarities. To begin with, methods of divining had important roots in Egypt, and divining was a craft the Gypsies were also naturally adept at, having carried it with them from India across troubled Asia. Gypsies were rather stubborn, like the Egyptians, and the Egyptians had always had a strength of spirit which tended to ignore political change, rather like the Gypsies. Above all, stories were told, just as they are today, of the mysterious power of the ancient Egyptians, who were every bit as psychically gifted as the Gypsies were. In turn, the Gypsies listened attentively, always partial to a good story.

The fact that the Gypsies had brought their own magical and shamanic crafts with them from India to Constantinople may or may not have been talked about in the lively market-places of this ageing city, but it is likely that the Gypsies would have remained

34

secretive about their homeland and what had happened when they had been forced to leave it. It was far better to hail from a people who were still held in awe and who had enough mystique in which to cloak a troubled past than admit that you were descended from common slaves. There can be no doubt that the Gypsies would also have admired the ancient Egyptians for their skills in the magical arts.

The common man in the streets of Constantinople who sat down in the market-place to have his fortune told by the Gypsies may well have been attracted by the secrecy and magnetic charm of these colourfully dressed dark-skinned natives, who wore kohl around their eyes like ancient Egyptians and who were painted with henna, which came from a plant growing in Egypt. Fortune-telling was frowned upon by officialdom, but there was a confident air about these people that was inspiring, for all their noise and childlike laughter.

The man might have muttered something about Egyptians to his wife as he joined them, and the Gypsies would casually have taken note, for they might already have heard others referring to them as 'Egyptians'. And in the end they would be happy to allow this man, any man, to tell them who he thought they were.

Thus the Egyptians, and later the shortened 'Gypsy', received the stamp of approval, and a new race was born. It was a name never chosen by the Gypsies themselves, but by those around them, yet it travelled with them further west, into Europe, nudged onward by the untiring Turks.

When the Gypsies found themselves taking up residence on the outskirts of Modon in Greece in sizeable numbers, headed by their chiefs and older wise women and guided by their shamans, there was a peaceful tribal structure to their social life again at last. So many of these natives were living in huts in this place that people began to call it 'Little Egypt', a metaphorical rather than a geographical place, the home of these secretive magical people with the dark skins and the healing powers and the ability to lift or lay curses, tell your fortune, cure your horse of its ills, cast spells, mix potions, charm wild animals, start fires or stop them - oh, and they could also mend your pots and pans while they were at it!

Indeed, many authorities will have us believe that the Gypsies happened to stumble upon fortune-telling and magic along their path as a means of 'conning' the public out of their money, but this is not the truth, for magical and shamanic traditions were always at the very heart of the Gypsies' social life and had been for many thousands of years. No one, after all, ever said the Gypsies were conning people when they mended their pots and pans, work which was always carried out to a high standard.

I believe that the Gypsies' magical side gathered power when they were able to band together in large groups again in Little Egypt. I think that after some 500 years of migration and the enslavement, near-starvation and near-extinction of their race, at that point the blood memory of these people was fully restored and they became empowered again. They were able to celebrate who they were, and what they had come through, yet they were still careful about keeping themselves to themselves and remained on the fringes of conventional society.

This could also have been another factor in their being nudged on further into Europe, for society was not going to tolerate anything smacking of paganism, sorcery and shamanism - unless, of course, it could all be tamed and tailored to meet the demands of the new all-powerful religion. In modern times the magical arts have to meet the demands of science in much the same way.

Also, in earlier days, the Gypsies' tribalism itself might have posed a threat, for they had come into Europe in very large numbers, in fact, in their thousands, at a time - the fourteenth century - when officialdom had already begun packaging the old pagan gods and customs as new Christian saints and values, and turning the tribes into neater, smaller, more manageable family units. The Gypsies had not exactly fostered and promoted a religion of their own, that is, something demonstrating political power and strength - if they had, given their vast numbers, Europe would certainly have taken up arms against them - but their tribalism itself had to be 'seen to', which wasn't too difficult, as European pagans had been dealt with before. Both tribalism and shamanism could easily be passed off as unfavourable pastimes of that much-feared designer-baddie the Devil - himself a creation of the Church.

It is said that the Gypsies' announcement of needing to wander for seven years through Europe whilst doing penance as Christian pilgrims at the same time was a plot hatched in order to procure them a safe passage. But bearing in mind the climate of Europe, which was socially muddled (this was the time of the Black Death, which took a heavy toll on Europe's population), and heavily religious, could a primitive people have done anything else?

Creating such a plot is well in keeping with Gypsy psychology, for Gypsies would rather play a game of pretence than sacrifice themselves to 'civilized' laws. But here we are obviously talking about 'lying' and one perhaps needs to understand how the 'civilized' mind was developing in order to finally understand what this 'lie' was all about.

I do not believe the Gypsies so much hatched a plot as went along with what everyone else was saying of them at the time, which many of us do today, although we perhaps don't always realize it. Perhaps the Gypsies only practised this to an extreme. Today, we might wish to keep our political opinions on an agreeable level to avoid confrontation; then, the Gypsies were keeping their religious ideas on an agreeable level for exactly the same purpose. They, after all, had much more to lose, so it was vital that they played their part well. So the 'plot' was a deliberate attempt to keep the peace around themselves and what the Gypsies themselves called the *Bari Hukni* - the Great Lie, or Great Trick.

The way they saw it, living without the Earth, or using the Earth, as opposed to borrowing it, was a sacrilegious act and living a lie anyway, and the masses were now living this way. Laws were created to take taxes from the poor, which the Gypsies saw as robbing the destitute and helpless, and the whole of civilization was about lies: lying to the Earth, lying to the spirits, lying to each other and, worst of all, lying to yourself. So the imaginative childlike Gypsy mind perceived the *Bari Hukni* as a necessary game, one needed in order to survive in a lying world. But at the same time there is no doubt that the tribes' shamans and elders, with their great sense of humour, must have enjoyed playing such games and teasing the 'civilized' mind - as a cat might perhaps tease a mouse! All this *gaujo* trickery couldn't, after all, be anything more than a joke - could it?

But also, in attempting to understand the *Bari Hukni*, it is necessary to understand some of its magical implications for the Gypsies, which are given in the number seven. Many researchers have been baffled by the very precise length of time the Gypsies chose to remain wandering in Europe and it is often assumed that they simply chose the number seven at random, as part of their own trickery and deceit. But why seven years? Why not four years, or 16 years? It is obvious that they could not retreat back whence they came, so were bound to spend longer than seven years wandering the new continent; moreover, by announcing this number publicly, were they not doing themselves a disservice by giving themselves limitations? What would happen when the seven years had expired?

For the Gypsies who were working with the *Bari Hukni*, the number seven would have been far more important than the content of the exercise! Seven is a powerfully magical number, and extremely lucky, if used in the right way, and the *Bari Hukni* was therefore also a spell, probably cast by some of the master shamans of the tribes. Those seven years were certainly lucky, for during that time the Gypsies received a warm welcome and plenty of alms.

But dark clouds were spreading across Europe, blackening and taming the once colourful, once wild and once free nature of this beautiful continent, and their magic was strong. According to the old Gypsies, Europe became enchanted by bad *gaujo* sorcerers. She had fallen under a spell - which has in fact lasted for hundreds of years. *Chovihanos*, female *Chovihanis* and elders would have frequently worked their own spells as antidotes and would have ensured that correct information about the *gaujos* and this great enchantment were passed down to successive generations of children as the tribes travelled on across the land. But the seven years turned into 70 years, and then into 270 years, until today we can see that Europe is still enchanted, still waiting to be set free.

Where the Gypsies' wandering is concerned, an interesting point arises concerning the word 'travel', as it dates approximately from the fourteenth century and was always associated with hard work, or a painful effort, being originally related to the Old French *travailler*, which in turn was related to an earlier word implying an instrument of torture! Travelling large distances in those days when roads were almost non-existent might well be something you would describe as 'torture'. From the formation of this word, we may also see that the Gypsies would not have been known simply as 'travellers' in those days, for in fourteenth-century Europe - providing you wanted to remain respectable, rather than being known as a mere itinerant - you could only be a 'pilgrim'. This was the age of the Crusades, the age when you walked hundreds of miles, dutifully, just to visit a holy shrine, and were tolerated, admired and given alms for doing so, whoever you might be. In his *Dictionary of Word Origins* John Ayto gives 'pilgrim' as a word being used back in the thirteenth century for traveller: 'one who journeys for specific purposes'. People continued to journey for specific and very religious purposes for a further 200 years - all, perhaps, except the Gypsies, whose idea of journeying was still attached to the old nomadic cycles structured by the Earth's seasons, a structure already largely extinct in Europe.

So when in the early fifteenth century a European official looked at the strange dark-skinned *sherrengro*, or Romani chief, with the battered hat and the even stranger colourful cloaks and robes, and asked him where he and his savage-looking people had come from, the chief was expected to say that they were all pilgrims - which he did - and that they were all Christians - which he did - and that they had all changed their primitive and heathen ways in favour of following the *true* religion. Then he received a reassuring slap on the back and was given alms together with a pass giving him and his people permission to remain and wander in the respective country.

The passes the Gypsies were given were presumed to be legal documents from people in high authority, including Pope Martin V. It is possible that they could have been forged. But historical evidence shows that the Gypsies were welcomed in Europe and given alms, so whether these passes were authentic or forged, we can be assured that the Gypsies were more welcome in Europe at this time than at any future date in their wanderings there.

The chiefs were able to settle their people in the many sprawling forests of this new continent by now, allowing them to roam freely in great bands across the new uninhabited wildernesses where they could practise their ancient customs in peace, as they had always done. On the face of it the Romanies appeared to have mended their heathen ways - but they had no intention of changing anything.

The realization soon came that they only wanted to live their own lives and mind their own business - which in these times would have been considered to be outside the law - and so tolerance wore thin. All this was so different from the laws of the caste system back home in India where tribes were expected to keep themselves to themselves. Now, when a Romani Gypsy was found by the common people in the forests whenever healing, magical guidance or a herbal potion was needed, this infuriated the authorities. The dark clouds quickly began to gather around the Gypsies as chroniclers, the press of the day, began their savage attack, labelling the Gypsies outcasts, thieves, beggars, charlatans and confidence tricksters. These labels, which were designed to turn the common people against the Gypsies, echoed all across Europe and have stuck to the present day, constituting an unfair burden which the Gypsies have long had to carry.

Tragically, this ignorant attitude eventually led to further persecution and slavery throughout the whole of Europe, particularly eastern Europe, where Romani men, women and children were auctioned and kept in chains even up to the middle of the nineteenth century, and where in the German Reich in World War II between a quarter and half a million Romani Gypsies were put to death in concentration camps. Sadly, persecution of the Romani race still goes on in many parts of Europe today.

Having landed in Britain at the very end of the fifteenth century, by the sixteenth century Romani Gypsies had arrived in vast numbers, which was when persecution of them in Britain reached its height, particularly under Henry VIII, under whose rule it became unlawful even to be a Gypsy! But the Gypsies were to remain in the woodlands of Britain for the next 500 years, practising their magic, a deep mystery to the rest of the population. In fact, for approximately 400 of those 500 years the ordinary person in the streets of Britain thought of Gypsies as being powerful supernatural beings.

My grandmother had told me that Jack Lee said it used to be auspicious for the common person to make contact with a true Romani Gypsy, for this native had powers which could link the common person to the Great Beyond. This is a somewhat different picture from that given by many history books, which have usually drawn information from the scaremongering Christian chroniclers who always made a feast out of attacking anything which appeared not to conform.

I believe Romani Gypsies enjoyed a better reputation than we might suppose in many areas of Britain, particularly among the ordinary people, but that the 'bad' picture gradually filtered through to our present age because of a social offloading which needed to be done by society, unfortunately an offloading which only took place because the Gypsies happened to be in that place at that time. Thus, the once helpful, once useful and once likeable wild people of our British woodlands, who cherished and guarded the trees, became the social outcasts we still know as 'Gypsies' today.

But by the sixteenth century the Romanies were well and truly 'Gypsy'. They had been 'Egyptian' (up until the early twentieth century), 'Gipcyan', 'Gipsen' and in more recent times 'Gippo'! And in other countries they were to become 'Gitan', 'Tsigan', 'Bohemian' and a host of other names. India was now well and truly history; India had been forgotten, as had the miserable trek across Asia in those turbulent years. Now, instead, Gypsies told fantastic tales of Egypt and pilgrims, embellishing the story with scenes of fairy-tale castles in the sky and giants and witches and fairies of the Underworld, which the common person would listen to with great wonder, for stories like this were not told any more.

Were the Gypsies again telling lies? It is quite natural for us to assume so. But their truth has always been something which the modern mind finds hard to

44

comprehend, and certainly difficult to tolerate. The Gypsies' definition of truth and lies springs fundamentally from another place in another era when humans lived by different values and walked the Earth in a very different way. And whether in the fifteenth century or indeed the twentieth century, we often find the Romani Gypsy using the same kind of language, embroidering a tale with so-called 'fantasy', when they are more often than not simply drawing from their own ancient legends and folk tales, simply telling the *truthful* story of their culture's past as seen through their eyes.

It seems that much of an ancient culture can be preserved when a people separate themselves from mainstream society whilst maintaining and practising their ancient traditions at the same time. It is, however, important when speaking of people who separate themselves from society to make clear the distinction between Romani Gypsies and a variety of other so-called social outcasts, for there are many people in our own society who are often confused with true Romani Gypsies, particularly those we may term 'drop-out', 'hippy', 'rebel', 'tramp', 'New Age traveller', and even the homeless. All these may be as much *gaujo* to the true Romani as those other *gaujos* who constitute the bulk of civilized society. The Romani race needs always to be seen as an ancient race in its own right.

Unfortunately, in more modern times, the old magical ways kept alive by the social interaction within Gypsy tribes and between Gypsies and *gaujos* seem to have died completely, as has happened in many tribal cultures all over the world. Many Gypsies no longer value what went on in their past; in fact, they are hard pushed even to remember what went on in their own grandparents' time, for their grandparents and great-grandparents have usually preferred to take their ancient knowledge to the grave than hand sacred knowledge over to those who may well abuse it. This is quite understandable in many respects, for many modern Romanies would indeed not respect their culture's knowledge. And so true Romanies who still carry the old magical ways are increasingly difficult to find.

But I believe that back in those earlier centuries in Europe people still had an instinctive memory of their own primitive tribal past. Colonization of the West would, after all, only truly begin in the sixteenth century. So between the fourteenth and sixteenth centuries people were not so disconnected from their ancient past as they are today. Even so, to the British and Europeans of the Middle Ages this distant past was beginning to seem more and more like a half-remembered dream. Folk tales and tradition still provided the connection to it, although it was becoming increasingly difficult to find anything from the ancient world which had not been relabelled or disfigured by Christian symbolism. Thus today we believe that many customs and traditions are in essence Christian when the vast majority of these had their beginnings in an earlier age. The Romani Gypsies, with their stubborn tendency to cling to ancient traditions, provided a vital link with the pagan past and refreshing glimpses into the old Otherworld.

And a Gypsy might have said, in an English market-place, in the eighteenth century: 'In the beginning there was *Kam*, the sun, a great Gypsy king who madly pursued *Shon*, the moon, his beautiful sister in the sky. And she had to keep evading him because if he caught her they would have an incestuous relationship. So she slipped silently over the horizon out of sight by the time he rose each morning. But one day he did catch her and they fought for a while, which caused darkness to spread over the Earth. And this union resulted in the birth of the Gypsy race.' And he may have nodded, adding, 'Yes, that is where we Gypsies come from.'

Perhaps his listener's eyes were wide. She wanted to believe him because he told this tale with such conviction. It brought comfort to her, for she knew this was the kind of tale that would have nourished all her ancestors in the past and she so longed to believe the way he believed. But officialdom had long put it about that these tales could not be found in the Bible and could therefore only be related by those who were 'wicked', those who were sorcerers and wizards and 'ventriloquists', people who conversed with spirits, those who were in fact practising the work of the Devil.

All this greatly confused the Gypsy, for he knew that his tale was anything but an untruth, anything but wicked; it was something his ancestors had been handing down for many centuries and was simply the story of all his people.

From where we are all standing in the modern world today it may be difficult for many to perceive the

Romani Gypsy mind as it has been over the last few hundred years. The fact that more people are attracted to studying tribal ways of life these days certainly helps us step closer to this ancient nomad, though, and slowly the Romani Gypsy can at last begin to emerge from a particularly dark past, as a member of a tribal people worthy of recognition.

Today, people have a need to believe in the old myths and this came home to me in a big way when the 1999 solar eclipse took place, which I called 'the sacred marriage of *Kam* and *Shon*'. So many people who were aware of this beautiful old Romani story of our spiritual mother and father mating in the sky experienced distinct changes in their lives at that time and this itself helps to link them to a primitive past, for they are thinking in the very same way that their ancestors would have thought. Those who looked at the eclipse taking place were in danger of subjecting themselves to bad luck, whilst those who respected what was going on up in the heavens and who didn't watch were soon enjoying good luck. Reports reached me of various 'good luck' and 'bad luck' stories, which I saw as a positive sign, for people were beginning, once again, to harness the essence of an old myth to everyday life and to see it as a powerful source of magic.

It is this simple act of belief which ultimately connects us to a more natural and what we might call a more primitive way of relating to each other and the Earth. There is magic happening all around us in the signs and symbols which regularly cut across our paths every day, if only we care to look and see what is there. And if we practise looking for signs about our future, every day, we will soon make a habit of it, which is exactly what the old Gypsies would have done.

Finding a small acorn, for instance, is a powerful symbol, if it is on your path. Your foot might kick it, but pick that acorn up, put it into your pocket and carry it with you. Then ask yourself what you were thinking when your foot touched that acorn. Were you thinking about a dream you have? The acorn symbolizes the oak, and greater things, so by picking the acorn up you are giving yourself its potential, the potential to become something greater than you are and to begin building your special dream.

There are far too many examples of finding symbols and omens to go into here, but by training yourself to work in this way, you are working as the old Gypsies would have worked, and you are reaching the core of that primitive psychology which all old Gypsies retained over the centuries and which ultimately helped them retain their traditions to this day.

The *Kam* and *Shon* myth is a particularly powerful omen, as the sun and moon are powerful spiritual beings to the Gypsies and they are with us all the time. We all know that a red sky at night can mean 'a shepherd's delight' - fine weather the next day - meaning that we can get out and do things, and we have remembered that, but equally we need to remember how a new moon can give us a boost of energy for the dreams we wish to fulfil and can therefore mean that we can work well at what we are trying to achieve if only we try.

The solar eclipse of 1999, I knew, was a powerful omen for marking the rebirth of the Gypsy culture and this rebirth is happening, as more and more people over the last few years have started to take my culture far more seriously. Even more will do so after reading this book. The solar eclipse seems to have provided that vital turning point which my culture so badly needed.

So if there is one thing which helped to preserve the Gypsies as a race, it is their ability to understand and practise constructive magic, and to keep practising it behind closed doors, throughout their many centuries of wandering. Many will say that they acquired their magic and healing ability from other cultures, but I believe this is often the other way about, for I have sometimes had little or no experience of other paths, only to learn that traditions being practised by some of the more modern religions are very Romani in essence. There are many similarities in pagan traditions and in spiritualist traditions, and I feel that the Romani Gypsies, having carried their own traditions across Asia and into Europe, may well have contributed much of their own culture to others on their travels over the centuries, particularly as they always practised it in its pure form.

Certainly, the Gypsies' ability to absorb other languages and encounter other traditions of the countries they passed through *without* losing their own, over an extraordinary length of time, is a quite remarkable exercise in itself. In Britain, the rest of Europe, and indeed the rest of the world, many Romani Gypsies now profess to be Christians, but they are also just as likely to practise Hindu-flavoured traditions as well, traditions which they undoubtedly carried with them from India. But if we dig deeper into their psyche we discover underneath the foundations of what they have been in their tribal/animist past. It is like stripping away layers, only to find that the bottom layer is as primitive as it has always been. It is somehow as if the Gypsies made a pact with their tribal identity never to forget who they truly were. For so long they were considered to have no religion and no real spiritual identity. They have said themselves that when prophets of old were writing down the laws of their religions on stone, wood and paper, the Romanies wrote theirs on cabbage leaves, which were promptly eaten by a passing donkey, so they could therefore not remember what their own religion was supposed to be!

This perhaps best illustrates their own Earth spirituality, subtly mocking the conventionally pious. 'You can't be *serious* about moving away from the old Earth spirituality, can you?' the Romani is saying, with eyebrows raised, even after all this time, for the Gypsy's magic prevails and will always be at the heart of any spiritual excavation that is carried out within the Romani mind.

For the true Romani Gypsies, no matter what religion is in vogue, at the end of each day there can be no laws except the Earth's laws. So they would tell you what you expected to hear if you asked them where they came from. But for me, as for all my ancestors, an old legend, such as the story of *Kam* and *Shon*, will still prevail and will always carry the best truths.

So I also believe, as my *boro dad* and many of my elders believed, that my race originally began with the incestuous union of two great spirits in the heavens, *Kam*, the sun, and *Shon*, the moon, who were themselves born of two yet greater spirits, Earth and Sky, and Earth and Sky are the greatest and most powerful spirits of all. This belief links me with all my ancestors of the past, because it has been passed down through countless generations, and I like to allow my mind to wander back to some of those ancestors and to reassure them that although many Romanies have fallen by the wayside, spiritually, I still *believe*, I still *know* the truths of these great stories. And I imagine those ancestors nodding approval and sighing with relief that there is someone in their future who - even though with the greatest of difficulty - has somehow managed to stay on the same path.

# 3

## BORROWING FIELDS AND FORESTS
## A Sacred Romani Law

Red-gold leaves fluttered down through misty funnels of sunlight around me as I lay on my side in the autumn wood. The ground was hard and somewhat cold beneath me, yet something kept me lying there, or perhaps prevented me from getting up.

I thought I was probably dying, for I had not eaten in 24 hours and I was at odds with myself and the world, an 18-year-old desperately attempting to piece his life together.

Two days earlier I had had a strange but very strong experience, having slipped off into what seemed to be a trance, like a very heavy day-dream, which the *Puri Dai* afterwards assured me was quite normal for the kind of person I might well become: a healer. The same had happened to Jack Lee in the past and was a means by which he had often conducted his healing sessions, she told me.

We had been sitting in a group talking about the Lowerworld of old and how in earlier times our people were extremely wary of disturbing the *Biti Foki*, or fairy people, who lived in the depths of the forest, for these powerful little beings had always fiercely defended all areas of outstanding natural beauty over the Earth and were a great force to be reckoned with. If you disturbed their ancient habitat unnecessarily, those sacred places where they came up to meet human and animal worlds, you invited trouble indeed. The legends and folk tales of old were rich in the trials exerted upon unsuspecting humans who had chance encounters with these formidable guardians of nature. But as a *Chovihano*, or healer, you inherited an inner key or pass which gave you permission to access their world, along with the rare honour of earning their respect. A *Chovihano* was unafraid of the *Biti Foki*; a *Chovihano* was unafraid of anything that was of the Otherworld, because he could accept challenges and knew how to meet things head on.

At this time in my life I didn't exactly know if I would achieve the rare qualities of the *Chovihano* which, among other things, called for high levels of courage and trust, yet I had an instinctive sense of being unafraid of the unknown, which at least furnished me with a head start.

Ever since I had been small I had wanted to take off on spiritual as well as physical adventures, which sometimes drove my mother to despair, but as time went by I would be meeting experiences which would serve to put these instincts to the test many times over.

Here in this red-gold wood, I was just at the beginning, learning to grope my way through subtle worlds of dreams and psychic experiences, worlds which few in the material world outside might understand. My family had taken a step back from me, which was quite normal, simply allowing me to get on with it all. So I followed my own hunches, as all *Chovihanos* had done before me, attempting to find my own *tacho drom*, or true path.

'Go into a field and lie there' was the only advice given me by my grandmother following the trance experience I'd had. She and my mother had both known what was going on when I had 'slipped off', for when I had opened my eyes they had been looking at each other in a rather knowing way. Jack Lee had also been told to lie in a field by his elders when he had been young and I felt privileged to receive the same instruction. I later discovered that this act was designed to help a potential healer connect with the Earth.

In earlier times young *Chovihanos* and female *Chovihanis* would have been told to go into the depths of the forest for a vision to help clarify the nature of their path, but in these modern times of land ownership it had become increasingly difficult to find potentially conducive wooded areas in which to work, so a young shaman might be advised to conduct the exercise in a field.

So I had found myself a comfortable spot in a nearby field where I could lie down in the uncut grass, looking at every blade stretching beyond my face to the sky above. There, for a short time, I connected with the Earth, for the grass soon seemed to be taking on a life of its own, cautious at first, but as soon as the grass began singing, it was as if I were, by degrees, being accepted back into its secret world. Then I could hear my *boro dad's* familiar musical voice: 'This is what borrowing the Earth is all about, Jasper.' He had always put over to me that if you didn't own or tame the Earth, she was more receptive to you and more inclined to talk, and I was indeed beginning to hear the Earth speak. *Dik ta shoon!* I thought. It wasn't long before I felt myself watching and listening on a universal scale. As the warm autumn breezes caressed my face and body, and as the blades of grass continued to shimmer against the sky, I could hear another voice whispering and I began to feel that same pulsing energy beating through me as my heart began to thump in a rhythm in my ears, just as it had before. I knew it was the Earth speaking.

But then there was a commotion at the edge of the field, rudely disturbing the new harmony I had found, and I sat up angrily, looking about myself. A middle-aged man, quite obviously the owner of the field, was gesticulating to me angrily, plainly letting me know that my presence offended him.

I held up a hand, acknowledging him, and attempted to tell him that I would soon be gone, but I imagined he hadn't heard me, for soon he was walking towards me.

'Did you hear what I said?' he was yelling. 'Trespassers will be prosecuted!' He was pointing to an obscure sign somewhere on the edge of the field, which I obviously hadn't seen.

Reluctantly, I stood up. This was not a man to reason with. In fact he berated me as he accompanied me to the edge of the field.

This was my first ever solo encounter with an angry landowner over the question of land and as I climbed the fence to the footpath it suddenly sank home that I was being forbidden to practise a custom my people before me had practised for thousands of years. In the old days when common land was abundant it would have been far easier to escape to rural places to carry out communions with the Earth. How little this man knew of the old world, I thought, as I glanced back, feeling an immense sadness that the field and I had had to part company just as we were getting to know each other.

As I walked away I heard the man following on behind me. 'Are you one of the Gypsies?' he asked.

I turned. 'No,' I answered, simply, and kept walking on.

I have mentioned before that we always walked away when someone challenged us. We played it cool and never made a fuss. There might be many occasions when Romani Gypsies might be thrown out of pubs or out of public places – and out of fields.

I walked, frustrated, in circles, for quite some time and ended up in the red-gold wood, feeling, as many young people can feel, that all was futile, that there was probably no place for me in the adult world, and also, as many Romani Gypsies have long felt, that there was no more room for our ancient race in the fields of England.

Ironically, although I had been advised to lie in a field, I actually ended up in a wood, which served to link me with all the Gypsy *Chovihanos* of the past in their search for a *tacho paramoosh*, or true dream, a glimpse of your own personal shamanic path. Over hundreds of years *Chovihanos* would have attempted to find their paths by going into the ancient woodlands and communing with the spirits there. The dream or the vision of your path is important. It stretches in front of you but also behind you and links you with that vital Earth energy with which you will be working as a healer and in your liaison work with the Otherworld. Being told to go into a field was by no means a 'standard' initiation for a *Chovihano*. It was more a test of strength for me personally, I discovered later, so that I would know how to handle relationships in my shamanic work. And now when I look back I see the relevance of encountering the man in the field. If I did not meet these experiences in my earlier days, how could I equip myself for the difficulties I might encounter, particularly in the *gaujo* world, where prejudice has been great and where understanding has been so limited?

I did a lot of thinking over the 24-hour period I spent in that wood. I was there for the best part of a whole night. It did prove to be a difficult exercise, as I wasn't always alone. Occasionally, someone with a dog would pass, or a group of children, but I kept out of their way as much as possible, determined to carry out my task.

As I lay there on the wood floor looking up into the branches of the trees, I soon had the same feelings coursing through me as I'd had in the field. But this time there was a distinct restlessness accompanying them, an electric energy which was hard to contain. It was as if I had been injected with some vibrant fluid which had suddenly been released in my veins as my heart again began a rhythmic thumping and my body wanted to convulse. I had ingested nothing at all in many hours and was not of course to know at that time that this very act would have contributed to a heightening of my inner senses. Thoughts became loud and I considered that I was probably going mad. I know for sure that had anyone seen me in that wood at that time, rolling and writhing about, they could have been forgiven for thinking that I was having a fit! Indeed, I thought I was having a fit as thoughts rushed into my head only to spin out of control, a strange and quite disturbing sensation.

In recent times I have come to look upon this and successive experiences as 'shamanic' because of what others studying shamanism have told me. Then I was not so much afraid as confused, and before long it became clear to me that these feelings and indeed this pattern of behaviour were necessary to the trance state when conducting healing. I learned eventually that if you know how to handle the weakest and the strongest conditions within yourself, you will know how to handle these within others, and quite simply nothing will ever be a surprise to you, so long as you can journey to these places yourself. To this day I believe that if a healer cannot meet the weakest and the strongest within him/herself, then that person is not a true healer, because a healer must be acquainted with all inner conditions, so that nothing is ever a surprise. At least this is so in my culture.

These highly charged surges of energy, then, or 'fits', became familiar to me, and certainly easier to manage, and they eventually became a feature of my healing work.

In that autumn wood when I was just 18 I instinctively knew I was on my way to meeting the *Biti Foki*, or fairy folk, on my way to becoming a *Chovihano* and to developing the healing skills my great-grandfather had long practised. I was on my way to my own *tacho drom*, that true path. But there was one basic principle I would need to learn before I could ever go further and that was to understand the true meaning of borrowing. This is essential for all Romani Gypsies, and all healers and users of Earth medicine. I was shown its importance by a vision of the past involving all the Gypsies of old.

In this vision, I was astonished, and indeed privileged, to be an observer of a great procession of Romani Gypsies as they moved in their tribes through the trees in front of me. I saw great armies of them with their carts, horses and donkeys, as when first entering Britain in the late fifteenth and early sixteenth centuries. They were so very colourful, wearing bright materials and adorned with bright coins on their clothes and in their hair.

It became a procession that moved swiftly through the ages, from this earlier period up until the present day, ghosts of the past, perhaps contained within every tree's memory, for the trees seemed to spit out the vision, as if regurgitating it, in order to show me what nature had been keeping to herself for so long. I thought, if human beings have not acknowledged these wild people of the woods as a major part of our woodlands' history, nature has, for the trees remember everything, trees still acknowledge their ancestors, and ancestor tree spirits pass memories and important experiences down to younger trees. I knew this because Jack Lee had told me so. The vision therefore became an exercise in learning that we are really all the same, all members of the same family, whether we are human, animal or tree. We all have ancestors and all ancestors are important in our lives, in a great many ways.

As these colourful bands of people continued to move through the trees, I saw the way they interacted with the trees and with all aspects of nature around them. I saw them sitting around their fires, carving, weaving and producing crafts with quick nimble fingers while they sang or talked; I saw them rounding up horses, carrying out repairs, busy with their smithing skills. They were acting in plays, playing the fool, laughing, crying, squabbling, sharing experiences, but all the time they were communing with nature, and nature was happily communing with them. In moving through the trees they were moving through an old ancestral world where they were never alone, in fact where they were always safe, for experience was rich in these places, and the atmosphere was thick with spirits, magic and sacred areas which gave access to the Otherworld.

By the time the vision had taken me on to the Edwardian era, the era of the decorative Gypsy wagon, however, things had changed considerably, for now the relaxed atmosphere in the forest had gone and fears abounded. The forests were now dark, ugly, menacing places where shadows lurked, so many shadows that nothing of the old ancestral world existed there any more, and what was worse was that the trees were afraid too, afraid of their own shadows, for they couldn't understand what they'd done to be punished like this by human beings. Was it any wonder, I thought, that the forests were all being taken away? They were no longer valued when they were seen as stark places of fear.

A mist then gathered, obscuring the vision until it was as if sucked back into the trees so that the scene returned to normal, or perhaps back to the way it had been when I had first walked into the wood.

Was that the end? Was that the vision's message? But there was more. Again, I was soon hearing my *boro dad's* words: 'Borrow the Earth, Jasper, *borrow!*' And I then found myself reflecting on his great prediction that the whole world would be living under a curse if it continued to indulge in ownership in such an unthinking way, stealing the magic from the forest and from the land. I realized how the whole idea of ownership, as my great-grandfather had seen it, extended far beyond the realms of mere possessions. Ownership was clearly a state of mind.

Reflecting upon the way the trees had spat out the vision and sucked it back in again, I began to see us all, trees included, as a giant vacuum cleaner, sucking everything up in a greedy fashion - possessions, people, animals, land, ideas, thoughts and the very soul of life. And we human beings had been the inspiration for this - which certainly made me feel ashamed to be human.

I saw it all as an inward-spiralling process and it became intensely uncomfortable to experience consciously, for I was left feeling queasy and irritable, and in desperate need of spitting the whole lot out of myself, rather as the trees had done. I eventually did this, spitting not once, but three times, as I had seen Great-grandfather doing during the magical rites of a ritual. Spitting was often a Romani's way of sealing something; the spittle of the Gypsy *Chovihano* was considered to be extremely powerful.

Afterwards I lay back on the ground. beginning to

feel a little more comfortable as I entered another phase of the vision.

A great peace then came over me and it was noticeably quiet - no sound of traffic, no noise but the breeze shimmering the red-gold leaves in the tops of the trees. I could even hear the sound of a single yellow leaf falling softly to the wood floor, like a light, crisp, crinkled piece of tissue paper. We have so much noise in our modern world, grating, unnatural noise, that we have forgotten what it is like to listen to nature as she lives, grows and dies around us. Hearing nature grow must have been very familiar to ancient ears and I felt that that was what I was doing at that moment in time: listening as I might have listened many thousands of years ago.

I then also caught sight of a single ancestor standing in the wood on his own, reassuring the trees that everything was all right, that many of their own family were suffering as much as they were. This old spirit *Chovihano* of the past was quite calmly telling them that nothing was their fault, and to be patient, and to understand that human beings were unfortunately at that time the most ignorant creatures on the Earth, but that there would come a time when things would change. He was very old and moved with the aid of his *ran*. This is the staff the *Chovihanos* carry and which they use to protect themselves and to cast spells. My great-grandfather had one, which he carried with him especially on occasions when vampires were present - or in today's language, those people who may drain your spirit or waste your time. This old ancestor fascinated me. I couldn't help feeling sorry for him. He seemed to be doing his job alone, the job of going about reassuring trees that it wasn't their fault that we were all the way we were and that better times were ahead.

I didn't know at this point whether I should speak to him, but I chose just to watch, as I instinctively felt that this vision was here to teach me as an observer. So I watched and simply waited for something else to happen.

A sharp wind then seemed to start blowing in the wood, as if out of nowhere. This is something I have since become familiar with when experiencing ancestral communications. It is as if the elements respond to and indeed wish to take part in what is going on, which of course is because they are a part of what we are: the greater family. 'They are, after all, living with us in the same world,' Jack Lee would often point out when the natural world came up in conversation. All aspects of the natural world manifested as beings, he said, and all these beings had a right to be listened to.

As this strong breeze blew, I had the moving experience of mentally expanding to embrace the immediate wood around me, becoming the wind and the Earth and even every small bird and insect who happened to step within the perimeter of this new existence. The old ancestor had gone now, and I gave my thoughts and energy to what was at hand as I became the very smallest and the very largest of creatures. I knew then that I was tapping into the actual workings of creation, an unforgettable experience that I was indeed privileged to have.

Within this, I could see clearly that we needed to reverse the inward-spiralling process if we wanted to get back to our natural selves. We had a bad need to exhale, to shout, to scream, to vomit, to get rid of, to be without and generally to let go of everything we had become so used to holding on to - or owning. I saw that it was a process we had been developing mentally and emotionally throughout more recent history, until now ownership was deep in our bones, until we had become dangerously skilled at practising the craft.

As I watched a blackbird pecking about on the wood floor, these thoughts were reinforced. The blackbird did not question his personal rights to the land, for he was a part of the land, as necessary to the Earth as a small sentence may be to a book whose text depends upon every single word for its completeness; it otherwise becomes sheer nonsense. This blackbird was not sucking everything up; he merely took from the land what he needed and no more, and it seemed impossible for him to do otherwise. Boundaries existed for him, of course, where other blackbirds were concerned, but these were based on respect and understanding, a system based on borrowing rather than ownership. Subsequent conversations with wild birds have revealed to me that their territorial rights have more to do with personal space than measurement of space. If this were not so we would long ago have been victims of a massive takeover by any number of species of bird and animal, who might consider it right and proper to have as much as we human beings have.

I learned then that the land was, and always would be, a personal place, rather than a geographical location. Nature had never intended us to 'own' on so vast a scale, and I reflected on the fact that the words 'own' and 'possession' had no equivalent in the Romani Gypsy language, for 'own' was only ever used as an adjective, whilst there was no equivalent at all for 'possession'. Even the verb 'to have' was not used in Romanes.

I soon found myself pondering on this principle in relation to nomadic life, i.e. taking what one needs when the need arises, which Jack Lee said was a universal principle. Many predators certainly responded to this law, which meant that when they were satisfied they left their prey alone and it was thus safe for prey to wander in the vicinity of a potential killer and come to no harm. That was what hunting was all about, and nomadic peoples, including my own, had long understood this.

Also, the nomadic art of resting, replenishing and moving on again not only sustained the Earth but also provided important guidelines on how to live in harmony with others. Borrowing each site you stopped at was tied up with the life/death process: that is, using the site only for as long as you needed before returning it to nature again. I had learned about this life/death process from my elders, who taught me that just as a small death occurs whenever a site is left behind, so a new life occurs whenever a fresh site is found. This is also the reason why Romani Gypsies always prefer black and white animals, their piebald horses being an example - life and death are constantly reflected in the dark and light shades of the animals, constantly reminding you that life and death (borrowing and relinquishing) are always around each corner, in their many different forms. We always kept animals who were black and white at home, whether they were horses, cats, dogs or chickens.

But the borrowing principle also extended to all things which came into your hands during your life, and by borrowing - which meant that you avoided clinging to things, particularly in a mental and emotional capacity - you were regularly in the process of accepting change. Romanies have always been good at doing this because as nomads they have never always been able to carry too many possessions along with them. But by accepting change we are able to move forward in our inner lives and to learn from experiences in the proper way.

I have always seen the act of name-changing as a typical example of this. Some of the old Romani Gypsies would change their names with every new site they stopped at! This, inevitably, seems a strange exercise to many people today, because we live in a world which thinks largely in terms of labels, measurements and geographical space. How many of us, for instance, could cope with a friend changing name several times in a year? We would find this very confusing. But if asked to remember the places we might have travelled to within that year, we would more than likely be able to reel them off; in fact, we would probably feel obliged to remember them. But if we are trying to get into the minds of the old tribal people, we will need to start thinking in terms of *personal* space and to spend time thinking about what we perceive it to be.

When I stood up and laid my palm on a tree on that occasion in that wood, I felt, as the old ancestor I had been watching had felt, that all trees everywhere had been denied the full, rich, happy life they had once enjoyed in our primitive past, when Romani Gypsies had been nature's guardians. I felt that the trees' wonderfully flamboyant characters – which my great-grandfather told me most of them had – had been suppressed, perhaps just as humans' free-spirited tribal characters had been suppressed, over hundreds of years. I felt a suspense, a tension in that wood, as the trees wondered what was going to happen to them; it was clearly a tension caused by changes in the natural rhythm of things. The *Chovihanos* were gone, and compared to earlier times all seemed so silent, controlled and prudish somehow. And all because we human beings had made the decision to own rather than borrow, under the illusion that by owning something it was more legitimately ours, when nothing can ever be ours, not at the end of the day, and never in the eyes of nature.

I knew it would be my *tacho drom*, my true path, to reunite people with nature. My work would be about restoring the old bonds between ourselves and the land, as all Romani *Chovihanos* had done for hundreds of years before me, and to educate people on the borrowing principle. And in doing this I knew I would also be working to lift the enchantment which had been placed on Europe, and indeed the curse which had been placed upon my family. I knew that there would be a hard road ahead and specific testing to ensure that I was fit for the task.

In that wood I looked up into the trees and felt the inspiring comforting feeling that all trees give you when you are standing with them. They are good-natured considerate creatures and always want to do their best for you.

Then from the corner of my eye I caught sight of the old ancestor, moving along with his *ran* again. He had turned to look at me and on his face I caught what I thought to be a knowing smile, as if he knew everything. His lips moved, although I could not hear what he was saying, as he was too far away from me. He was old, so very old, or so it seemed to me at my tender age. At that time I somehow took his presence for granted. He seemed almost a part of the landscape itself as he moved about it so naturally. It was only when I arrived home and described him to my grandmother that I realized who I had been in the company of - the Ancestor. *The* Ancestor, the man who had guided my great-grandfather from the Otherworld, and my great-grandfather's father, and many of our fathers stretching back into infinity. My elders had expected him to appear as he did. It was a sign to them.

I sat down in the chair, numbed, unable to believe what had happened. My grandmother was meanwhile singing my praises. I was destined now to follow the old path of the *Chovihano*, she said. I would perform healing on many levels, I would one day enter the world of the *Biti Foki* and I would follow a path different from most paths, a sometimes harrowing and painful path.

Her predictions were right, for the path has been different, and certainly very harrowing and painful, but it has also been special, and I am indeed privileged to have the Ancestor as my guardian, for he has shared with me so many insights about the Otherworld and about the way life used to be for the old Romani Gypsies. But he is also a vital link with my distant past, something rare in these modern times, especially in the Western world. He has worked with me to help restore ancestral awareness between people in our modern age and their distant blood cousins of long ago, something that is not only deeply healing but, it seems, a necessity if we wish to move forward in our understanding of the way life used to be.

At that period in my life I returned to that wood many times, but I didn't see the Ancestor again in the same way. But I often spoke to him, nevertheless, as I sat there, sometimes out loud, asking for his guidance and frequently telling him my problems. I had the feeling he was waiting for me to live through certain experiences and to mature before he could work with me in a more significant way, which indeed happened.

I emerged from that vision in that wood realizing that the art of travelling was - and probably always had been - a spiritual exercise. It was of course also a mental, emotional and indeed a physical one. But the art of travelling used a currency, rather as we might use money to acquire possessions today, a spiritual currency involving the higher human qualities such as courage, trust, wisdom and respect for all things. The nomadic art of borrowing and life itself was all about personal circles and cycles: the human's personal circle/cycle in a relationship with the land's circle/cycle.

I was to discover later in life elements which seemed to justify this, particularly when I began studying the history of words. The word *jal*, for instance, meaning 'to go' or 'journey' in Romanes, is closely related to *Jol* in Old Norse and the Anglo-Saxon *Yule*, both which signify a cycle of the year, or in more modern times the Christmas period. *Jahr*, 'year' in German, and even 'year' in English are both related to *jal*. A journey, then, was for the old nomad of the deeper past a cycle or circle, a sojourn with the sun through the seasons within the greater personal space borrowed from the natural world.

I have also reflected on the fact that there is no word in the Romani language for 'borrow'. A word which has sometimes been used for it is *chore*, which means 'to steal'. I have heard some Gypsies saying that they have only *chored* something, when what they really mean is that they have just 'borrowed' it. A friend of mine who is French told me that a word used for 'steal' in the French language is *chourer*, which she believes might well be associated with the Romani language. It has led me to believe that perhaps long ago the Gypsies forgot the original meaning of this word, hence using it for 'borrow'. Or perhaps the verb 'to borrow' has always been somehow inextricably linked to the verb 'to steal' in their language. Perhaps, like many words, and indeed traditions, in the Romani Gypsy culture, the essence of it all is buried deep in a time when personal space was more important than measurement of space. There may just have been an age when you could not steal from the Earth because to take more than your share was unthinkable.

I still go back to that experience given me by the wood and the field, and to those very solid images of the Ancestor moving with his *ran* and his knowing smile through the trees. He has since encouraged me to converse with trees, which is difficult to do in these times when more land is privately owned in Britain than ever before. But I carry a lasting and fond memory of that borrowed wood and that borrowed field and what they both taught me, and I never pass a tree, or walk across a field now, without engaging these spirits in some kind of conversation - a promise on my part that I will do all I can to help things change.

# 4

## LIFE AND DEATH BEYOND THE HEDGEROWS
## THE GYPSY WAY OF LIFE

My *Puri Dai* told me that once, before I was born, everything that was on the mantelpiece in a house they had been sitting in suddenly fell with a great crash to the floor, apparently of its own accord. She said that Jack Lee had leapt out of his chair and had rushed to the other side of the room with his eyes blazing in terror. He had then run outside to the garden, where he had fallen to the ground, remaining there for some time, lying against the Earth.

This had been an omen, my grandmother said, a warning that a curse might well be upon the family if it continued to live in houses and indulge in ownership in the *gaujo* manner. Later, they discovered that at the precise moment the phenomenon had occurred, a relation had died. She had been in another house, dropped an oil lamp after falling over and tragically burned to death. This marked the beginning of the curse which has remained in the family to this day.

As a *Chovihano*, Jack Lee attempted to carry out purification rituals to charm away the bad energy, but the bad luck considered to come out of *gaujo* living was strong and it was finally decided that the *bengesko yak*, the evil eye, was well and truly upon them all. My grandmother said that Jack Lee left the house and went away for some considerable time following that event; he thought that his sorcery could not work any more.

Living and dying, or rather how you live and die, was always an important issue for the Romani Gypsy. The general belief is that if the old ways are not observed you lay yourself open to bad luck which will weaken you, thereafter inviting harmful magical influences in the form of curses and enchantments to enter your life. These can be a severe threat to health and well-being if not taken seriously.

When the objects on the mantelpiece took their mysterious unaided dive to the floor that day, my family saw it as a warning to protect themselves. An ancestor's spirit was not at rest and this is a very serious matter, for it subjects the family to what is probably one of the greatest fears for the Romani Gypsy: the *Mulo*.

The word *mulo* is related to the Sanskrit *mrta*, 'dead', also to the English words 'murder' and 'mortuary'. It covers many aspects of the spirit in death in Romani lore and like all spirits, it manifests as a benevolent or malevolent force. When benevolent, the spirits of the departed are seen as trustworthy, and in many ways alive, but alive in another world. They can guide and help those in the flesh in many ways. But if malevolent, these spirits are still considered to be living in this world and are what we might call vampires, zombies or the walking dead, a belief which dates back many thousands of years and which may well have its roots in vampiric traditions in India.

From my own family I learned that the spirits of the dead are extremely vulnerable just after death, rather like newborns. I understood that after death you returned to Grandmother Earth, the source, and entered places that are often beyond the comprehension of those left behind, as only the *Chovihanos* have access to these obscure realms. Providing you made your transition back to *Puvus*, the Earth, through the grave, all went smoothly, and you could move on to other dimensions with ease. But if something interfered with that process, you might well become a ghost, a lost soul, haunting those left behind. Only a *Chovihano* could then find your soul and bring it to rest.

It has been common in modern times to associate exorcism with Christian ministers, but post-death soul-retrieval was a common task for the Gypsy *Chovihano* in earlier times. The word *drukerimaskro* was used to describe a Christian minister who had the power to lay ghosts to rest. *Drukerimaskro* originally meant 'soothsayer', an art which was linked to the *Chovihano*. Certainly it was always impressed upon me that a healer must be prepared to help the dead as much as the living.

The healer's role will lie not only in rescuing a lost soul, but also in *experiencing* that soul's misery and pain, thereby 'capturing' the curse or spell responsible for keeping the dead person out of the grave.

Perhaps new ideas of death, or more correctly the loss of the ancient value of death, have created a fear in our modern times of being buried or contained in the Earth - almost as if at death we are being buried alive! Since the Earth's soil is no longer the 'source', no longer the 'mother', it is no longer considered to be healing and it is no longer considered to be clean. It has become unhygienic and constantly needs washing away. So the Earth's soil has become 'dirt', a term I find deeply offensive.

Romani Gypsies have used the soil in many ways in their rituals and to break spells, throwing it over themselves or even into their mouths on occasion. Jack Lee threw himself on the soil when the objects fell from the mantelpiece as a means of protecting himself and asking the Earth's forgiveness. Many Romanies who drop food on the soil outside will pick the food up and eat it, but if food is dropped on the floor inside a house it is considered to be *mokado*, or ritually unclean, and is thrown away. In early times when humans moved into dwellings the soil moved in with them, household dust being linked with good fortune, and its removal only ever being carried out as a ritual.

Some Gypsies have been rather preoccupied with cleanliness, which has been attributed to high standards of hygiene, but this is, in fact, a corruption of the old way when washing was a means of washing away magical impurities.

For instance, Gypsies' modern habits of using several different bowls for washing have their roots in fears of magical cross-contamination, where bad luck will be passed on through the flow of water. Several washing bowls will be designated for different purposes, i.e. clothes can never be washed in a bowl that is normally used for washing dishes, and a man's clothes and a woman's clothes have to be washed in separate bowls. Children, who are considered to be naturally pure and therefore incapable of passing on bad luck, can have their clothes washed in anyone's bowl.

For the Gypsies, magic has always been far more important than 'dirt' and dust; bad magic alone provides the greatest obstacle to sacred living.

Contact with *gaujos* has often been considered to leave a Gypsy in a *mokado*, or unclean, state of mind. (Interestingly, the word 'mokkers', as in 'to put the mokkers on something' comes from the word *mokado*.) But death, and its *mokado* effects, has always been given special attention in Romani lore, for there are no compromises when your time comes. You may walk about in your physical life dragging your soul and your past behind you, but at death you must relinquish all, particularly if you wish to become a wise and respected ancestor – and most Romanies prefer this option, as their fear of the *Mulo* is so great. The borrowing principle – accepting something and being able to let it go when nature demands – holds true once again.

There is no doubt that Jack Lee knew all this, but he was only too aware that the old traditions were rapidly being devalued as *gaujo* magic was becoming stronger. Most other Gypsies were experiencing the same discomforts. For instance, although many were still practising the death ritual, which requires the deceased's belongings to be burned, buried or destroyed, it was humiliating for Gypsies to have the great ritual blaze of a flaming tent or wagon brought under control by concerned firefighters! With fewer places than ever in which to conduct this old ritual, loved ones risked suffering the horrors of not having their needs met at death and were therefore susceptible to the *Mulo*.

Such fears caused Romani families a good deal of anxiety, which many ordinary people failed to understand. The death ritual itself would, of course, have been much simpler in earlier times when Gypsies moved about with fewer possessions. The decorative wagons, or classic Gypsy caravans, first used in the early nineteenth century - which are the inspiration behind the holiday caravans we have today - and then the motor-drawn trailers brought Gypsies more fully into the civilized world, but they also brought space for storage which meant an inevitable increase in possessions. Understandably, the fewer the possessions, the less one needs to relinquish when departing from this world.

Many resisted the horse-drawn wagon at first, as they did the motor-drawn trailer which took its place, preferring to stick with the prehistoric bender, which had after all served them and other Asian and European nomads for thousands of years. The decorative wagon was in fact favoured mostly in Britain, the patterning becoming very dense and colourful as a means of preventing bad luck filtering through to the inhabitants within, such as in the winding vines which were painted on most wagons, symbolizing continuous uninterrupted flowing life. In Europe the wagons remained plain and some Gypsies there were inclined to live sedentary rather than nomadic lives.

I believe that the era of the wagon was detrimental for the Romanies' spiritual lives, particularly at death, as possessions were being passed on in the *gaujo* manner rather than being destroyed, which also meant that the old nomadic values of letting go were not properly adhered to and souls were becoming lost. Ownership was taking over in a very big way.

There is far greater meaning in burning elements of the natural world, a few hazel rods and animal pelts or blankets, rather than 1,001 man-made or

factory-produced items which make up an individual's personal world. In fact, I don't believe it is
possible to practise the old death ritual in the modern
world with so many accumulated possessions. It is
better by far to set aside a few treasured personal
items which must be destroyed and which will represent the sum total of the image of your physical self
which you will need to let go of; that is, after all, what
the death ritual is all about. Needless to add, I have
one or two personal items of my own which must be
destroyed when I reach the end of my life. One's personal drinking cup is usually among these. But it can
be a rather strange request to leave in one's will!

My great-grandfather practised old ways belonging to
an era which preceded the classic Gypsy wagon, an
era when clans travelled on foot with horses, donkeys,
benders and an awareness of the borrowing principle
and the ancient ancestral world. This, to me, is the
*tacho Romani drom*, the true Romani way, as it should
be followed. I have known many an individual who
has wished to emulate the Gypsy lifestyle by acquir-
ing a piebald horse and decorative wagon and taking
to the road, but these things will no more make you
a Romani Gypsy than putting on a white coat will
make you a doctor.

When Jack Lee passed away, the *Puri Dai* sadly carried out her own ritual. She made a fire in her back
garden and stood with a few close relations burning
some of his things. She thought it a very unfitting end
to a man who was well loved and who was a great
*Chovihano* of the old kind.

Once the death ritual is over, the protective fires have been lit during the all-night vigil when the body is watched over, a rite which is linked to the Irish 'wake', and the body has finally been burned or buried, there are other customs to observe, such as not using the name of the departed one. This can last anything from a few months to a few years. If your name happens to be the same as that of the deceased, you might well be expected to change it! This practice is not uncommon in other tribal societies, so important has it been to give the dead a clear road home. The spirits of the dead should remain in the next world and their bodies in their graves, and nothing should be done to encourage them to return. Similarly, for a short period following a death Romanies might well avoid food enjoyed by the departed one. Many Gypsies planted thorn bushes on graves - a deterrent for any restless soul who might favour resurrection! Flowers may not always be chosen for graves, as they contain a special power and must not be abused, being governed by the all-powerful fairy people.

Although the departed are encouraged to remain in the Otherworld, it has been common for *Chovihanos* to communicate with them, either guiding the 'lost' back to their rightful home or acting as a spokesperson for the ancestral world. Certainly my great-grandfather spent a good deal of time communicating with the dead, for there seemed to be many who had become lost and were wandering about this world aimlessly. But he also regularly communicated with the Ancestor, the man I had been privileged to become acquainted with in the autumn wood in my teenage years and whom I communicate with regularly today.

The Gypsies' ability to communicate in many ways with their dead was recorded by the old chroniclers, who described the craft as 'ventriloquism'. This was the art of producing spirit voices, or more aptly, a state of trance. It was associated with sorcery and has also been known as necromancy. But most Gypsies are not embarrassed to talk openly, alone, to their departed ones at the graveside, as that is where they consider such communication should take place. I have vivid memories of my grandmother talking to her husband quite as if his soul had melted into the gravestone itself, which has grounding, for the Gypsies believe stones to have great power, the stones of ancient circles being called *rakerimasko bara*, or talking stones. The stone helps the soul travel up or down into the Earth - as stones may well have done in ancient times - and provides a medium for regular contact. Needless to add, Romanies would be especially careful when meeting an ancient circle of stones, ensuring that they gave the stones their utmost respect, because those stones might contain the souls of many who have passed down into the Earth through the ages.

The *Chovihano* is trained to know good spirits from bad spirits and in my work as a Gypsy healer I have laid many ghosts to rest, escorting the departed to places which are often referred to, collectively, as 'the other side'. This is a place which some tend to speak about with great geographical exactness, when it is rather a state of mind, a place, I believe, which has been created out of modern perceptions of death, which I will explain more fully later. But I also see the post-death world as many worlds. There is always a world within a world within a world,' the Ancestor has told me and it is always as well to remember that whatever world we believe exists always provides a gateway for another.

I believe that there was a time on Earth when death was as important as life, when we didn't choose to ignore it until it was staring us hard in the face. I believe life and death were once both intertwined, for many ancient cultures. This is expressed in the Romani word *meriben*, which means 'life', but also 'death', and 'existence' and 'soul' as well. Perhaps this also illustrates just how much language can play a part in preserving our spiritual lives, for too many words can take the simplicity out of something sacred and can water it down considerably. Thus, if I say the word *meriben* to myself, it has the power to conjure up many sacred elements within life and death, preserving meaning, but in the English language, the words 'life', 'death', 'existence' and 'soul' can mean so many things they invariably need other words to clarify their meaning.

But being born into the flesh is quite frequently as important as departing from it within Romani lore and there are many customs for an expectant couple to observe during pregnancy and birth, and even during courtship and marriage. Adhering to these customs ensures a smooth passage through life for all concerned.

When my parents decided to marry they eloped - with parental approval. This was normal. A couple runs away and returns again and nobody minds - for what purpose I do not exactly know, except perhaps to strengthen a sense of responsibility between the two people concerned. After all, they have to live with one another, so it is quite likely a dress rehearsal for survival in a sometimes anti-Gypsy society.

A couple may marry in church but will usually carry out their own ceremony, Romani-style. Few in the past have taken the Christian wedding seriously. In fact, just as you are not considered to be properly dead unless you have observed the old customs, so are you not considered to be properly married unless you have conducted your own special intimate ceremony, which can be as simple as holding hands and swearing to love each other. This is enough to seal a bond between two Romani Gypsies. Marrying in a Christian church, like burial in a Christian graveyard, has merely served to reinforce the Gypsies' 'standing' in the *gaujo* community.

To this day my mother looks back on her church wedding with great amusement, often recalling the ceremony as one might recall a trip to the circus. She has spoken in the past like an excitable child of the way she continuously giggled as the minister wrapped up her hands and those of my father in a cloth whilst speaking his 'important words', and how the name 'Rosalind' instead of 'Rosaline' was put on the marriage certificate, meaning, she believes, that she and my father were probably not legally married after all! This, to her, merely demonstrated the futility of religious custom.

With more relaxed attitudes concerning marriage in modern times the official religious seal is no longer so necessary. Lizzie, my partner, and I carried out our own ceremony, and my *Puri Dai* always said that if you cannot express your own affections for each other and mean it, how will a minister or registrar be able to do it for you? With today's divorce rates, I think she had a point. Marriage or a close relationship is more likely to work in a community which attaches no rosy stories to what is otherwise a very serious pact between two people who are choosing to live together. Romanies are told that life together will be tough and are encouraged to enter the relationship with their eyes open. But they also observe the happy side and always know how to celebrate weddings and other special occasions.

If a couple decide to end a marriage, they simply announce their intention to live apart and both are free to marry others. Some Romanies were appalled to discover that *gaujo* divorce involved a little more than a simple announcement to live apart, and where divorce laws were deemed to have no value there were a few cases of bigamy.

In North Wales, where my great-grandfather's family lived, Romanies jumped over the broom to marry. This may well have been a Welsh custom before becoming a Gypsy custom. The ritual for the Gypsies involved laying a branch of flowering broom on the ground with the bride and groom leaping over it whilst holding hands. If their clothes didn't touch the broom it was considered lucky. If flowering broom wasn't available, then a broom handle would suffice. All heathland plants were respected by Romani Gypsies and brought good luck, with heather perhaps being the best known for this. Divorce for Welsh Gypsies simply entailed jumping backwards over the broom. Both parties were then free to marry others.

Where there was unfaithfulness, however, things could be very different. Women who took lovers might well have a slit cut into their ears by the elders of their clan. Wives might be returned to their own clan in disgrace and given no mercy.

As punishment for infidelity was more severe for a woman than for a man, we may naturally assume that Gypsy laws are chauvinistic and very one-sided, but if we examine the magical implications of these laws, we see a very different picture. My grandmother said that contrary to what many believe, many women took lovers deliberately, holding power over their men in a magical way, because Gypsy women possessed a unique magic since very early times, and most of their men knew it. People to whom magical power is absolute can easily be reduced to quivering wrecks if they believe that some unseen force has a hold on them and a Gypsy woman only had to brush a man lightly with her skirt in a certain fashion to wield power over him and make him unclean. An unfaithful husband, therefore, could fear all manner of disasters crossing his path should his wife give him that fateful swish with her clothes.

My own father once had a brief affair with a woman behind my mother's back. He was good-humoured, had a good helping of Gypsy charm and inevitably attracted the women. Once my mother found out about the affair, she tormented him in the old way, largely by making him believe that nothing would go right for him ever again. He was always nervous if ever the subject was brought up in conversation, which my mother saw fit to do on a regular basis. His fears focused around what she had the power to do, if she chose to, rather than what she was actually doing. This was woman's power in Gypsy society. It cut deep and must have caused many Gypsy males in the past to look upon even the briefest affair as a very regrettable incident.

Gypsy women were considered to be as delicate, mysterious and as powerful as *Shon*, the moon, who is, after all, the original mother of the Gypsy race. She has passed her ways down through the generations and both the moon and a menstruating woman carry great power. So the powerful Gypsy woman could render people and things *mokado*, particularly around menstruation times. When a girl reached puberty, her powers became strong and didn't lessen until after the menopause.

In earlier days menstruating women often wore a *mokado poktan*, menstruation smock, to let others know that they were menstruating. Menstrual blood itself always carried great power and some women used their own blood as an ingredient in spells and recipes when wishing to attract a man. A man who unknowingly ate a cake containing a woman's menstrual blood would be loyal to that woman forever.

My mother was always very open about her menstrual cycle and always informed the family when she was menstruating. This is because women usually refrain from touching certain foods, particularly meat, during menstruation times, purely because of their increased power. My mother never wore a *mokado poktan*, as this would have been considered old-fashioned, but her openness certainly encouraged the males in the family to respect and understand women's ways a little more.

A man was always protected by fire, but if a woman passed between him and the flames of a fire her shadow might magically attack him. A woman who stepped over drinking water in a stream had enough power to stop a man from drinking from that stream, even if he was dying of thirst. And if a woman wanted to prevent a man from enjoying his dinner she only had to step over his plate and he would invariably throw the whole lot away.

Many of these customs still prevailed in my own family when I was young but were never carried to an extreme; they were in fact sometimes practised with an air of fun. Some do believe Gypsy women to have had a bad deal, but there is probably far more respect for women in Gypsy society than in *gaujo* society in general. In my own community, wife battering was unheard of, as was child abuse.

A Gypsy woman might either use or just assume magical power where men were concerned. When a female cousin of mine married, for instance, she announced openly on her wedding day that she had a date with someone else on the following evening. She was addressing the females in the party at the time, but word naturally filtered through to the males, including her husband to be, probably deliberately so. I doubt if she ever kept her engagement, or even if the meeting was ever due to take place at all. It was merely her way of flaunting her feminine power and getting off on the right foot in the marriage.

It is only in modern times that I dare speak openly about the power of Gypsy women. In my own life-time such silent power has been strong, and is never questioned, even by the *Chovihanos*, who never inter-fere with domestic affairs unless invited to. I have heard it said many times that Romani Gypsy fami-lies are male-dominated, but this has not been my own experience. A Gypsy male knows his place when in the presence of a Gypsy woman - particularly if she happens to be a *Puri Dai*. Similarly, women do not interfere with men's affairs. The males usually strike up the business deals in the tribes and are con-sidered to know what they are doing. However, they will invariably seek matriarchal approval if any major decisions are to be made, or at least an agreeable nod from the *Puri Dai*. It was not uncommon for me to see my own *Puri Dai* occasionally cuffing the ears of her menfolk - including her own husband when she thought he was not behaving in the appropriate manner! The *Puri Dai* is, without doubt, the most wise and revered person in any Gypsy clan, and is rarely crossed.

As an illustration of this, a friend of mine visited a Gypsy encampment some years ago and was shown around by the resident *Puri Dai*, who also happened to be a member of the Lee or *Purrum* clan. She was proud to show off the inside of the wagons, in one of which was her son, busy having a shave. The power of the *Puri Dai* is absolute, so her son did not question being pulled out of the wagon, his face covered in foam, to wait for an age while his mother and her visitors continued their tour.

In another instance a Lee male was mending the roof of his wagon when he accidentally fell off, which, true to the spirit of a Lee male, resulted in hysterical fits of laughter as he lay on the ground - fortunately he hadn't hurt himself - but only his wife could put an end to his frivolity, by clouting him on the head!

Lee women are usually small but fierce. But although my grandmother had a strong warlike side to her nature, she was also extremely gentle and caring towards her brood. I still miss her dreadfully. A Gypsy child, particularly a potential healer, is often closer to grandparents and great-grandparents than parents.

We are all familiar with the stereotype Gypsy female, the Carmen-like figure who will always play with men's affections, and there has always been a strong sensuality deep in the Romani Gypsy spirit, which I believe is related to distant tantric ways back in India. I certainly believe this natural sensuality has contributed to the romantic picture we have built of the Romani Gypsy in more modern times. Female Gypsy dancers, such as Spanish Flamenco dancers, can be very openly provocative, and young Gypsy women commonly flaunt their 'come and get me' message to both Gypsy and *gaujo* alike, but the provocation usually starts and ends there. Their open sensuality has long caused people to believe they are free and easy with their affections, but we Romanies have always said that the female spirit is very sensuous and flirtatious in her nature. The provocative woman, the provocative moon, the provocative Earth - it is a spiritual matter rather than a purely physical matter and Gypsy women have long allowed the essence of all that is naturally sensuous in the spirit to shine through. Romani males usually understand this; unfortunately *gaujo* males merely see women whom they think will be an easy catch.

The power of the Gypsy woman naturally extended in a big way to the female *Chovihani*, who already had a head start in magic just by being born a girl.

It is not difficult to imagine how powerful Gypsy women could be when gathered together. In some cases, power was increased when two women took one husband. I put it this way round because it is more common to say that one man has two wives and to assume that the man must inevitably be in the more powerful position. This was not quite the case in Gypsy society. Any man who married two Gypsy women was considered to be courageous indeed, for he was taking on a double helping of magical power! Although polygamy has never been common in modern Gypsy society, it was practised up until the Edwardian era by some tribes.

At the beginning of the twentieth century unfaithfulness in couples increased when artists and intellectuals like Augustus John made a fashion out of emulating the Romani Gypsy lifestyle. In turn, many Gypsies emulated the lifestyle of these influential members of high society and began keeping lovers - and sometimes wives - in many parts of the world and abandoning the old ways which dictated that the sexual act was also a sacred act. In the hills of North Wales Gypsy males who had been isolated from Western civilization for so long and who were ordinarily deeply respectful of their women were suddenly taking off and developing carefree relationships with *gaujo* women. The modern romantic idea of the Gypsy male had truly been born, a role many Gypsy males played out with ease, because of their charming, artistic and somewhat intelligent characters. This image of a mysterious and aloof lover who hadn't a care in the world was attractive to many upper and middle-class women, but it was also an image which would eventually contribute to the splitting of many families in Gypsy society, though many Gypsy males simply preferred not to talk about their sojourns away from their families, Jack Lee being one of them.

A Gypsy woman's power was also evident at the time of giving birth. In earlier times she would have had a special tent erected for her where she could give birth away from the rest of the tribe. Surrounded by lucky charms, such as bits of gold and silver and perhaps particular stones or leaves she might have picked up along her path, and protective herbs, such as rosemary, mugwort and garlic, and also effigies, perhaps little animals or people representing protective guardian ancestors, she would manage her own power within the tent, while a fire was kept burning outside as protection for everyone else.

As soon as mother and child were up and about, the tent and all its bedding would be burned to ensure that no strong magic filtered through to the rest of the clan. Mother and child were so powerful just after a birth that not even the child's father would risk venturing into the tent. If he did, others might well avoid him, for he could pass on his *mokado* state.

Women and newborns could cause those around them to become magically vulnerable because the child was considered to have only just stepped out of the Otherworld; in fact, the baby could very well still be attached to it. A door was open to the Otherworld whether you were going into it, as in death, or coming out of it, as in birth. The Romanies considered the Otherworld to be the most powerful place of all and it therefore always deserved the greatest respect.

Certainly, my own birth was watched somewhat cautiously, as Jack Lee foretold that a child would come into the family who would carry on our traditions, and my grandfather, Gladdy Lee's husband, therefore took it upon himself to ensure that my mother wanted for nothing while she was pregnant with me, not only because she needed looking after at such a delicate time, but also to ensure that the spirits of both mother and child were appeased. My mother has told me how he carried this to an extreme, often nervously jumping to attention whilst in her presence and sometimes holding up traffic whenever she crossed the road - which she found extremely embarrassing.

Despite this, nobody seemed very certain that I would be eligible material for the role of *Chovihano*. I was born with a twisted arm and hand, which everyone thought would be a deformity, until it righted itself. This was the first sign that I was able to use a power to put things right and, coupled by the unusual characteristics I displayed as a toddler, it sealed my fate.

My grandmother, ever a follower of the old ways, gave birth to her children more or less on her own, resisting medical attention. My mother, who allowed medical attention at the birth of her children, admired my grandmother's strength and loyalty to the old spirit.

In fifteenth-century Europe a Gypsy woman is recorded to have given birth to a child in the middle of a market-place and then remained there for three days - a magical number for the Gypsies - before she rejoined her clan. Being surrounded by the *gaujo* community at this delicate time would not have troubled her, for it used to be said that if you passed bad luck to *gaujos* it was not as bad as passing it to your own kind! This is because Romanies perceive all people as belonging to separate tribes, each tribe having a basic need to preserve its separate identity - a primitive idea, but one that has moved with the Gypsies into the twentieth century. So a Gypsy would have looked upon *gaujos* as one might look upon a different species.

I have given a good deal of thought to this subject, which links with the caste system in India, and which, in its roots, also links human instinct with basic animal instinct: i.e., we all stick to our own kind, get on with our own business and leave everyone else to get on with theirs. This instinct works in accordance with natural law, where no one species is higher or lower than another, all just existing alongside each other.

Of course, this instinct is no longer honoured in India, nor anywhere else in the modern world. A 'class system', to both strong and mild degrees, has now ousted the old tribal animal instinct in more civilized communities. Such an instinct is still very much acknowledged in the animal world, however, as you may put many species of animal in a field together, or many species of bird in a cage, but each separate species will stick to its own kind.

Romani Gypsies have long had a reputation for simply ignoring the *gaujo* population around them in a very animal-like way and sticking to their own kind, which brings to mind quite vividly something Jack Lee told my grandmother many years ago - that it can be bad luck for one species of animal to interfere or interbreed with another. He maintained that animals saw it that way, too, and that was why they always left each other alone. There are doubtless scientific reasons behind this instinct. But it is obviously a natural law which the Romani Gypsies honoured through their generations.

On a deeper level, marriage and birth for the Gypsies re-enact a powerful drama set in the sky hundreds of years ago when *Kam*, the sun, mated with *Shon*, the moon, something which I believe to have been an eclipse. Whether this occurred when the Gypsies first came out of India, when tribes first interbred, or even hundreds of years before this, I do not know.

Romani Gypsies describe an eclipse as 'the moon blackened the sun' and in these words I also hear the Gypsy male saying, 'My wife made me *mokado*. She put her powerful shadow over me.' The moon would doubtless say that the sun should have taken care when chasing her in the sky!

An eclipse is clearly a time when primitive people see all things on Earth as being extremely vulnerable to great magic, and *Shon* was seen to have practised her great magic on *Kam*, her brother, and given birth to a whole new race of people who were destined to travel the world as no other nomads had, perhaps enacting this incestuous drama over and over again with every Gypsy marriage.

If you grow up with such strong primitive customs dominating your daily life these naturally colour your thinking. As a teenager, my 'different' views caused a few bumps and bruises along my path on social occasions.

When young, my sojourns into the *gaujo* world were few and far between, and the ways of men and women were therefore often strange to me. As an older teenager I found myself exposed to a new set of rules which tended to highlight my ignorance regarding social interaction. I found myself confronting unspoken laws and, for want of a better term, 'rituals', which were sometimes alien to me. It had been instilled in me never to let down my shields too eagerly in the presence of *gaujos*, otherwise they could plot and scheme and deceive, and if they got to know you were Gypsy, you would become vulnerable to their magic - which wasn't considered to be too healthy! They were considered to be somewhat 'out of control' and even 'out of touch' with their understanding of magic, so they could therefore weave spells and not know they were doing it.

Although the subject of food is never an issue for Romani Gypsies, in my earlier years it could well have appeared to be a problem. A friend and I were musicians and had formed a band together with others, but I was reminded by my elders that, nice as these *gaujos* were, they were *gaujos* none the less and that I should take special care that their 'unhealthy' magic didn't influence me - particularly at the table! So on each occasion that I was invited to dinner at my friend's house I was under strict instructions not to eat the food provided and always arrived with a can of soup which my mother had packed up for me. I would sit in embarrassment eating the soup, while others around me partook of the delicious home-made meal that my friend's mother had prepared for them. Never did this friendly woman tire of trying to entice me to eat what she had made and never could I tell her why I wasn't able to eat it. No one present even knew I was a Romani Gypsy at that time and I did not dare mention the fact, as I naturally feared the worst.

Fortunately, my friend's mother was a very far-sighted and persistent lady who eventually became one of my dearest and closest friends, and I am always grateful to her for her patience and for introducing me to the ways of the world outside.

The Romanies can be fussy about their food, not because they are conscious of good health, but because food, like everything else, has magical properties and when it is eaten you either become what it is or may be influenced by the magic of the person who prepared it. This was so deeply ingrained in me that I was able to introduce aspects of this very old way of dealing with food into my healing retreats some years ago, which proved to have very beneficial effects.

Some Gypsy habits with food die hard, though. When my mother and grandmother were on the road they carried evaporated milk with them for their tea, both because they could not always find fresh milk and because they considered it to be a treat. To this day my mother still thinks it a treat to drink evaporated milk in her tea, but she also believes it is a treat for everyone else! Many of my friends have had to suffer her 'rich' cups of tea and she never seems to understand that some people have no taste for it.

Some foods not only choose to be with you but also talk to you - which I will deal with more fully in another chapter. Often when I invite someone to dinner I will automatically prepare something which I feel will be relevant to that person, for food symbolizes elements within nature which we need for our inner well-being. At least that is the way I have been encouraged to look at food.

The magical potential of food can also be enhanced by numbers. In fact the number of vegetables in a meal may often be as important as the type of vegetable. The counting also extends to serving food. I frequently infuriate my partner by counting when I am spooning out soup - which she would favour pouring - and she waits patiently while I count out an uneven number of servings with the spoon: first five, then seven, then three and five again. This is behaviour which some would doubtless consider to be 'obsessional'. But I am counting because the numbers can form a lucky combination and such luck will pass into the soup when we eat it. Forget to count out those lucky combinations and you could find that luck will forget you!

Stews, broths, rabbit, hare, deer, 'tickled' trout and in earlier times wild boar would often have been on the Gypsies' menu, mostly cooked over the fire. Many people know of the Gypsies' preference for *hotchi-witchi*, or hedgehog, baked in clay. Some indeed prepared this special delicacy that way, but the method of cooking would usually depend upon the area a band of Gypsies happened to be in. After all, you couldn't bake food in clay if there was no clay to be found. But all food took a long time to prepare, however it was cooked, because Gypsies were dependent upon natural means for cooking it, and it always had to be eaten in daylight. My grandmother told me that on the road you needed to prepare your meals well in advance of darkness, not only because otherwise you would not be able to see what you were eating, but also because you never actually knew what magic might attack your plate if you couldn't see it! Such rules could be as important as basic table manners at Romani Gypsy mealtimes.

Gypsies ate certain foods sometimes just to be able to wear, use or carry the skins, teeth, claws and seeds of those foods, or the fellow beings they had hunted, so that they would take on aspects of what had been absorbed. The word 'health' rarely came into the picture, yet Romanies have usually been healthy enough and many have lived to a great age.

The hunting skills were developed over thousands of years and invariably involved a deep respect for the animal concerned. 'Hare-charming' was something my great-grandfather practised regularly. This involves mesmerizing the animal so that she is completely enchanted by you. Whistling or singing to a hare will captivate her if it is done in the old caring, sensitive way. Gypsies of old would slowly encircle a hare for a very long time, gaining her confidence before finishing up right beside her and maybe gently tossing a coat over her head.

Similarly, not so long ago Gypsies would wait patiently for hours outside rabbit holes for rabbits to appear. If you sit there long enough you become part of the surroundings and rabbits will ignore you - far better than giving chase or shooting or trapping them.

Invariably, animals who were hunted came to a Gypsy, rather than the other way about. Perhaps that is hunting in its most natural form, for there is an easy rhythm about it all and the animal is at liberty to choose his own destiny. But it always means that a lot of patience has to be exercised on the part of the hunter.

Gypsies believed that whatever was on your path was volunteering to give something of itself to you, and that included food. If an animal didn't appear and you went hungry, it was a matter of fate, the animal's choice not to be there at that particular time.

If anything in the area of food was to be avoided it was unweaned animals and animals who had died a natural death. This also had to do with magic. Unweaned animals, to the Romani, are as magically powerful as human babies, because they too are close to the Otherworld. And animals who have died a natural death might well have been contaminated with the *bengesko yak*, or *evil eye*, and could therefore render you *mokado*. The *Mulo* and bad magic could lurk in the most unlikely places. If you hunted and killed the animal yourself, you were more likely to know that the meat was 'clean'.

In fact there is no word for 'animal' as such in Romanes. Animals are creatures of the Earth, like ourselves, and all are addressed by whatever species they happen to be. This is perhaps a more respectful way of viewing the fellow creatures who share our Earth. Many animals are given names which simply describe what they are, such as *rukengro*, or squirrel, which means 'tree fellow', and *puvengro*, or mole, which means 'earth fellow' – but there again, *puvengro* is also used for 'potato'!

The Romani Gypsies have always been big meat-eaters, for many reasons. Among other things, meat is a nourishing way of sustaining yourself, particularly when you may be forced to live for a number of days on what you find. Hunting is never easy on land that is 'owned' and Gypsies therefore developed stealth when looking for food. Watching and listening in hunting became as important an accompaniment as the knife you might take with you to kill your prey. Interestingly, some Gypsies called a pocket a *poachy*, which perhaps speaks for itself.

Some Romani words have been swallowed up by the English language, just as many English words have been swallowed up by the Romani language. But some Romani words can be helpful in highlighting certain meanings for us in our own language. *Dosh* is one such word, the word some of us may use as slang for 'money'. When Romanies could no longer hunt because there was no free land left to hunt on, they were forced to buy their food. Interestingly, *dosh* in Romanes means 'harm' or 'evil', stemming from the Sanskrit *dush*, 'bad'. There is no doubt that some of us see money as being the root of all evil. And when we use the phrase, 'What's the damage?' when asking for a bill, we may see a connection. My grandmother always used to say that a caught fish was always luckier than a bought fish!

Romanies were always fiercely protective of their own language in earlier days. It was a language spoken not only in Europe, Asia and its native India, but in Australia, America and Canada as well once Romani Gypsies travelled further afield. Gypsies who had been in the Welsh hills since the seventeenth century managed to preserve this native tongue for an astonishingly long time, but in other areas of Britain it soon became diluted as Gypsy and *gaujo* merged, culminating in a somewhat comical version of the original.

Gypsies today will still at times use words picked up by their ancestors in places like old Persia some 900 years ago, *Chovihano*, meaning 'witch, sorcerer, magician, shaman', is the best example and also stresses the importance of shamanic practice to the Gypsies whilst travelling through that country. In England it was once thought that Romanes was an 'invented' language, enabling Gypsies to speak to each other in code. However, a great many words have passed into English as slang, *pal*, meaning 'brother', being one such example. The word has its roots in the Sanskrit *bhratr*, stemming from the Proto-Indo-European word *bhratar*, from which English also gets 'brother'. The old Romani word for 'brother', *prala* , was a step on the way from *bhratr* to 'pal', the latter being used so frequently that *gaujos* adopted it, giving it the meaning 'friend'. This is because anyone who becomes a good friend to a Gypsy automatically becomes a brother, and the same is true of 'sister', *pen*.

Another Romani word frequently used as slang is *posh*, which in Romanes means 'half'. A Gypsy might be *posh*, or a *posh rat*, if the product of a Gypsy/*gaujo* partnership. *Posh rat* may appear to be describing a toffee-nosed rodent, though it is pronounced more as 'pahsh raht', but actually means 'half-breed'. Some Gypsies would sneer at their half-breed cousins for being the offspring of someone who had become a member of a society which refused to live in the old proper manner and it didn't take long for *posh* to be absorbed into the English vocabulary as slang to describe anyone who assumed airs and graces because they thought they had more than anyone else, particularly with regard to owning rather than borrowing. There are other theories behind the word 'posh', but I think the Gypsy theory is significant.

Most are of course familiar with the word *diddikai* and many people ask me to clarify what this word actually means. If *posh rat* is a half-breed, a *diddikai* has only a small amount of *kalo rat*, or black Gypsy blood. The older Romani Gypsies would say they were 'black' if they were true Gypsy. My mother used to tell me I was behaving in a *kalo*, or black, manner if I was being very Romani in my behaviour. The word *kalo* is of course connected with Kali, the female Hindu goddess.

The old Romani Gypsy language was spoken almost musically and the language would therefore have best been preserved in Wales where the accent is naturally lilting. Most Gypsies in earlier times would undoubtedly have spoken with an Indian accent, and if one thinks of the Indian accent and the Welsh accent, it is possible to hear a similarity, particularly in pitch, resulting in a rich sing-song effect. For those Gypsies who settled in England and who adopted some of the many English accents, there resulted a more comical sound to some of the words, purely because of different tensions. Those who can speak with an Indian accent will probably be best suited to speaking Romanes in the old way!

But curiously, the old Romani language has also helped to preserve some old English words which are no longer used, something I only discovered more recently when looking through some of the words recorded by John Sampson in the early twentieth century and collected in his *Dialect of the Gypsies of North Wales*. There I discovered the word *houfe*, an old English word meaning 'cap' or 'bonnet'. The Romani word for this is *hufa*, which I immediately recognized, for at home we always used the word when our cats rubbed their heads against us in affection. My grandmother always told us that when the cats were *huffing* us they were giving us their bonnets! I still use this word to this day and my partner has now become so familiar with it that she now refers to cats as 'huffkins'!

Another old English word was 'urchin', which was always used for 'hedgehog'. This word, now associated with scruffy, unkempt little children, was retained by the Gypsies, who once called the hedgehog *urchos*. I believe that the name 'urchin' was transferred to scruffy children because of the Romani Gypsy children, who were not only scruffy, but also ate 'urchins'! This is perhaps an example of the way Romanies preserve things, words just constituting one small area.

I still conduct my rituals in Romanes today, because I believe it gives a ritual far more power and purpose, and I still hear my *boro dad's* musical voice and my *Puri Dai's* sometimes squeaky voice speaking in the old tongue. I believe that by continuing to use the old language in the old way I help to evoke the spirits of old, who still live beyond the hedgerows, in that special secret magical place where all old Romani souls still dwell.

# 5

## THE WHISPERING FOREST
## THE ROMANI WORLD OF WOODLAND MAGIC AND FAIRIES

My experience in the red-gold wood was only the beginning of a long and exciting relationship with trees and the magical elements within the natural world which I had been taught to use in a respectful way. But the more I journeyed into *gaujo* society, the more I was to discover just how much people tended to separate themselves from nature, preferring to see the splendours of Earth as something to be explored

## as a leisurely pastime rather than a backdrop for all our experiences.

Our history books, in fact, do not always give us an accurate picture of life in our British woodlands in days gone by. Rarely do they mention the ribbons of smoke curling up from clusters of wagons or bender tents, seen from nearby lanes or roads by passers by, and rarely do they mention how the wild woodland people were frequently consulted for any number of medicinal and magical cures. One is usually reduced to seeking out more obscure reference sources in order to discover such information.

A Gypsy healer of 200 years ago might have been one of three very different people: a *Patrinyengri*, a herbalist; a *Drabengro*, which accurately translated means 'man of poison'; or a *Chovihano*, the tribe's shamanic trance healer, who was usually concerned with the Otherworld life of the patient.

The *Patrinyengri* and *Drabengro* could often work alongside the *Chovihano*, depending upon the kind of healing required, but all three had a special and unique relationship with the forest, which was ulti-mately governed by the formidable *Biti Foki*, the fairy people. Any plant removed from the forest or anywhere on the ground usually demanded a sacri-fice of some kind on the part of the healer, some-thing that could be offered to the plant and also something that could be offered to the *Biti Foki*. The *Chovihano* was perhaps the best equipped for making these offerings as he had undergone initiations with the *Biti Foki* down in the Underworld and knew the way they tended to think and behave. He might even know the *Biti Foki* personally, in any of the areas he camped in. But anyone seeking out a plant for medicinal or magical use was wise to make an offering of some kind. This was, after all, a polite thing to do and would preserve good relations with the natural world. This is no different from doing good deeds for family, friends and neighbours. It is a politeness which we have sadly forgotten in our modern times when we rip plants from the ground without a thought for their feelings. In the past it was unthinkable to expect an aspect of nature to do a good deed for you if you were not giving something back in return.

Milk was sometimes offered to the *Biti Foki* when it was available, or a favourite piece of food would be given. The Romanies often gave offerings of beer, mostly because they enjoyed beer themselves. My grandmother told me of a Romani *Chovihano* who was criticized by *gaujos* for wasting beer, because having been given some by them he promptly took it into the wood and gave most of it to the *Biti Foki*! Doubtless, it was believed that he was just throwing the beer away. But such is the *Chovihano's* devotion to the Otherworld and the woodlands.

The *Patrinyengri - Patrinyengro* if male - was a very popular person in the Romani Gypsy tribe. This Romani herbalist was not always a woman, but many women seem to be naturally equipped as herbalists as they care and attune themselves easily to Grandmother Earth. The *Patrinyengri* was consulted regularly for all kinds of ailments, particularly if those ailments were minor. It was also common for her to work alongside the *Chovihano* during in-depth rituals if the patient's soul was at all troubled or at risk - which usually meant that there were some emotional or inner disturbances accompanying the sickness.

The *Patrinyengri* usually develops an instinctive rapport with plants as a child, rather as the young *Chovihano* develops an instinctive rapport with the Otherworld. The young *Patrinyengri* is attracted to spend time with plants, learning about their worlds, usually from an older *Patrinyengri* in the tribe, sometimes the child's mother or father, who will take the apprentice under his or her wing for a good many years.

One of the first rules the child is taught is respect for the plants. Several methods are employed as teaching aids, such as encouraging the child to converse with the plants, so that eventually he or she will get to know them on a more personal level, developing a rapport with one in particular, who may then become an adviser. This has happened with my partner, Lizzie, a *Patrinyengri*. She is not Romani by blood, but practises the craft in the old way, having developed a strong rapport with parsley, sage and rosemary plants, all of whom have very strong personalities and are aptly suited as advisers. These herbs then advise their *Patrinyengri* on how best to use other herbs for various conditions.

Alongside respect, the apprentice must also learn of the strong magic that accompanies plants and herbs. This is perhaps one of the most fundamental rules for every *Patrinyengri* to learn, because if the magical essence of a plant is not fully recognized, the healing properties are not activated and simply will not work, and this can ultimately mean a loss of power for the *Patrinyengri* concerned. This is something many people do not understand when practising herbal medicine today. Most fully expect a plant to heal them in some way, but if they have been trained to ignore its magical power - and unfortunately most people have - the plant will not give of its best, for it will feel most unloved and uncared for.

Many people might wonder why some tribal people say it is bad to use different parts of a plant rather than the whole plant itself. The only answer I can give to this is that once you attune yourself fully to what I would call 'whole-plant magic', you will never look back to doing things in the old way. Using bits of plants is not only highly disrespectful to that plant, but is also much like being on a side road to healing instead of on the main road! It is all about communication and understanding the fundamental needs of plants, much as you would understand the fundamental needs of any children or animals you care for. Many wouldn't dream of disregarding the needs of their children and animals; when using 'whole-plant magic' you are not disregarding the needs of *Puv*, the Spirit of the Earth. Does she not give to us every single day? I think it is not too much to ask of ourselves to care for her plants in the same way that she will care for us. Perhaps it is a matter of reintroducing older habits, which we all once had in earlier times, and bringing ourselves home to her laws again.

Many Romanies believe that a plant may in fact fear a human just as much as a human may fear a plant, for the magic can be very strong in either species. Jack Lee always defended plants and trees by maintaining that human magic was far more harmful than plant magic, because humans, in creating their own magic, often go against all the rules of the old natural laws, which plants will never do because they know better. Also we perhaps expect too much of a plant when we only choose to see it broken down into scientific components. I have always thought it cruel to extract and process what one needs from a plant, scientifically, whilst ignoring the powerful being that it is. It is like slicing an arm or a leg off your doctor when you ask for his or her medicine!

In past times great power was rightfully ascribed to plants, so much so that they were once revered and worshipped, and treated as gods. We perhaps still worship aspects of alternative medicine as gods when using herbal treatments, but we may sometimes be worshipping the scientific components alone. Only tap into that golden magic and you will see how a plant will not only work for you, but will work a lot more quickly, being your friend and only too pleased to help you. It is certainly a matter of talking to your plants, and also of always remembering to ask them what you require of them and thanking them for their trouble. After all, you wouldn't dream of walking into your doctor's surgery expecting medicine without bothering to thank anyone for it.

The *Patrinyengri* knows this perhaps more than anyone else. She is aptly qualified to administer herbs to sick people, for she has spent so much time living with the souls of herbs, in their world. Every *Patrinyengri* who has ever used a herbal cure has carried out a personal ritual before making up a remedy because every true Romani Gypsy knows the rewards that come from respecting nature in this way.

It is quite possible that the Romani *Patrinyengri* gave much to the image of the old witch living in her remote cottage in the forest with her herbal brews. This female figure features in many old Romani folk tales, as do her powerful herbs. She is sometimes an ethereal figure, with supernatural powers, an expression of the plant or tree itself, as she is considered to dwell within them. Most Gypsies, particularly the *Patrinyengri*, saw a need to appease the spirits contained within nature, which were sometimes referred to as 'witches', for these might otherwise escape and wreak havoc upon humans and animals. It is possible, therefore, that a 'witch', as seen by the *Patrinyengri*, was more like a member of the fairy race than a member of the human race. The image of the 'witch' and the image of the *Patrinyengri* must often have been greatly intertwined in past times.

Romani folk medicine is popular today when we are all seeking natural remedies for our ills, but there is in fact a good deal that this ancient craft has given to the remedies we already use in modern times.

Some years ago a Romani Gypsy *Patrinyengro* in my family's part of the world made up a herbal remedy for a baby who was severely distressed by a skin complaint, which we thought was eczema. The mother didn't like the ointment because it smelled and was 'a horrible dirty grey', but having known the Gypsy and his family for a long time, she trusted him and persisted with the treatment over several days, and slowly, she watched the baby's skin heal. The woman was elated and wanted to thank the Gypsy, but typically, he had disappeared. (Romanies seem to have a habit of doing that!) The local chemist, however, had discussed the ingredients with the Gypsy himself and was so impressed that he made up the ointment for others suffering from similar conditions. The Gypsy, though, was never seen in the area again.

The ointment was doubtless made up of tar from pine-tree bark - which possibly caused the strong smell - and skin-healing herbs such as marigold and chamomile. These tar-based applications were often used in cases of eczema. A cream would have been made by pulverizing the bark and heating it with fat, which turned it into an ointment. Goose or pig fat was commonly used by *Patrinyengris*, along with hedgehog fat, for mixing up these potions.

It wasn't always common for Gypsies to reveal the secrets of their remedies, but they would be inclined to do so where they had built up a trusting friendship with local *gaujos*.

The Romanies practised herbal medicine in Britain and Europe for more than 700 years and it was usual for people to ask them for cures, as their folk remedies could always be trusted, but sadly nowadays only people in their later years can remember incidents like the one above. Yet many Romani remedies are still being used today. It is only a pity that those wild people in the forests who worked so tirelessly to preserve herbalism are not always credited with the origins of this ancient healing art.

I have stressed that the magical elements within the plant are more important in Romani folk medicine than anything else, and this is true not only when ingesting herbs or plants, but also when interacting with them, as part of the cure, which is sometimes a requirement in certain conditions.

For instance in cases of toothache, the herb groundsel is dug up and has to touch the tooth a magical number of times, in this case five. The patient is then required to spit a magical number of times, in this case three. The plant is then buried again exactly where it was found and the toothache heals.

The number five in this instance relates to change and uncertainty and to working through doubts and fears about the self. If this is recognized, then the number three will provide a relevant method of sealing what has been accomplished between yourself and the plant, brought about by spitting. By burying the plant again you are returning your pain to the Earth, who will deal with it for you and turn it into something positive.

Problems like toothache can be dealt with in a great many ways by Romanies. Sometimes toothache is cured by driving a nail into a tree so that the tree takes the pain away - naturally with the tree's permission - or by chewing the foot of a *hotchiwitchi*, or hedgehog, who is considered to be a powerful animal.

But numbers, as mentioned before, play a very important part in the Romani Gypsy culture, and many people still go back to such old magical practices when they find themselves counting stairs or cracks in the pavement or in the back of their minds doing things a certain number of times to avoid bad luck.

Doing something three times is particularly lucky, but it is also a test. The old saying 'three times lucky' has great meaning. If you become aware of working with natural laws, you will find that the number three will play a prominent part in your life. For instance, something special you may be attempting to achieve might be difficult to bring about. Doing it three times can ensure that it stays with you and brings you luck in the future. Also, the Romani Gypsies would consider something worth having if it had tested you three times before it came to you! You need to have patience indeed.

Because we live in a very 'instant' world where we want everything to come to us without delay, we perhaps do not have the patience to work with the universal law of numbers any more, but this is our loss, because many of us are busy moving from one thing to another in life, without success, without waiting to see if the magic of numbers will work for us.

Number nine is probably the most testing number of all and a very protective number. If you do something nine times, you are tested to the hilt. This, to my mind, is easily explained when you think of trying to achieve something over and over again. If you are trying that hard, i.e. nine times, you deserve to win! Such is the foundation upon which spiritual initiations are laid. How keen are you to achieve what you are aiming for and to work with the greater energies around yourself to bring it about?

The *Patrinyengri* will use numbers as part of her skill. She may wave a herb over your head three times or nine times. It is important to remember that she does not just dose patients with herbal teas or herbal pills. The plants need to communicate with the patient themselves and the *Patrinyengri* will see to it that they are given every opportunity to do so.

The *Patrinyengri* is a walking encyclopaedia of herbal lore and no one in the old Gypsy tribe would suffer so long as people like her were around. Of course, the *Patrinyengri* today would have the greatest trouble procuring natural herbs along the hedgerows, simply because there are no hedgerows.

We are all fond of ingesting a natural remedy when we feel ill, but for the Romanies - the *Patrinyengri* as well as the *Chovihano* - the mere presence of a herb, part of a tree, or even a piece of food, can serve to drive an ailment away, largely because the herb, tree or food is seen as a powerful being which will therefore have some effect on the ailment and the person who is sick. This is very difficult for many of us to comprehend in a world where everything that is considered to be healing must be scientifically tested to justify its use as a medicine.

As an example of this, a lady Lizzie and I were treating had a sore throat and a suspected cold on the way. We had been educating her to understand herbs and foods as sentient beings and she had been learning to talk to them over a period of time. On this occasion we had recommended lemon, ginger, honey and some coltsfoot tea, drunk with a little whisky. The lady acquired a large lemon and some root ginger and put them in her kitchen, talking to them about her condition in the old Romani way as she went through her day. She intended to make a drink with the lemon and ginger the following evening, but by that time her throat was better, the cough had eased and it seemed that she no longer needed the medicine. She told us afterwards that she strongly felt that the spirit of the lemon and the spirit of the ginger had heard her speaking about her problems and had come to life. They seemed to understand her. It seemed that the more she believed in them as *real* beings, the better she felt.

It is always important to acknowledge the spirits of all the natural things we ingest if we want a plant's powerful magic to work for us. It is because these spirits are so very powerful that they can sometimes offer healing to us. However, some foods and herbs have lost their magic, especially when they have been picked in the wrong way, stored for too long, or else simply ignored. In such cases a *Chovihano* and *Patrinyengri* may need to work together to bring their spirits back so that they may 'live' again.

By far the best way to treat yourself with herbs is to grow them in your own garden. But make two rules: never forget that they are thinking, feeling beings who need to be talked to and respected, and never forget that they hold great magic.

In modern times, it is perhaps hard to comprehend the animist view Romani Gypsies have had of life and the universe. As already explained, we live in a world of geographical space, where a cup on a table, directly in front of us, is considered to be part of our world, while a star that is a speck in the sky, millions of miles away, is thought to have little or nothing to do with our immediate personal worlds. But the old Gypsies considered that anything you could see or hear or touch or sense or smell was without doubt contained within your own personal world, otherwise you would not be experiencing it, and everything within your own personal world must inevitably contain life and a spirit of its own. It is a sad fact that in modern times even a tree which might be directly outside our window can have little or nothing to do with our personal world. It therefore doesn't have a being or spirit of its own and therefore cannot talk. This is not so in Romani tradition. Absolutely everything you are experiencing at this moment in time is able to talk to you, wherever you are, whoever you are with!

So for the old Romani healer, life was all about seeing the world as a living, breathing, thinking, talking world, and the natural world had a lot to say and was considered to be the most important world of all. For the Romani *Chovihano* and *Patrinyengri*, life still is all about seeing all things as containing individual spirits, because there is nothing more powerful than the linking of spirits during the process of healing, whether those spirits be human, animal or plant.

The *Drabengro*, however, is a different story. This is a man - or a woman if *Drabengri* - who existed in older Gypsy tribes and who worked in a way that was vastly different from the *Chovihano* and *Patrinyengri*. The name *Drabengro* was often given to *gaujo* doctors who administered poisonous drugs, for the word, literally translated, means 'man of poison'.

In earlier times, when it was easier to bypass the law, poisoning was a means of permanently finishing someone off if you didn't think they should be around any more! And who better to acquire the poison from than a Romani Gypsy, who lived in the forest, whom nobody knew, and who had an excellent knowledge of natural poisons. You could visit him and tell him everything and your secret was safe, for he usually had little contact with *gaujos*, and little time for them.

The vengeful *gaujo* who entered the Romani encampment asking for poison to polish off a spouse would have been offered other remedies first, however, such as a spell to entice the spouse to move away or some other such magical and more humane remedy.

Romani Gypsies were not in the habit of using their
herbal knowledge for negative purposes; in fact, it is
true to say that murder has rarely been known in
their own society and Gypsies in earlier times who
might have committed such a crime would certainly
have been turned out of a tribe. To them, murder was
an entirely *gaujo* creation - they had had personal
experience of that - and it never ceased to amaze
them how *gaujos* could do such things to one another
so unselfconsciously. But it is necessary to remember
that all Gypsies in earlier times would have seen
*gaujos* as a very strange and quite unfathomable
breed, and many would have accepted that they
behaved in these peculiar ways as a normality.
However, it is interesting that the word *drabengro* was
soon being used to describe a *gaujo* doctor when
Gypsies learned that medical doctors administered
dangerous drugs to people!

Similarly, Romanies were often consulted when
farmers wanted to be rid of vermin, for Gypsies were
able to provide the relevant herbs to entice vermin
away. Interestingly, the Pied Piper of Hamelin is a
good example of this, for he used the herb valerian
to carry the rats away from the town. It has been
suggested that the Pied Piper may well have been a
Romani Gypsy, even though the story is recorded as
having taken place long before the Gypsies officially
entered Europe. Who he actually was will probably
long remain a mystery.

In earlier times, entering the forest specifically to
find Romani Gypsies was not the easiest thing to do,
for if you were not already familiar with a particular

tribe you might well need to make a few visits before even finding them. Gypsies have always been clever at being invisible and in the forest they were kings and queens of their magical domain, for they were unafraid of the evil spirits, ghosts and wild animals that the *gaujos* said lurked in the forest. Driven by their protective instincts as nature's guardians, Gypsies were, in fact, inclined to play upon this idea. There was an advantage in strengthening the ignorance that was developing about forest life - at least it kept the *gaujos* away.

A Gypsy walking in the forest, alone, between 100 and 300 years ago, would have been in a place very different from the one we might imagine him walking in today, for it would have been rich with the voices of ancestral spirits whispering in the trees, and rich in signs and omens all along the path, such as the shapes made by the branches of trees, the activities of birds and a good many other things besides. The *Chovihano* would often have walked alone, observing the signs and communing with the spirits of trees and, of course, the *Biti Foki*.

The *Biti Foki*, or fairy people, as already mentioned, are a race of beings who have long been in the Romani Gypsies' lives and from the Romanies' point of view they have long been a race of beings who have been grossly misunderstood. The two words *Biti Foki* came from the English 'small folk'. Strictly speaking, these two words give the singular and not the plural form, the plural being *Bite Foke*, but I have long used the singular spelling to describe the plural, because of the pronunciation, which is 'Bittee Fohkee'.

I have always found where the Romani language is concerned it is far easier to use phonetic spellings and I always remind students of the language that no Romani Gypsy ever wrote the grammatical language down. In eastern Europe the word *Kashali*, sometimes pronounced as 'Keshahlen' in western Europe, has been used to describe the *Biti Foki*.

For all Gypsies, though, the *Biti Foki* are really a part of the old ancestral world, for in Romani lore they have inhabited the forests since the beginning of time. It is said that in earlier times, when they were recognized as protectors of the ancient woodlands, they were able to move about the forests more visibly and freely than today. But now, like many wild animals, it has been important for their safety that they separate themselves from humans, because humans became hostile towards them, so hostile that in recent centuries it became far too dangerous for them to reveal themselves. They therefore needed to remain in a place where they knew they would be safe: deep under the ground. But it is also their deepest wish to return to us one day and again be part of our culture and society. This is how it was all explained to me in my younger days, and I fully believed what I was told, as my elders believed it all without a shadow of a doubt!

When I was small, perhaps about five years old, I had my first encounter with a member of this ancient and fascinating race of beings. He was called Tom and was really a miniature man, perhaps about a foot tall, nothing like the 'Tinkerbell' variety of fairy we are ordinarily accustomed to today, for he had no

wings and he was not a pretty-faced being at all. His
features were in fact rather heavy, more like a
grumpy old man, and he was rather thick set in build,
with a large head and face. But he was extremely
intelligent, very wise and wickedly humorous; he
could play tricks on you and he also talked a lot
– which is something I had been warned about.
Members of the *Biti Foki* clans could, in the words of
my elders, quite easily 'jaw your head off'! I can still
remember my family complaining about these little
people rather as you might complain about a gossipy
neighbour!

We perhaps need to remind ourselves today that the
fairy stereotype we might be accustomed to – the
sweet-natured, delicate and innocent little-girl being
with gossamer wings – is really a creation of the
Victorian era which had its roots in the sixteenth and
seventeenth centuries when flower fairies became
popular due to fashionable and wealthy young ladies
spending more and more time in their flower gardens. These images were possibly created to counter-
act some of the rougher, tougher versions of fairy
people who had been known in earlier times and
who were reputed to have superpowers beyond
human understanding.

Perhaps there is also a deeper social issue at work
here where the feminine image is concerned. The
innocence enforced upon women in these eras of
great social change was an attempt to curb their
Otherworldly powers, and this also extended to
fairies, who have really suffered a similar fate.
Anything which had its own mind and, moreover,

Otherworldly powers, was doomed to be tamed and spoon-fed a whole new set of rules.

I first met Tom in our local library - a most unlikely place to meet one of the fairy people! I used to go there when I was about five years old to look at the picture books, as I wasn't terribly interested in reading, and Tom would be there, usually leaning on the books or just standing somewhere near me. Although he talked a lot, I cannot remember much of what he said now, probably because I was too young, but I do remember that it was always very interesting and I returned to the library many times, really just so that I could spend time with him, as I found him a truly fascinating being.

One may wonder why he always appeared in the library and not in a more natural setting, such as a woodland area. This, as it was later explained to me, was because of what I was to become later in life. The *Biti Foki*, it seems, make it their business to get to know a *Chovihano*, just as the *Chovihano* will make it his business to get to know the *Biti Foki*, and they will do this in any way they can. If there is an opportunity for them to be listened to, they will take it.

Tom did appear in other places a little later on, particularly when I was older and undergoing some quite tough initiations along my path, but he still talked my head off, usually about how difficult it was to be a member of his grand old clan. Like the Ancestor, he inhabits a personal space, a place which has no geographical location and therefore bears no name, in the depths of the Lowerworld. Nowadays he might just appear near a clump of bushes, or near a specific tree, or perhaps a wooded stream, or even in the library when he is desperate to make contact with me. Just as the Ancestor always protects our people and the Otherworld, so Tom always protects the woodlands and forests, sometimes with a ferocity that would indeed trouble many people, which is why some Gypsies have wanted to avoid the fairy people of old. Many Gypsies have also disliked the *Biti Foki* because the appearance of these mysterious magical people usually foretells an ordeal, which will soon test your courage and endurance. There are many instances where Gypsies resisted materializations of the *Biti Foki* in the woodlands by shouting abuse or hurling stones at them - which to any passing *gaujo* seemed strange indeed if all that could be seen was an irate Gypsy shouting into thin air!

There are many Romani Gypsy stories of the trials and tribulations of the unfortunate human victims who unwittingly happen to stray into the territory of these little people. These are stories which have long been told around Romani camp-fires in the depths of forests on dark evenings and have sparked fear into the minds and hearts of the primitive Gypsy who understood only too well how dangerous and unlucky it could be to harm or injure one of these ancient people and the wild natural places they inhabited.

I have already mentioned that flowers are very much protected by the *Biti Foki*. Many Gypsies have super-stitions about bringing them inside the home and my mother had personal experience of this when she once brought some bluebells into the house and developed a severe attack of hay fever as a result - something she had never suffered before in her life. She was in no doubt that she was suffering because she had unthinkingly brought these wild flowers into the house, for wild flowers, as every Romani Gypsy will know, are very much like wild animals and also wild people - they do not warm to being suddenly captured and confined, and they will give off their bad magic instantly, rather as a skunk might give off an unpleasant odour when it believes itself to be under attack. Also, if you remove flowers from their natural places without permission, the *Biti Foki* will be especially annoyed and will see to it that you have bad luck as a result. Needless to add, my mother never brought wild flowers into the house again!

Of course, flowers can be used positively for healing if treated with respect and used in the right way. I have used flowers many times to carry away a sickness. As they die, in your house, so your sickness will die, for they will carry all that is bad away with them, but to do this successfully, it must be prearranged with the *Biti Foki*, and of course with the flowers themselves. The *Biti Foki* will, however, invariably become your friends if you have proved yourself worthy and respectful of them.

It has been said that only special people pass the test to become a *Chovihano*, for the *Biti Foki* will always ask for a great deal in return for the knowledge and protection they can give. In many Romani Gypsy stories it is common for them to ask for 'meat' when testing human beings - that is, actual flesh. This always represents facing all the things you would really prefer to avoid. It is, collectively, all the fears and dark spots within you, which you will be called upon to sacrifice for the sake of developing your ancient craft - not an easy thing to do. I have seen many walk away from the shamanic path when realizing what will be demanded of them. In my own culture, and indeed in my own experience, it is not for the faint-hearted.

But once a *Chovihano* has exhibited the courage to face his fears, the *Biti Foki* will look upon him kindly. And there is a sunny, golden, magical world deep down in the Earth where the *Biti Foki* reside, waiting for him when he has finally made the grade. The *Biti Foki* will then be his friends forever and will stand by him whatever happens. Tom has stood by me for many years and I am also extremely protective of him, for he has become a member of my shamanic family.

The life of a fairy person and the life of a tree usually go hand in hand, at least in Romani lore. Of the many trees I have developed relationships with over the years, a handful stand out as having taught me a good deal about their lives, but I have never learned anything about them without the help of a fairy person - or two.

Many people do not imagine that trees can have characters as diverse as human beings. I was introduced to this fact not only by my great-grandfather, who impressed upon me the need to approach trees as politely and as sensitively as one should approach people, but also in my young adult life, when I happened to be lodging with a friend, an older lady named Julia.

In the garden of Julia's house there lived four trees, forming a square at the edges of a well-kept lawn. When I was first shown around the garden, I didn't know of the complex relationship which would ultimately develop between myself, Julia, these four trees and a most protective female member of the *Biti Foki* race.

One of the trees was an apple tree, a James Grieve, which Julia told me gave an excellent yield of fruit most years. She spoke very proudly of this tree, who stood very upright and tall. Almost immediately, though, I observed how the other three trees, two of which were silver birch, were leaning away from the apple tree, almost as if they would run away had they the legs to carry them.

As Julia talked on about the apple tree, singing his praises, I walked around the tree and was instantly aware of a most overwhelming, not to mention unpleasant, feeling of superiority coming from him, as if he were looking down on me - even though he wasn't really that tall. I had never quite experienced this in a tree before, although I recalled many instances when my great-grandfather had said that trees were in danger of becoming as self-centred and as arrogant as some human beings. He had talked of trees he had encountered in his youth, particularly in large and extremely well-kept gardens where they were given far too much attention and where far too much was expected of them. He always lamented that the older he became, the more the trees were becoming what our Ancestor referred to as 'incurably individualized' - and that was how the Ancestor usually described human beings!

On that morning I circled the James Grieve slowly, while my friend talked about him. And I knew then, as I fixed my gaze on the tree, that he knew what I was thinking. I felt his immediate expectation of my adoration; in fact, I knew that he was accustomed to being worshipped with no less attention than one would lavish on a spoilt child, but I was also aware of his underlying confusion. This was not a tree as the old ones would have described a tree in ancient days. Old Gypsies spoke highly of trees, but if I closed my eyes and used my senses alone, the tree I was with now felt not so much a tree as a human being.

I said nothing to Julia, but observed her over the next few days as she frequently went down the garden to talk to the James Grieve, bothering little about the other three trees who were so obviously having a hard time of it that they were straining to lean as far away as they could go. When I spent some time with them they pretended to be indifferent, but were in an obvious agony. Eventually they confided that they hated the James Grieve because he not only got all the attention from my friend but also assumed a superiority which was quite difficult for them to tolerate and all in all it was a most unpleasant situation for all four of them to be in. Trees are usually friends with one another when they live side by side, but these were distinct enemies and I recalled my great-grandfather telling me how difficult it was for trees who felt uncomfortable or threatened, for trees could not run. They simply had to sit out a situation, no matter what the outcome was.

The picture I was receiving was quite different from the one Julia was busy painting of her garden. A person with strong feelings for trees, she enjoyed encouraging people to talk to her trees and to go out into the garden to hug them; consequently, the feeling many of her visitors were getting from the trees wasn't the feeling I was getting. I watched many people going into her garden and spending time with the trees, but spending most time with the James Grieve, as he greedily fed off their attentions.

A great battle was raging in this otherwise peaceful and picturesque garden, the like of which I had never heard, or experienced, before. I found myself with a quite difficult situation on my hands. After some two or three weeks of watching Julia feeding and petting the apple tree, I could stand it no more and thought that before I said anything to her I would first confront the tree myself, so that I might begin dealing with the situation on a more shamanic level. So I did this while my friend was out shopping one day.

On the face of it the James Grieve was adamant that everything was in order. So then I put my hand on his skin - the Romani word for tree bark is *mortsi*, or 'skin', and my elders always told me that if you remember to think of the bark of a tree as being as sensitive as human skin, you will understand how trees feel when you touch them.

'I know what you're up to,' I told the tree firmly. 'I know you're feeding off Julia's attentions and giving these other trees a hard time. I know what she's doing to you and how hard it must be.'

I was angry. I couldn't help feeling angry. There was so much anger flowing between all these trees and my own didn't help. But to watch this one tree acting like a spoilt child and the other three living their lives in misery was as much as I could bear. But then I began to feel the apple tree's own confusion and despair because I had spoken to him in that way. So far he had been living in a cossetted world and having someone challenge him was something of a shock. He also recognized that I was a Romani *Chovihano* and this hit him hard.

But then I reeled backward in shock as a loud piping voice spoke just as angrily to me in return. It was a little fairy woman, about a foot high, looking up at me with fierce dark eyes, her hands on her hips. She wore old-fashioned clothes with dark reds, blues and blacks prevailing, and in her little battered hat she looked a little like a miniature witch. She seemed almost as fierce as my own grandmother could be when riled.

'Julia!' she sneered, in a sing-song voice. 'Julia! All we ever hear is Julia! Are you going to go on about Julia too? Do you know what this tree is called?'

I quickly shook my head. I hadn't expected a member of the *Biti Foki* to appear like this and was immediately respectful - and naturally fearful - as I'd been taught to be. 'No,' I tried to say, gulping nervously, and as the fairy stared at me she seemed to have the power of a woman who could easily have been some six feet tall!

She looked up at the James Grieve, towering above her. 'Have a guess.'

I hoped she wasn't going to play games with me, as all the *Biti Foki* could if you had something special to learn - as I obviously did. I begged her forgiveness and told her I couldn't possibly guess his name in a million years.

'His name's *Julia*,' she said, again with a sneer on her tiny face, and I stared at her for some seconds in disbelief. I might have laughed had the situation not been so serious. I certainly wanted to laugh, as the little woman went on to tell me that all four trees bordering the lawn were also called Julia.

'But why?' I asked, thoroughly confused by this time. She went on to explain something which the Ancestor was later to emphasize, something very important in Romani lore - that if certain creatures on Earth are given names, they assume too much of a personal identity, which isn't always good for them, particularly if these names are permanent, as they then become far too egocentric for their own good. The trees were called Julia, the little woman said, the house was called Julia and in fact everything else round about had assumed the name, because Julia had long been an extremely important spirit in the area and was actually sucking the natural life out of all the things she came into contact with, ultimately - within nature's language - turning them all into Julias! The trees, the little woman said, understood Julia to be something special; she had almost become a goddess!

As the little woman looked at me I knew instantly that were I to stay around the place for very long I too would be in danger of becoming Julia. The whole thing seemed to have escalated beyond control. I knew that the trees could not be blamed for any of this, for they lived on an entirely different plane, mentally, and their comprehension of names and individualization was clearly very different from ours.

But all this also reminded me of a story my great-grandfather had passed on about the way we human beings could so easily adulterate elements of nature by infecting them with our own patterns of behaviour. It was all a lesson. If we didn't live by the borrowing principle and by understanding that we were *sharing* the Earth, we would be living in a very egocentric and lonely world indeed, a world which was individualized to an extreme, both limited and limiting. Hadn't this already happened in our human society?

I felt extremely sorry for the little woman as she sat down at the base of the tree with her hands squashed in her cheeks and a pout on her small face. It was always difficult for the *Biti Foki*, sandwiched as they were between the human world and the natural world, and often trying so hard to encourage those two worlds to join together in harmony. But I also felt sorry for the James Grieve, who was now feeling rather ashamed. Trees, like animals, are quick to feel shame when they feel they have done something wrong. It wasn't, after all, his fault that everything had developed like this. I felt saddened that I was learning this valuable lesson at the expense of these ancient beings.

The little fairy woman knew who and what I was and she therefore saw fit to remind me that it was my duty to learn this lesson and also to do something about this situation. I promised her I would.

At the next convenient moment I cautiously broached the subject with Julia. She knew that I had been trained as a *Chovihano* in the traditional way, although neither of us had told many who were around us at the time, yet initially it was hard for her to comprehend my experience; she could not quite believe that trees could become so like human beings. The 'individualizing' of our environment is a science that relates more to the Otherworld than the physical world, but it is something we will need to understand more in the future if we are at all to understand the natural world around us and the way it is inclined to function. In this case Julia and I eventually carried out some healing work on the trees, literally healing the garden and the environment of its 'Julia'!

It has always been the Romani way to seek permission before making contact with any aspect of the natural world. I sometimes wonder whether we ought to be hugging trees, as some people like to do without even asking permission! After all, would we do this to a stranger in the street? Checking that our actions are not an imposition is the first rule in successful communication with all other species - and indeed each other - but this is particularly true of trees.

As well as learning about the difficulties some trees can experience when under the influence of human beings, I have also had many opportunities to learn about the difficulties human beings can experience when under the influence of trees.

Trees' influence on human beings would indeed have been far more common in earlier days when people in many cultures looked to trees to teach them. These were days when all Gypsy *Chovihanos* deliberately put themselves in the care of trees when wanting to learn the Earth's secrets.

As a teenager I began to feel the strength of the trees that lived about me in my environment, whether I walked about in the wood near my home or whether I was walking down one of the tree-lined streets which led to my home. I often experienced what I can only describe as a 'presence', as if the trees were fully aware of my existence because of some predestined attachment we had to each other. This awareness became so strong when I was a young adult that I soon began giving trees a wide berth when I walked past them. They could whisper to you and either guide you or misguide you. And if the moon were full, you might be caught off your guard and might just walk home the wrong way. When returning from a night out, neighbours might see me zigzagging down the centre of our road as I attempted to pass trees cautiously - on the face of it I must have appeared to be intoxicated!

On my way I often heard the trees whispering, passing on some message - or perhaps even a joke - to each other in their own language, which I often imagined went something like this: 'Look at him! Doesn't he look funny? He's young; he hasn't learned anything yet. But he has special powers. What will he do with those powers? Will he be courageous enough to learn our ancient secrets?'

You might be very easily influenced by trees' whispering, especially by those trees who lost their leaves in winter, for they were the ones who could not always be trusted. This was considered to be the mischievous side of a tree's nature. My grandmother told me that her elders had impressed upon her how Gypsies in the old days had sometimes become lost in forests, particularly when spells were 'in the air', as she put it. She told me that on becoming lost, some Gypsies would remove their clothes and put them on again inside out, because while you were lost you were vulnerable and you would need to fool any evil spirits who might take advantage of your delicate situation. The trees might just tell all kinds of spirits about your weaknesses if they didn't like you. To this day I still turn some of my clothes inside out, not only when I feel lost but also when I feel low, and I certainly use this old custom when I conduct a healing session. It can be particularly beneficial sometimes to reverse one's clothing during the phase of the old moon or at the height of a full moon. Today some of us may be loath to perceive negativity as an evil spirit, but negative experiences do nevertheless occur at these delicate times. If you examine your calendar you may be able to trace your 'highs' and 'lows' and how they may just coincide with significant phases of the moon.

It is also wise to take care when you are out with trees. My grandmother explained that they were powerful beings, far more powerful than humans, and you therefore had to take them seriously, because if they wanted to teach you something, their teaching would be of the highest quality - which meant that it might sometimes hurt! This is why if you think in the old way you will always think twice about walking up to hug a tree, for it is a strong, powerful and extremely ancient spirit you are dealing with, one that should never be taken lightly.

I have found the best way to look upon trees is to see them rather as you might see a dog - a dog can roll over and be played with, but is also capable of savaging you. I often advise people to think like this when approaching trees. Use the golden rule: approach with a reasonable amount of caution, and also the greatest respect, and you will in turn receive the best a tree can give you, and you can probably tell that tree all your problems and hug away to your heart's content.

Trees may seem very passive, and so they are much of the time, for they are generally very wise and good-natured creatures, but there is a deep and unfathomable, and sometimes also a quite playful side to their nature, which we humans don't always understand, and we should always be assured that most trees will know far more about us than we will ever know about them. Remember that they are not just thousands but millions of years ahead of us in time, and indeed experience.

I have heard trees whispering in many ways. I have heard them laughing, crying and also screaming when they are torn down. If you know a tree is to be felled, then it is a good idea to go and talk to that tree, to explain what is happening and why. The tragedy occurs when condemned trees are marked on their trunks for the chop, for these ancient creatures in all their innocence often only see the markings as decoration, for in earlier times when trees were revered they were hung with rags, adorned with seasonal ornaments and left offerings. Some of them still think in this simple ancient way today and will not always understand what is happening – and why humans can be so cruel. So it is a good idea to tell them what is going on and to console them. That is the least that we humans can do if a tree's end is on its way. Don't forget to add that it isn't your fault, that you are well and truly on the tree's side.

Some humans will undoubtedly laugh at you if you think like this. But Romani Gypsies have done so for many hundreds of years. They feel it very deeply when woodland is destroyed, for it is the destruction of their very foundation and a great crime committed against Grandmother Earth.

Needless to add, the more you develop a rapport with trees, the more you will grow to love and understand them for their own sakes. It is a sad truth that many humans only see trees as unthinking, unfeeling objects or as a reflection of what they perceive nature to be.

I heard the trees whispering to me in the red-gold wood when I spent that special night there and I have often listened to their whispering in the early hours of quiet mornings when I have been journeying through my shamanic visions, as *Chovihanos* often do. Many people will never have heard this because in modern times there is far too much noise. The whispering grows out of a deep rich silence, within which, in earlier times, Romani Gypsies heard nature singing - and trees, along with the *Biti Foki*, always had plenty to sing about!

There have been a few trees in my life who have been very special to me and who have provided a gateway to much that I have needed to learn. These trees have also become friends, and although all of them have been deciduous and therefore beings who might reveal my innermost secrets, I have been able to trust them implicitly and to call upon them for advice whenever I have needed it.

One of these trees has been an oak, whom I affectionately call *Puro Moosh*, or 'Old Man'. He lives by the river and is gentle, wise and kind. I often think that in human form he would be a sweet old man with a long white beard who might enjoy simple home comforts. He has taken me on many long journeys, down into the Earth and elsewhere, and I often introduce him to many friends and visitors when we take walks beside the river, purely so that they may meet him, because I am extremely proud of him. Some of them will come away carrying small pieces of his bark or perhaps one of his fallen leaves. These are given by him voluntarily, as all trees will give something of themselves to you if they are treated with respect and provided it is an appropriate time in your life for you to receive something.

Once you have made contact with a tree, it is best simply to move around the trunk, feeling the bark - or skin - gently with your hand. The tree will allow you to do this if you politely inform him or her of what you are doing. The tree may even know you are coming and will prepare something to give to you. A piece of bark may peel off in your hand if the tree wishes to make friends with you or develop some kind of relationship with you. Remember never to pull any of the bark off forcefully. This is a crime, for the tree needs to give you the bark voluntarily. Remember also that a tree likes to befriend human beings for a substantial period of time, if not forever, not just for a fleeting moment; trees do not make good fairweather friends.

Considering this, it is also polite to develop the habit of taking an offering to the tree now and then, perhaps something you enjoy, perhaps beer or milk; something in liquid form is particularly appreciated. Trees have been receiving such offerings from human beings for thousands of years.

I have a collection of many pieces of bark given me by various trees I have been fortunate enough to befriend and work with shamanically. These pieces are borrowed, not owned, for I intend to return them to the land one day. But the biggest piece of bark I have in my possession comes from the skin of the Old Man down by the river. I have known him for a good many years and our relationship has grown.

Not all trees of the same species will have the same characters. The Old Man, like many other trees in the West Country, where he lives, is, as already mentioned, very gentle and calm by nature, but in the south-east of England, which was where I encountered the James Grieve apple tree and his friends, trees are quite different. I discovered this when meeting another oak tree, this time a massively powerful one.

This oak tree was very large and dwelt with great princely pride in a garden near to a friend's home. Squirrels would scamper playfully up and down the great tree or else lie basking in crevices on his branches in the sunshine. So small in comparison, they could seem like insects, for the oak's trunk was huge with an almost muscular form. Compared with the Old Man with his long beard and quiet contentment, this tree was like the strongest gladiator poised for action.

Every time I looked out at this tree from the window, I shivered, and remarked to Lizzie that I would not cherish the idea of being under the guidance of this oak during shamanic training, as I was with the Old Man back in the West Country. I should have known that I was secretly inviting his response. Such is the nature of trees; we perhaps forget that they know more about us than we think.

We also forget that all trees take on the flavour of the land they happen to live upon, which can vary in temperament just as much as human beings can. Just as Africans may be different in temperament from Scandinavians, because of the influence of their land, and just as people living in southern England may be different in temperament from people living in the remotest regions of Scotland, because the land holds many varying characteristics, so trees differ according to where they live. The land has character and it influences everything which lives and breathes and moves upon it, whether those things are aware of the influence or not.

Even the water in the ground can be affected by the land, being in some places hard and in some places soft. Where it is hard, the land will often have a stronger temperament and will give you lessons that are far more adventurous in content and often 'to the point', as well as being a good deal more concentrated; where it is soft, the land will be gentler and will give you lessons that are of a more diluted and sometimes more diverse nature. Yet, strangely, these lessons may also come to you in a much heavier disguise, as softer landscapes and softer water can often be deceiving. So a lesson in a hard-water area may be short and sharp, but a lesson in a soft-water area may be a long time being learned.

The oak living in the south-east started to watch me, because he knew that I was also watching him. And it wasn't long before he had taken me into his mighty embrace and one night I had a most powerful dream about him.

In the dream I was having to walk backwards around his trunk - which is very wide indeed - singing a special sacred song. This was a test, because I was wanting to learn more about him. And as I was walking backwards I couldn't exactly see where I was putting my feet, so I had to go very carefully, trusting that firm ground was behind me on every step. I knew that if I succeeded going backwards around the tree three times I would be shown something special, one of his innermost secrets, so around I went, singing and trusting - as much as I dared.

I had almost completed the whole course when I suddenly found myself hesitating, sensing that I shouldn't put my foot down behind me on my next step, and when I glanced behind, which was the first time that I had done so, I saw that there was a perfect drop stretching down into infinity directly behind me. Had I continued stepping backwards I would certainly have fallen down into this deep chasm, which would have sent me flying down into the dark recesses of the Earth - not a very pleasant experience, as it had happened to me once before. But this fall would also have meant that I would probably have failed the oak's test. He was a hard and strict teacher, but not without good cause.

Hesitating, I just balanced precariously for a while, waiting to see what would happen next, and then as quick as lightning I was suddenly transported into the inside of the trunk itself, where there seemed to be a happy reunion going on. Many animals were celebrating together and the whole dream then took on something of an *Alice in Wonderland* flavour as I joined rabbits, squirrels, cats, dogs, mice, insects and also larger animals in this one great trunk.

'You all come from me,' the great oak then told me. 'You all come from trees, for all creatures are built of the same substance and come from out of the Earth.'

It was a wonderful end to the dream and I was honoured to learn this and to have passed the test, but I felt even more privileged to have had this experience with that oak, for that is perhaps the most important part of learning shamanically.

Romani shamanic training is both a subjective and objective exercise, for you need to know how to balance the introspective with the actual, which is a hard thing to do. Knowledge and experience must always go hand in hand and must form a partnership, because it is through such a partnership that they each become valid, so that we may more easily embrace the wider spectrum of ancient secrets and the cryptic trails they are likely to leave. It is sometimes as if a conclusion has to seep down into the depths of our beings in order to be fully comprehended and appreciated, and that is what I feel happened during my time with this particular oak tree.

I have stressed that trees have different characters. They are also male and female, perhaps not as rigidly as we human beings are, but just as some trees have masculine traits, such as the oak, others have gracefully feminine traits, such as the birch. You will need to spend time - lots of time - with these trees before you understand the kind of masculinity and femininity they are likely to express. In human terms the oak is a rather strongly built man, usually firm and gentle - especially if he happens to live in the West Country! But the birch is elegance itself. She is a real lady who loves to surround herself with soft veils and delicate things, and she is so naturally exquisite that everyone who passes her cannot help but remark upon her beauty.

I have spent time with both oak and birch in their masculine and feminine forms, and when they take on a human aspect - which all of them can do with ease, because the human form is a lower life form and therefore easy for them to personify - they are beautiful indeed, perhaps the prototype of the human being as it could be if it allowed itself to rise to such noble heights. This is perhaps what could be termed 'shape-shifting', which needs further explaining elsewhere, but it is enough to say here that trees are excellent practitioners of this ancient craft. Perhaps they know more about the true positive qualities of a human being than we do, since we deliberately removed ourselves from the natural beings we once were.

There are a great many other lessons and dreams I have experienced whilst in the company of trees, in many different places, but there are few experiences more powerful than those in which the *Chovihano* receives his *ran*.

The *bakterimasko ran*, or magic wand, as a spirit in its own right, was always an important accomplice in the healing work of the Gypsy *Chovihano*, and it is the highest honour when a tree selects a branch to work with you as a magic wand. My great-grandfather informed me that a *Chovihano* would only be given a wand by a tree when he was ready to begin his healing work properly. Traditionally, the wood has been birch, but many factors need to coincide for the wood to be charged with magical energy, such as your finding the wood at a specific time in your life and while on a specific path. The season in which you find it in can be relevant, as can the position of the moon, and sometimes other factors. There is certainly nothing spooky or dangerous about a magic wand, so long as you know how to use it and respect it.

I have been given a handful of wands in my lifetime, but two special ones, a large one and a small one, came to me at a relevant period in my life, when I was being more open about my native roots and therefore able to practise my shamanic healing more positively. It was as if the birch trees who provided me with the wands were celebrating the fact that I could at last come out about who and what I was, and they were fully in support of me. I had earned my right to work with them. These wands were certainly far more powerful than any I had ever been given before and I began to hear my great-grandfather's words echoing back through the years, telling me that the healing craft of the old Gypsy shaman is a sacred craft and it can only ever properly be carried out with the assistance of trees.

The larger of the two *rans* was given to me by a cat, Ollie, who had become a close friend. I returned home one day to find him lying on the wand, a paw draped across it, and as he looked up at me I knew this beautiful piece of birch was meant for me. The smaller of the two was given to me by the birch tree herself. I stopped and spoke to her, and was encouraged to look up into her branches. There, within easy reach, was a small loose branch which had fallen down from the top of the tree and which I could easily untangle from all the other branches.

These two *rans* work with me in many ways and bring something of the old forest life into my healing sessions, speaking their own ancient language, which is simple and straightforward and easy for most people to understand once they begin to care for trees.

—

The spirits of trees and the *Biti Foki* were a major part of life in earlier times, when people were happy to put the natural world above themselves. Romani Gypsies have retained this natural relationship through the many centuries that Europe has been 'developing', or 'progressing'. The trees, and the *Biti Foki*, are happy to build these same relationships again, should we have the courage and patience to step forward - or perhaps backward - and begin to make friends with them again.

Many of the *Patrinyengris* have now gone, the *Drabengros* have almost certainly disappeared and even the Gypsy *Chovihanos* remain a very rare breed. But this is because many forests in western Europe have also disappeared, taking the human wildlife with them. But the *Chovihanos* know that there is an ancient world which was forced to move underground in earlier days and they also know that it currently still lies there sleeping. It will be part of the *Chovihano's* work to continue to protect that world while it remains in the Lowerworld, with the objective of helping it rise up again from its slumbering depths when the time is right for it to emerge – which I feel is certainly upon us.

As a *Chovihano*, I am able to guarantee that the whispering forests of western Europe are still whispering. If you put your ear to the ground in the woodland, then close your eyes and grow very still, you may just be able to hear their ancient songs being sung deep beneath the Earth.

# 6

## THE ANCIENT POWER OF GYPSY HEALING
# THE CHOVIHANO'S SPECIALIZED CRAFT

It is nineteenth-century Britain. Victoria is on the throne, the Industrial Revolution has begun, steam trains are travelling from one end of the country to the other at breakneck speeds and the British are a powerful nation of explorers and colonialists, settling in many parts of the uncivilized world where tribal people are undergoing mass religious conversion and education in the modern sciences.

IN THE THICKEST PART OF A FOREST IN THE BRITISH COUNTRYSIDE A NON-LITERATE *CHOVIHANO* SQUATS ON THE WOOD FLOOR, CONDUCTING AN ANCIENT HEALING RITUAL. HE CONVERSES WITH THE TREES AND WITH THE SPIRITS OF SUN, MOON, AIR, EARTH, FIRE AND WATER, ASKING FOR THEIR ASSISTANCE, AND WITH THE AID OF HIS *BAKTERISMASKO RAN*, OR MAGIC WAND, HE 'CONDUCTS' THE FLOW OF ENERGY WHICH IS BEGINNING TO FLOW ALL AROUND HIM, JINGLING THE WAND'S BELLS TO KEEP AWAY UNSAVOURY AND UNTRUSTWORTHY SPIRITS, WHO MIGHT JUST TAKE AN INTEREST IN WHAT IS GOING ON AND BRING BAD LUCK. THIS HEALER IS LIKE THE LEADER OF AN ORCHESTRA CONDUCTING HIS MUSICIANS. HE MUTTERS WORDS IN THE ROMANI LANGUAGE, SPRINKLES SALT AROUND TO PROTECT EVERYONE AND FEELS THE SPIRITS GATHERING ALL AROUND HIM. HE IS IN COMPLETE COMMAND OF OTHERWORLDLY ACTIVITY.

HAVING BEEN ALONE FOR SOME TIME, PERHAPS FASTING, PERHAPS PARTAKING OF VARIOUS STIMULATING HERBS AND SOME ALCOHOL, THE *CHOVIHANO* NOW SEEKS GUIDANCE FROM THE SPIRITS OF THE NATURAL WORLD, HIS SPIRIT GUARDIANS AND HIS ANCESTORS.

THESE ARE IMPORTANT INFLUENCES,
FOR THEY UNDERSTAND HOW SICKNESS
IS MADE AND THE ART OF REMOVING
IT. HE SMILES AND TALKS TO ALL
THESE SPIRITS, AND IT APPEARS THAT
HE IS TALKING TO HIMSELF, BUT THE
GYPSIES GATHERED AROUND HIM
UNDERSTAND WHAT IS GOING ON, THAT
THERE IS A CONVERSATION TAKING
PLACE BETWEEN THEIR *CHOVIHANO* AND
HIS GUARDIAN SPIRITS. THEY ARE ALL
GATHERED AROUND THEIR FIRE WITH
THE *PATRINYENGRI*, WHO IS BURNING
HER SACRED HERBS, ROSEMARY AND
MUGWORT, FOR PROTECTION AND
VISIONS, AND SHE TOO MUTTERS
SACRED WORDS IN ROMANES.

IT IS TIME NOW FOR THE HEALING TO
TAKE PLACE.

THE *CHOVIHANO* JINGLES AS HE GETS UP
AND WALKS, LADEN AS HE IS WITH ALL
MANNER OF TALISMANS, AMULETS,
CHARMS, COINS WHICH FLASH IN LIGHT
AND BELLS WHICH JINGLE WHEN SHOOK.
THESE HE WEARS FOR PROTECTION.

THE MOON IS IN HER NEW PHASE AND
SOMETIMES GLOWS WANLY BEYOND
THE TOPS OF THE TREES WHEN SHE IS
NOT HIDDEN BY CLOUD. THIS IS A
GOOD SIGN FOR THE *CHOVIHANO*, FOR IT
MEANS THAT GOOD LUCK CAN FLOW.

OWLS HOOT AND NIGHT CREATURES SCUTTLE ABOUT ON THE WOOD FLOOR, ALL SOMEHOW A SACRED PART OF WHAT IS GOING ON IN THE WOOD TONIGHT, ALL CONTRIBUTING THEMSELVES AS RELEVANT OMENS.

THE CHOVIHANO, BY DEGREES, THEN WORKS HIMSELF INTO A HEALING TRANCE, WITH THE AID OF HIS RAN, HIS VASTENGRI, OR TAMBOURINE, HIS LUCKY CHARMS AND HIS SPIRIT GUARDIANS. HE ROCKS AROUND, MOANING AND MAKING STRANGE NOISES, AND THIS MEANS THAT HE IS MAKING CONTACT WITH HIS SPIRIT GUIDES, WHO WILL KEEP EVERYONE SAFE. HIS AIM IS TO STAND IN THE SHOES OF THE SICK AND THE TROUBLED IN THE GROUP AROUND HIM AND TO TAKE ON ANY OF THEIR PROBLEMS, SO THAT THE PROBLEMS MAY PASS THROUGH HIM AND AWAY INTO THE OTHERWORLD, WHERE THEY ARE CONSIDERED TO BELONG.

HE IS WILLING TO GO IN SEARCH OF PEOPLE'S SOULS, SHOULD THEY HAVE BECOME LOST, OR TO TAKE ON MUDDLED, MALEVOLENT SPIRITS WHO MAY HAVE BEEN INFLUENCING PEOPLE WITHOUT THEIR KNOWING IT. ANY MALEVOLENT SPIRITS WILL ENTER THE CHOVIHANO'S BODY, BELIEVING THAT HE

IS THEIR FRIEND, AND HE WILL THEN
ENTERTAIN THESE SPIRITS, FIRST BY
CHARMING THEM AND ASKING THEM
TO LISTEN TO THE BELLS OF HIS MAGIC
WAND, WHICH THEY WILL FIND
ENCHANTING, AND HE MAY PERHAPS
EVEN START SINGING TO THEM, SO
THAT THEY START TO TRUST HIM. BUT
HE WILL THEN ATTEMPT TO ENSNARE
THEM AND TO DELIVER THEM TO ONE
OF THE POWERFUL GUARDIAN SPIRITS
WHO IS WORKING WITH HIM. THIS MAY
BE A HUMAN SPIRIT, AN ANIMAL
SPIRIT OR EVEN THE SPIRIT OF A
STONE, OR IT MAY EVEN BE *YAG*, THE
SPIRIT OF FIRE. WHOEVER HELPS THE
*CHOVIHANO* WILL HELP TO CARRY ALL
THE BAD SPIRITS AWAY, BACK INTO THE
OTHERWORLD WHERE THEY BELONG.

AS THE TRANCE PROGRESSES, THE
FOREST TAKES ON A DIFFERENT FEEL; IT
BECOMES A FOREST THAT IS SUDDENLY
HALF IN THE OTHERWORLD, AND ALL
THE PEOPLE AND CREATURES WITHIN IT
ARE ABLE, IF THEY CHOOSE, TO CROSS
THE BRIDGE THAT IS BEING CREATED
AND TO STEP INTO THE OTHERWORLD.
THEY KNOW THAT NO HARM WILL
COME TO THEM FOR THEY HAVE THEIR
*CHOVIHANO* BESIDE THEM TO PROTECT
THEM. HE CAN CONVERSE WITH ALL
SPIRITS IN ALL WAYS AND NOTHING
BAD WILL HAPPEN WHILST HE IS

IN THEIR PRESENCE, PARTICULARLY
WHILST HE IS ENTRANCED.

THUS, THE WHOLE FOREST RINGS WITH
THE SMACKING SOUND OF THE
TAMBOURINE AND THE VOICES OF THE
GYPSIES AS THEY MOAN, YELL, LAUGH,
CRY, SCREAM, SING, ROCK AND DANCE
TO THE RHYTHM OF THEIR RITUAL,
THEIR HANDS CLAPPING ALL THE
WHILE. THE PEOPLE, THE FOREST AND
ALL THE GUARDIAN SPIRITS ARE NOW
IN HARMONY, AND THERE IS NOTHING
MORE POWERFUL, NOR MORE HEALING
FOR THOSE GATHERED AT THIS RITUAL.

AFTER MUCH FIGHTING AND WRITHING
AND SHOUTING, THE *CHOVIHANO*
EVENTUALLY COMES OUT OF HIS
TRANCE, AS IF HE IS COMING OUT OF A
VERY HEAVY SLEEP. HE SITS UP AND
AT THIS TIME IT CAN SEEM AS IF NOTH-
ING HAS TAKEN PLACE AT ALL, FOR HE
APPEARS TO BE REFRESHED, VERY CALM
AND QUITE NORMAL. HE IS SMILING,
AND PEOPLE NOW LAUGH TOGETHER
AND QUICKLY BEGIN TO RE-ENACT THE
DRAMATIC PARTS OF THEIR RITUAL,
EMBROIDERING MUCH OF IT WITH
THEIR OWN INTERPRETATIONS, WHICH
THEY WILL DO FOR MANY DAYS,
PERHAPS EVEN WEEKS, TO COME.

THE *CHOVIHANO* TAKES A DRINK,
THROWING BACK HIS HEAD AS THE

LIQUID DRIBBLES OVER HIS CHIN.
THIS WORK MAKES HIM VERY THIRSTY,
AND INDEED HUNGRY, BUT RARELY
TIRED, BECAUSE ALL THE GOOD
SPIRITS HAVE HELPED HIM. AND AS HE
LAUGHS AND TALKS WITH HIS PEOPLE
HE THINKS HE ENJOYS NOTHING
BETTER THAN A LONG DRINK OF BEER,
SOME BREAD AND CHEESE, AND A GOOD
CHAT FOLLOWING A HEALING RITUAL.

The above account of a Romani Gypsy shamanic healing session is typical - I have drawn material from numerous accounts and experiences - but in the nineteenth century it was by no means common. Gypsy healers of this kind were scattered around, but were rare, usually practising in very small groups and only practising aspects of the craft. In North Wales, where Romani Gypsies were more secluded, the craft was probably more widespread, although still carried out in great secrecy. We can at least assume this, as Jack Lee was able to emerge from North Welsh Romani stock to pass these ancient traditions down to me, with the very clear message that they should always be practised with a degree of reserve and the utmost respect. It is ironic that while the British were busy 'developing' other continents in the Victorian era, the Romani Gypsies were still practising their ancient shamanic and magical skills on their own doorstep, right under their noses!

The healing ritual was always an important part of Gypsy society. A Gypsy healer was careful to conduct the healing in the strictest secrecy and, according to ancient tradition, might have taken any number of hours or even days to prepare for a healing session - providing there were adequate means of doing so. The length of time devoted to the pre-healing ritual and the ritual itself would also depend upon the severity of the condition the healer was being asked to cure. More and more, though, the social climate needed to be taken into consideration; thus, healing sessions became not only shorter by the Victorian era, probably limited to two or three hours, but were soon severely desensitized, robbed of the earlier vibrant energy that ordinarily accompanied such ancient practices.

These practices served to bring people together in a way that is seldom experienced in our society today, but when they are used, there is a distinctive feeling of togetherness which is undeniably strong. As I have seen it, healing practised in such a community, in the presence of Otherworld spirits, has a lasting effect, because it is all about 'community' and sharing problems on a more meaningful level. There is support from all corners of a very active universe and this helps people to feel that they are not quite so alone.

I still believe that it is important to conduct healing within a supportive group environment, generally among people who are mostly familiar with each other, people who are not too troubled by feelings of self-consciousness and who may be willing to observe appropriate behaviour. This is really no different from using fitting manners at the dinner table or being generally polite in the street when you meet someone you know. Showing respect in many places in our society calls for a certain self-control, because it is simply what we have become accustomed to. We might say that it would be inappropriate to walk into the waiting-room of a doctor's surgery shouting and singing and banging a drum. It is equally inappropriate, in a Romani healing ritual, to sit noiseless and motionless when the *Chovihano* enters his trance. It could almost be described as extremely disrespectful if you did not acknowledge his somewhat eccentric behaviour, and applaud it, and sometimes even find it openly amusing! And yet though Gypsies appear to be so relaxed during a healing ritual, there is no lack of attentiveness.

An example of this is a memory I have of my grandmother and a female companion in discussion over the name of a particular brand of biscuit whilst Jack Lee was busy going into one of his healing trances. As the trance progressed the two women volunteered various names which might well solve the mystery and this debate continued on and off throughout a large part of the session - but in no way did it detract from the energy created in the session, because they also talked openly about what they were sensing during the heat of the ritual, i.e. what they were seeing, hearing and feeling within and around the environment and within and around Jack Lee himself.

In another instance, an old man who regularly joined me for my healing trances had been talking about the price of tomatoes to another member of the group and half-way through the session, some 40 minutes or so later, he sat forward, summoning the attention of the other member of the group with the words, 'What price did you say those tomatoes were?'

This is quite typical behaviour in a Gypsy healing session. It may seem trivial, or irreverent even, in the presence of the *Chovihano* and his healing spirits, but this relaxed attitude is necessary, it contributes to results. Members of the group are just as likely to mention that they are able to see certain spirits collecting around the *Chovihano* as they are to talk openly about the price of tomatoes!

My grandmother invariably brought her knitting or crochet work along to a healing session. A lady member who joined my group at a later date also followed this trend, with no lack of concentration; in fact, the employment of a craft, if executed in a relaxed manner, can sometimes increase concentration, for it encourages natural spontaneity. Much of the time in my own family a healing session would become completely riotous, with all of us laughing at ourselves and at each other because of some comment or other. Our humour often proved to be the best medicine for us all.

Sadly, there are no direct relations with whom I can practise the old healing traditions now, so it is necessary to train people to assist me if this ancient craft is to survive. Expressive, unselfconscious people are often preferred assistants, as most Gypsies are by nature fairly raucous and outgoing, and their energy is plentiful - which is just as well, as energy is needed from everyone to make a healing session work.

We perhaps sometimes need reminding that the quite restrained and solemn silences we may believe we need to adopt during ancient rituals are a rather unnecessary modern creation and largely the result of religious influence, which over a considerable period of time has replaced the more unrefined and expressive habits of the tribal individual. Indeed, I know of no indigenous tribal people who practise their ancient rituals without a light heart and a grin. In my own family, if you were ever to grow quiet or stop moving for just a short period of time, you were likely to be asked if you were feeling ill! There are undoubtedly appropriate times to be serious, but the shamanic healing session is not always one of them.

Learning to relate to, and relax with, the more outgoing, untamed parts of ourselves in our somewhat passionless society has certainly been something I have needed to introduce into healing sessions, purely because it is enormously beneficial to our health. The wild, exotic and romantic passion of the old Gypsy spirit, which so many can relate to, is given more meaning once we realize that in our recent history we have *all* been 'tamed'. On reaching that wild and natural spirit within, we reach who we truly are. To our surprise we usually find that this spirit doesn't feel quite as 'wild' as we thought it would, at least not in the 'running crazy' sense of the word. We discover, instead, a powerful but gentle healing part of ourselves, which we hadn't quite realized was there before. This part is simply waiting to be reawakened, in the right way.

I have often said that the Gypsy is the greatest actor, able to remain upon the stage of life for an extraordinary length of time without becoming fooled by the role. The *Chovihano*, then, must be an Oscar winner! For his craft could be likened more to a good quality stage-play than anything else!

This has to do with shamanic ritual and theatre being linked. 'Performance' skills are part of the shamanic healing craft the world over. I believe that shamanic ritual, which the *Chovihano* conducts with no lack of expression, must inevitably contain the true origins of drama, the most primitive form of theatre, where players renew their spiritual acquaintances with the natural world against the backdrop of an uncertain Middleworld where all creatures are vulnerable to weakness.

By using performance and creativity, and particularly by expressing ourselves more openly, we can start to free up our receptive and sensitive inner powers, so that we do not block any new thoughts and feelings that need to come in to help us initiate change. I often attempt to get people to move about whenever I conduct a healing session. My feeling is that they need to rock, or move about in some way, so that they are not resisting change. Sitting rigidly, waiting for something miraculous to take place has never, in my experience, helped anyone. Jack Lee was quite dramatic when practising his healing craft and rocked about quite considerably. In fact, some kind of dramatic activity was usually expected of him.

In earlier times Gypsy healing sessions were rarely limited by time. Some of us might find it difficult to imagine a healing session lasting anything from two to six or even eight hours, but in days when clans could remain relatively undisturbed, *Chovihanos* were able to go on working throughout the night.

An end result when the *Chovihano* is at work is the personalization of a sickness. In today's language the healer is saying, 'This is what your sickness would be like if it were a person.' It otherwise slumbers in the deadened void created for it by the patient, a thing without a soul, a ghostly embryo of some formless, timeless, shapeless power, which steals life away. I believe there would be far less fear of sickness if we could only accommodate the idea of personalization.

The old Romani art of 'offloading' sickness on to insects and animals is perhaps one way of personalizing a sickness efficiently enough to be able to see it for what it is, talk to it and send it on its way.

In the old days many Gypsy *Chovihanos* used slugs and spiders for more minor sicknesses. A slug would be given a person's sickness and then pinned on to a thorn bush. As he died, so the sickness would die. Likewise a spider would be wrapped in silk and worn around the neck; once the spider had died, your sickness would have died with him.

My great-grandfather used an earthworm, which he always maintained was an extraordinarily advanced creature - which in evolutionary terms he is, being millions of years ahead of us. He would dig up this small creature and bring him into the healing circle or group. A ritual would be performed over him and by magic my great-grandfather would transfer the person's sickness into the earthworm, sealing it into the creature by spitting three times on him and asking him to take the sickness back down into the Earth and thus away into another world.

I also use an earthworm for this ritual and even though I never kill him, the simple 'offloading' process can still sometimes bring a good many questions from those who have animals close to their hearts. Is it right to perform such a ritual? Should we be using any animal in this way?

I have already explained that the old Romani Gypsies related to animals very differently from the way we might relate to them today. Insects and smaller animals who live close to the soil or underground are considered to have access to the Lowerworld, just as birds who live close to the sky are considered to have access to the Upperworld, and these insects and smaller animals are always considered to be greater beings simply for being able to live in the Lowerworld without being taken over by the darker forces there - something no human beings are able to do. These creatures are therefore *biti Chovihanos*, little shamans, and have the power to absorb bad spirits of sickness and remove them on your behalf.

It is difficult for us to comprehend such thinking these days when animal welfare is such a huge concern. But perhaps if we understand that a worm was far more prized in Romani Gypsy society than it might be today, we might indeed begin to question our own ideas about these small creatures, though the majority of us may see them simply as the long wriggly things that live in our gardens and make us squirm!

I learnt when young that a worm or any other small creature was extremely pleased to be of service in any healing work. Certainly, the worms I have used in my own healing rituals have always performed their task with the utmost skill and also the greatest pride. As I understand it, this is a task worms have been performing with Gypsies for thousands of years.

Likewise for thousands of years animals were sacrificed for healing and good luck, and considering that human sacrificial victims were once highly prized and cherished - and knew they were, because to be sacrificed was the greatest honour - animals would have felt exactly the same. Slaughtering them in the abattoir is, I think, far more cruel and exploitative in many respects, as it is very impersonal - as sports like fox-hunting and shooting for pleasure are. The Gypsies never performed any of their healing rituals with animals for pleasure. It was always with the animals' permission. It saddened me once to hear a pig say, 'Am I not good enough to be sacrificed for special purposes any more?'

At the end of the day I think the question of animal sacrifice in ancient healing rituals will always raise objections - until, that is, people develop their own bonds and shamanic relationships with animals and the natural world.

I have already mentioned that I was encouraged to talk to the spirits within 'things' at home, whether these took the form of tables, chairs, cups, food or even a single hair on a piece of clothing! Everything had the capacity to speak. Constant practice of this ancient craft, which has long been called animism, will safeguard you against the many spirits of sickness who roam around looking for trouble, spirits such as viruses, who will, if you don't talk to them, invade your privacy or take you over without your knowing. This doesn't mean that you have to talk to them all the time, but if you know colds or the 'flu are 'doing the rounds', just start talking to these 'bugs' in a child-like and light-hearted manner, even if you can't see them or know where they might be located. By doing this you will be 'charming' them or, in straightforward modern terms, 'personalizing' the sickness, so that you are talking *to* something, rather than seeing it as a vague, empty space over which you have no control.

If a malevolent spirit of sickness sees that you can already see through it, it will not bother to fight for the right to inhabit you; there will certainly be plenty more gullible people who will be fooled by a spirit's formlessness and who will be only too pleased to accommodate it. This is particularly true of viruses.

Viruses are strange creatures. If human, a virus would join you for a drink at the bar and then crack you over the head with his glass! Humouring these spirits is the best thing you can do. But if you laugh with them rather than at them they will not be able to fault you and will seek their 'sustenance' elsewhere. To some, this may all sound like sheer nonsense. But just try talking to them for just a little while and you may surprise yourself, because they will suddenly leave you alone.

Many find it extremely difficult to know exactly where a spirit of sickness resides. Perhaps the question is not so much how we talk to things but why we *forget* to talk to things. Children talk to things spontaneously, not because they are children but because they have a natural ability to communicate, and when we reach adulthood we are encouraged to leave our childhood and all that goes with it behind. Perhaps the Gypsies never grew up, for they communicate in a very childlike fashion.

Healing, in my view, has always had a good deal to do with communication, whether that communication be between people, animals or indeed 'things'. So, it is good to begin practising with all the things you have around you, so that you can accustom yourself to talking openly to things which are considered to be inanimate. Some find this embarrassing and also quite 'silly' at first. It should indeed be fun, but the longer you keep practising it, the less awkward you will feel. Understand that you are not mad and that this craft has been practised for thousands of years by many Romani Gypsies and many other tribal peoples.

To the *Chovihano*, every small pocket of the universe is alive and personalized, a global network of powerful signals being broadcast around us every single minute of every single day. Of course we have telephones, televisions, computers and other

WE BORROW THE EARTH

sophisticated forms of communicative equipment, but even if these were taken away there would still be a great hubbub going on around us day and night, not only from organic beings, but also from so-called 'inanimate' objects. A cloud in the sky might speak to us as he passes us by; a bend in the road might have something direct to say to us as she takes us on to something new; a pebble on the path might speak to us as he is accidentally kicked by our shoe. Indoors, the bed might say, 'Ouch!' when we accidentally stub a toe on her in the darkness! Quite literally, these inanimate things feel much the same as we do, because we have given them life.

There are also undoubtedly times when the *Chovihano* will see the purpose of a sickness, which must then run its course within the individual before being 'exorcized'. These are the most difficult cases for the *Chovihano* to heal, for he sees that there is an obvious need for the sickness to inhabit its host. Perhaps it has come along to teach a host something important about life. Of course, we *all learn something* from sickness. None of us are excluded. But the spirits of sickness can sometimes be employed by our guardians - those knowledgeable ancestral spirits who guide us from the Otherworld - to teach us something we might otherwise not have a chance to learn.

During my training for my healing career, I was taken on a long journey by my Ancestor down into the Underworld where the spirits of sickness ordinarily dwell, so that I could understand the hows and whys of disease, which had always baffled me. I was told to find a cave, which I did, and as I stood at its entrance I saw how dark and sinister it seemed to be inside, and I knew I would be in for a bit of a rough ride.

I was introduced then to three people: a man who was the spirit of heart disease and heart-related problems, a woman who was the spirit of emotional and mental problems, and a child, a little girl, who was the spirit of cancerous growths. There was also a fourth spirit, the spirit of change, and this spirit was neither man nor woman but somehow both.

First, the little girl, who appeared to be about five years old, came up to me and held my hand, looking up at me with big bright eyes, calling me *boro prala*, 'big brother'. There seemed to me to be nothing the matter with her while I was standing with her; in fact she was laughing and seemed bubbly and strong. But then as she pulled me further into the cave, where it became unbearably narrow, she suddenly changed into a large ugly black shadow which ran the length of the floor, wall and ceiling; a rather chilling experience at the time.

The same thing happened with both the man who represented heart problems and the woman who represented mental and emotional problems. In and out of the cave we went, all of them taking turns to pull me further inside, where all of them shapeshifted into large ugly black shadows in the most compressed part of the cave.

After a time, however, I observed that the fourth spirit there, the spirit of change, didn't move. This spirit, who seemed to be sometimes young and sometimes old, stood there just watching us while we were all busy going in and out. Concentration on this spirit soon helped me to see that change was what we really needed to be focusing upon whenever we were beginning to develop signs of sickness, otherwise we could not grow, and if we could not grow, our spirits would weaken, because we were not doing what we naturally should be doing - like fulfilling specific goals in our lives, or even taking well-earned rests when we needed to. If we did not entertain these necessary changes, we became vulnerable to magic attack by any number of black shadows who dwelt in the dark pockets of the Underworld.

I saw many people - men, women, children and even animals - going in and out of those caves during my time there. The dark shadows of bad spirits took them there largely against their will and very few noticed the lively spirit standing alone at the door, the spirit of change. Those who did notice this good spirit, however, naturally began to change themselves and the shadows thereafter left them alone, because black shadows could not live with the spirit of change.

In all my healing work I now attempt to help people understand and cope with the changes their souls ask them to make in order to get well. These can often be a big wrench, but change is often the turning-point, the start of a happier, healthier life.

But what exactly do we change into? And how do we undergo such a challenging metamorphosis? This is something we can only discover for ourselves, but usually it involves making plans to do the things you really want to be doing with your life. Much of the time we say, 'I can't, I shouldn't, I mustn't, I daren't.' But much of this has to do with having had our souls hammered into shape by people who have had theirs hammered in exactly the same way.

Because of this kind of conditioning, with the passing of time we can end up fearing our very own souls and instead of detaching ourselves from the troublesome entities, we instead detach ourselves from our bodies, which tends to make us sicker than we would perhaps ordinarily be, and soul-loss becomes the inevitable result. In my view, soul-loss has risen to epidemic proportions in our modern times. I will go more deeply into this a little later.

In these earlier days of practising my healing craft I was getting very little support from my parents. Jack Lee was dead, my *Puri Dai*, although still very much alert, was growing older, and the realization was slowly dawning on me that I would soon be totally alone.

My parents felt more and more threatened whenever I attempted to mix with *gaujos*, especially if I happened to talk to them about our guarded healing practices. Not only would bad luck catch up with me, my mother warned me, but probably the police as well! They were always knocking on the doors of Gypsies, she claimed. She filled me up with plenty of scary stories, but finally, when an opportunity arose to work abroad as a musician, I seized the chance to leave.

This didn't mean that I was deserting my family, although they inevitably interpreted it that way. Their anxieties ran high at this time, as they knew that I would continue practising my shamanic skills wherever my travels took me and also that I was not exactly travelling with my own kind.

By the time of my departure my mother had taken to her bed, dying with a kidney infection - or so she said. She seemed to have become something of a hypochondriac and a recluse at this time in her life.

I remember standing in the hall preparing to leave, with my father standing behind me, telling me how bad I was for going whilst my mother was so ill. Because she was dying I had to stay. As a *Chovihano* it was my duty to help with her passing. She had already said that the *mulesko doods*, the 'death lights', had come to collect her; they were all gathering around the bed, and if I left now, at such a critical time, she would remain in this world and would become the *Mulo*, and it would all be my fault.

I knew, as they all knew, that she was not dying at all, that she would not become the *Mulo* and that this was just her way of saying she didn't want me to go. Although it was unspoken, we also knew that nearly everything in our past was simply crumbling away because we could not stop the modern world - and its curse - seeping into every nook and cranny of our lives.

I kissed my mother and father goodbye, closed the front door and walked slowly away, feeling as if I had betrayed my clan, which of course I hadn't. There had already been fierce quarrels between us all, my mother was often heard shouting at people who came to the house, if not someone on the end of the telephone, and my father eventually numbed himself to the whole situation by beginning to live more and more in his own world, while my brother simply spent more time in the pub drinking. So in my view, the spirit of the clan had already been betrayed.

I believe this deterioration to be due to the splitting of the larger family, but I also believe that what was left of the smaller family worsened because my grandmother was no longer able to hold us all together. It is true that it is part of the *Chovihano's* job to keep everyone connected, to weave the spiritual or Otherworld lives of the tribe into a colourful, meaningful tapestry, but ours had already broken down and what remained of the family deteriorated further after I left. At this time, the curse was exerting an especially strong influence, and my great-grandfather's warnings about it were often echoing loudly in my head. My ancient skills had helped to heal many, but now I knew I had to use them to heal myself and ultimately the spirit of the Romani Gypsy race. Perhaps this was the next step along my lonely path. It was really all that was left.

Soon, my mother was stubbornly refusing to forgive me for leaving her while she was dying - even though she lived on and is indeed still living to this day. She was, and still is, an intensely passionate and dramatic woman, as many Gypsy women can be, and her influence on the rest of the family was strong. So, following her lead, the others behaved as if it had been necessary to turn me out of the clan - as used to happen to Gypsies in earlier times, particularly if one of their number had become embroiled in *gaujo* activities.

My grandmother alone did not blame me for leaving home. In fact she understood my actions very well and after she died she eventually became a guide to me from the ancestral world and, together with my great-grandfather, encouraged me to talk openly about my culture. There was, after all, no other way the culture would be preserved.

Thus the prophesy Marie had made all those years before when she told my mother that I would be working at something unusual with the *gaujos* finally came true and is still coming true today. This has always been a comfort to me, confirming that I am on the right path and am not violating any of our ancient laws but in fact helping the Romani Gypsy spirit to survive.

Perhaps my only real grievance in those earlier days was that my family refused to let me know that my grandmother had died. This indeed brought me a good deal of pain, and still does. Gladdy Lee died and was buried before I was told that she had gone, and I was left alone to mourn her in my own way as best I could. This was not an appropriate way for my parents to behave and was in fact their way of punishing me and shutting me out. Romanies can be firm in their convictions and fiercely stubborn if they want to be.

I, however, do not believe that my family would have committed a crime so great as this - least of all against a *Chovihano* - had we all still been living with our old natural ways. I do believe that the full force of the old curse was upon them when they made this terrible decision to exclude me, and they would therefore have been influenced by its dark and ugly spell. I have heard many similar stories of Romani Gypsy families acting out dramas in this way, stories of those who are normally so loyal to their blood suddenly turning against their own. Such is the curse upon indigenous peoples everywhere. We are left asking the question: is the need to 'develop' really worth such suffering?

But I also believe that my family was experiencing what many others have experienced in our difficult modern times: the problem of soul-loss.

Perhaps soul-loss can best be defined by likening it to a television whose channels are not fully in tune, even though appropriate measures have been taken to ensure the normal functioning of both picture and sound. The pictures are foggy and perhaps flicker or blur, and the sound comes and goes and may be extremely distorted. Basically, the outer casing for the television is there, and it is plugged in and in receipt of sufficient power, but even when all the right buttons are pressed, it does not function as it normally should.

The biggest symptom of soul-loss is when a person both looks and sounds normal but feels as if something vital is missing (though in many cases the person may not even know that something vital is missing). You may feel as if everything around you is foggy and flickering, and indeed distorted, especially if in the past you have known what it is to be alive and kicking, in full command of your own spirit, wits and senses. You may also feel extremely frustrated and that nothing goes right for you.

Most see soul-loss as 'losing' the soul and I believe it was once like that. But because of the way we live today I believe that we do not so much lose our souls as *withhold* them. We are familiar with holding on to, or owning, our emotions and so many other things in our lives. We all too easily tuck our souls away in a corner somewhere, where we think no one will be able to find them, but we are not able to say exactly where that place is. This is because that place is quite timeless and faceless, with no true personal identity. There our souls will slumber, as if entombed, sometimes for a whole lifetime.

One lady I worked with once described this timeless place as being something like a washing-machine, in which all her muddled thoughts and feelings were constantly swirling around, a wash programme operating its own cycle. And she was powerless to stop it because she felt so disconnected from it.

In Romani lore, such circumstances may well contribute to the soul becoming lost to darker Otherworld forces, and sickness, or a mania of some kind, may be the end result.

Traditionally, the *Chovihano* searches obscure Otherworld realms looking for people's souls, held prisoner there by unsavoury entities, but today it is far more common for the *Chovihano* to find most souls locked in the past. In fact I discovered during the many healing retreats I conducted over a period of seven years that associations with the past seem to be the greatest obstacle to living in the present. This, very clearly, brought me up against another important area of healing within Romani lore, something that is sadly given no place in our society today: the world of ancestors.

For Romanies and a great many other indigenous cultures, it is unthinkable to live without a consciousness of the dead. The ancestors guide, guard and heal, They are the vital links in the chains bonding a people's spirit and they certainly act as guardians during Romani healing rituals. Remembering and honouring the ancestors is as important as remembering and honouring our immediate mothers and fathers.

In these modern times I see so many reasons why we should restore this old form of worship, especially when many people feel so isolated and cut off from their roots. I believe many of us would feel far more connected and grounded were we walking with those ancient relations at our sides. Then we would never become trapped in the past, for we would associate the past with wisdom, honour and devotion.

In my experience, many factors add up to making a healing ritual successful: protecting oneself with lucky charms and also plenty of salt, personalizing a sickness, restoring the wild self, surrendering to the spirit of change, honouring ancestors and being especially aware of the reality of soul-loss. There is also the art of bringing oneself to the edge of the dream world, where our imagination is restored and we are no longer afraid of what is considered to be the 'unreal' within ourselves. I introduced all these things on my *Devlesko Dikkiben* programmes.

*Devlesko Dikkiben* means 'sacred vision' or 'sacred sight'. In earlier days I referred to the process in English as 'Deep Visioning', which is similar in essence to the vision quest, where journeying and a short spell of fasting is used, together with sacred plants, for encouraging clarity of vision and sense of direction. I conducted these *Dikkiben* programmes with people from all over the world and was able to carry out much exploration with this Romani way of working in order to promote healing.

In our modern times there has been much use of the fast in connection with visions. It has long been thought by many tribal communities that deprivation, particularly when it applies to food and water, promotes a stronger awareness of the self.

In earlier days, people would draw up a treaty with the *Chovihano*, so that whilst fasting he could serve as a guide on their travels through Otherworld landscapes, where visions would leap into the spirits of those who were ready to receive them. I discovered, however, over the seven years that I was fasting people, that there are many factors we have to consider today if we wish to help and not harm ourselves during the fasting process, for this is a very powerful healing art with its own unique and indomitable spirit.

I soon discovered that most people could not work through 'visioning' programmes in the way I and my elders had done. Modern social disciplines seemed to be the strongest deterrent in preventing people from acclimatizing to this process in the natural way. I met many health conditions in the people who came to me from all over the world, but in these earlier days there were a great many who did not consider that psychological and physiological changes brought about by our modern times might just make a difference to results. I therefore soon found that it was necessary to re-educate people before they began a programme, and certainly before they began a fast. They were otherwise in danger of trying to run before they had learned to walk and the consequences could be detrimental to health and well-being.

My methods did not involve a complete water fast. I discovered that a water fast could only be successfully employed - or perhaps endured - by those who were already accustomed to going without food for long periods of time, such as people who were already suffering to some degree with eating distress. Home-prepared fruit and vegetable juices were given, which affectionately became known as 'brews'. These contained healing herbs and spices, and made extremely pleasant-tasting drinks. Sometimes even light broths were given, depending upon the condition of the person, for the aim was less about depriving than stimulating the senses. The spirit of the modern 'tamed' individual itself needed to be healed before we could go any further with healing as the ancient ones would have done it. I had to find ways of inspiring and motivating people, so that they would make contact with the Otherworld, where healing was more likely to occur.

Deprivation alone, I discovered, was much too severe, at least for those in our own society, for it tended to call upon more punishing or masochistic ideals in more modern civilized individuals, an approach which has its roots in the early Christian period when monks and the more devout fasted to thrash the animal out of themselves - both because of the animal's strong associations with shamanism and paganism, and also because animals were held in great esteem, *above* human beings. So I could soon see that what we needed was to reverse this process by encouraging rather than repressing the animal within in order to lessen the intense sense of discipline which we had inherited from civilized forms of living.

Although we could not fully return to expressing the natural wild self as we had done long ago, it nevertheless became important to help people acclimatize to the idea of a wild self by talking openly about how they saw this ancient part of themselves. They also learned to understand its place in our history and to express it where they could, with the help of Romani shamanic song and dance, which has always allowed for more wild, colourful and passionate expression.

But I did not send my participants out into the wilderness to sit for long periods alone with their thoughts, for it was evident that they were doing this much of the time in their everyday lives! Most, if not all in the civilized world, live in a kind of desolate wilderness within, which is nobody's fault, but people desperately need to reconnect with others of like mind in order to feel that they *belong*. If we restore this sense of belonging, then we ultimately restore our relationship with the whole of life. Only then can we begin to take ourselves out into a wilderness, because then we will be able to contrast the outer wilderness with what we have inside. Tribal people who have lived in the natural way and who have 'belonged' have a very different way of relating to the wilderness, and indeed to their own inner selves.

It was most important to put over to participants that natural wilderness wasn't a bolt hole, nor was nature something upon which one could project one's personal ideas about life and the self. The Earth had her own exalted ancient being and also her own sacred language, but this was a language very different from that of modern human beings. Nature was, like the trees, commanding, and full of mischief and great surprises, and you needed to learn how to approach her and how to be polite with her at all times before you could ever dream of taking yourself out into her wilderness. Otherwise, she was liable to lead you in circles, test you to the hilt or else just laugh at you. And that was something few modern individuals could understand!

Many found the healing they needed on the *Devlesko Dikkiben* programmes and when I could talk openly about the shamanic healing methods I was using it was naturally all the better. Some participants stand out in my mind as making quite remarkable recoveries, in particular, Lizzie, my partner, who had a quite serious health problem when we first became friends. Apart from feeling that she had a great lack of direction in her life, she had not menstruated for nearly 10 years, having been told by doctors that she had a growth on her pituitary gland. Following a scan she was also told by doctors that she had no ovaries, something which shocked and depressed her a great deal, and which also took away a good deal of her self-confidence. Medication was prescribed, but Lizzie remained miserable. I suggested she try one of the Romani *Dikkiben* healing programmes, which included an individually tailored fast, and all the rituals that are normally within the Romani healing process. Within a month she had started to menstruate again and soon began following her own personal path, rediscovering her love of herbs, which took her on to follow shamanic training in her vocation as a *Patrinyengri* and to become my assistant in the programmes I now provide.

On the reverse side of the coin there was a man who came to me with a very bad chest complaint. Coughing blood, he had been diagnosed with possible tuberculosis. After going through one of the *Dikkiben* programmes, he returned home feeling a good deal better and planned to return to me again at another time to continue. I had neglected to tell this man who and what I was, and when he finally asked to return again I thought I could trust him, telling him openly that I was a Gypsy *Chovihano*, only to find that he refused to have anything more to do with me, on the grounds that I was now 'preaching' something he didn't want to know.

This gives an illustration of the reputation Romani Gypsies have tolerated over the centuries. Once I have admitted that I am a Gypsy, many have - although I can't honestly think why - seen me as 'religious', as if I belong to some strange cult, as did the man above. Others have developed an immediate distrust of me, while yet others think that I am some kind of hippy! In the old days I needed to work undercover for my own good. Sadly, what many of the participants on my healing programmes didn't realize was that if it were not for my Gypsy culture and for the elders and ancestors, and indeed Jack Lee, who so devotedly passed these ways down to me, no participant would ever have experienced healing in this very effective way.

Now I am able to be open, for more people are only too pleased to learn about and support these ancient healing traditions, which have been practised on the doorsteps of Europe for many hundreds of years. People are now far more ready to understand magic and the reading of omens and the physical phenomena which may sometimes occur as a result of a healing ritual, so they have a head start where the healing of their souls is concerned.

I once gave a very battered rook's feather to a lady, a feather I had used quite a lot during healing sessions, and at the end of this session the feather was as good as new again, quite as if it had just been plucked from the bird. This was a clear message to the lady that she was being healed by the spirit of that bird whose feather I had borrowed for my ritual.

The physical phenomena which occur during this kind of healing often happen as a result of all the spirits of nature - and sometimes even the spirits of objects - taking part in the healing process. Occasionally, breakages will occur during healing sessions or rituals. I have had ceilings caving in, plates cracking and glasses shattering. I have known plants and animals to behave strangely, while machines have either broken down or repaired themselves. It has been commonplace in my life for machines at fairs and exhibitions to cease functioning when I am near them, and cars have reacted by threatening to break down when I am in them - or have even decided to go back on the road when they have been off it for some time. Once an empty jug a lady was holding had the bottom fall out of it suddenly, even though it contained no water. Also, like Jack Lee, I have listened to raps at the front door when there was clearly no one waiting to come in. Always one can read omens in these things and one can look for the spirits within such things and hear them talking.

Once I learned that an acquaintance's telephone had been wiped clean of numbers that had up until that time been stored in the phone's memory. This occurred at a time when I had just held a very powerful healing ritual. The incident gave a clear message to me that the lady was having difficulty communicating with me and accepting what I was doing regarding my healing practices and I soon 'lost communication' with her, so we could say that the spirit of the telephone knew about this before I and the acquaintance did, and was ready to reflect what we were experiencing.

If people are beginning to accept these occurrences now, it is surely a sign that they are also beginning to open their eyes to Otherworld magic in a big way and to communicate again with the spirits of *all* things, which is certainly not abnormal or unusual, or *even* weird, but extremely natural for us all.

Sadly, my family never really warmed to my attempts to preserve the *Chovihano's* art and our old healing practices. It was really some considerable time before I began to realize that I was probably the last remaining *Chovihano* to be practising in Britain, and possibly in the whole of western Europe. I was the very last link in a chain of *Chovihanos* that easily stretched behind me for thousands of years. My healing work in the *gaujo* world has therefore become more urgent these days, and certainly a good deal more adventurous.

In more recent times I have had a series of very powerful visions, which were healing in themselves, for they revealed to me that I would soon be on centre stage with my culture and that this path would be rescued from near extinction. I would meet many people who would clearly benefit from this culture and these people would learn from me, first hand.

This was no exaggeration, for in 1998 I found myself sitting in a conference room at Newcastle University in front of a bunch of academics and eminent people, all knowledgeable on shamans and indigenous healers, all looking at me and waiting for what I had to say. This came about when I got to know a literary agent who believed in my indigenous lineage and suggested I write a book. She also suggested I attend the conference on shamanism. It was suddenly so refreshing to me to discover that people were not finding my practices strange any more and, more importantly, were not taking them as yet another 'New Age' pastime. I talked nervously but openly at the conference, perhaps more openly than I had ever talked before in my life, though I had never given a paper at a university before - in fact, until the day before this event I hadn't even known what a paper was.

I also gave these people a healing demonstration. This was really the first time that I was able to bring a worm into a public setting and speak openly about its incredible healing powers, which many of these people had never seen or heard of before.

From the *Chovihano* who sat in the early forests preparing for his healing rituals to the *Chovihano* that I am today, who must give demonstrations of our craft in workshops or as part of university conferences, there may seem to be a wide gap, but this gap is not all it seems. For I still conduct traditional Romani healing rituals in the old way, or as close to the old way as I can, for I believe that the old ways hold the key to helping us discover more effective ways to heal ourselves.

The forest *Chovihano* and I have both looked out at the modern *gaujo* world and we have both seen it mirroring a spiritless life. But we have smiled at each other across the barriers of time, as only Romani Gypsy ancestors and their children can, when they know that their ancient spirit is still intact.

# 7

# LEARNING TO UNDERSTAND THE HUMAN IMAGINATION

I looked down at the sparkling water and saw that it stretched a long way below me. I had to cross this river in order to get to the castle beyond and to pass the test. If I didn't cross the river now, the giant I had left sleeping behind me would wake and find me and probably eat me up. I trembled with fright.

BUT I TOOK THE MAGIC BUTTON FROM
OFF MY COAT, SAID THE MAGIC WORD
AND BLEW ON IT THREE TIMES, AS THE
WIZARD HAD INSTRUCTED ME TO DO.
THE BUTTON BEGAN WINKING IN THE
SUNLIGHT AS IT TURNED GOLD AND I
COULD FEEL THAT THE SPELL WAS
WORKING. SO I BLEW ON THE BUTTON
ANOTHER THREE TIMES AND I COULD
THEN SEE MY FACE IN ITS SHINE, JUST
AS THE WIZARD HAD PREDICTED. AND
THE BUTTON WAS GROWING BIGGER,
AND BIGGER STILL, UNTIL I KNEW
THAT, JUST AS THE WIZARD HAD
SAID, ANOTHER THREE BLOWS WOULD
FINALLY TURN THE BUTTON INTO THE
BRIDGE I SO DESPERATELY NEEDED TO
HELP ME GET TO THE OTHER SIDE.

SO I BLEW AND I WISHED, AND BLEW
AND WISHED AGAIN, VERY HARD,
BRAVELY RISKING EVERYTHING AND
THROWING THE BUTTON RIGHT OVER
THE RIVER IN FRONT OF ME AND
WATCHING IN SHEER ASTONISHMENT
AS IT TURNED ITSELF INTO A LONG
GOLDEN BRIDGE, HOOKING ITSELF
FIRMLY AND EASILY TO THE OTHER
SIDE.

AND I RAN ACROSS THE BRIDGE,
LAUGHING, ECSTATIC, KNOWING THAT I
HAD ESCAPED THE GIANT YET AGAIN,
PULLING THE BRIDGE IN TOWARDS ME

ONCE I WAS ON SAFE GROUND AND
SAYING THAT MAGIC WORD WHICH
HELPED REDUCE THE BRIDGE TO THE
SIZE OF A BUTTON ONCE AGAIN.

AS INSTRUCTED, I THEN HELD THE
BUTTON CLOSE TO MY HEART, WHERE IT
HAD ORIGINALLY BEEN, AGAIN SAID
THE MAGIC WORD, AND THE BUTTON
ATTACHED ITSELF TO MY COAT, A
GOLDEN BRIDGE NO MORE BUT JUST
THE SMALLEST, SIMPLEST, DOWDIEST
BUTTON. BUT THE LESSON HAD BEEN
LEARNED. FOR I HEARD THE WIZARD'S
WISE VOICE SPEAKING LOUDLY INSIDE
MY HEAD AGAIN. 'THERE IS MAGIC IN
ALL THINGS, BOY,' HE SAID, IN HIS
GENTLE OLD WAY. 'DON'T EVER FORGET
TO *BELIEVE.*'

The magic word used to turn the golden bridge back
into the dowdy button in that little story was, in fact,
'believe' – perhaps the main ingredient for understanding the Romani Gypsy journey.

This small piece, taken from a Romani shamanic
journey, contains many symbolic elements which
usually make up the Romani folk tale, but it also
quite typically demonstrates the Romani Gypsy
shamanic journey of old.

Generally, 'shamanic journeying' is the term we use
in modern times to access the Otherworld. For many

of the Romani Gypsies in my great-grandfather's time this was called 'spirit trav'lin''. It is common for people who follow tribal cultures these days to practise journeying in order to link with the spirits of 'power animals' and 'guardians', so that these can be employed to instruct and guide one's journey through life, and this follows a very similar pattern in the Romani Gypsy culture.

Much in the Native American culture has set a trend for the craft of shamanic journeying as we know it today, so much so that most students who come to me to learn about journeying have invariably learned something of the craft through a teacher of Native American ways. In the West this ordinarily involves learning how to reach Upper and Lowerworld 'states', which the novice will usually learn to do in very early sessions. In my own culture this is only done at advanced level, that is, when the individual has understood exactly what he or she is likely to be encountering when travelling about in the Otherworld.

The Romani Gypsy Otherworld consists of Upper, Middle and Lower worlds, and the physical world we live in is considered to be just one of the realms of the Middleworld. All that takes place within the Middleworld, in terms of natural law, has to be learned before we can ever feel safe in exploring further. In Romani lore, the Middleworld is traditionally all about balance, so it follows that if during journeying we remain in the Middleworld before venturing further afield, we establish a good balance within and learn the strengths and weaknesses of our own imaginations, thereby understanding the whole imaginative process even more.

This is an essential lesson, much like learning about the gears and pedals of a car before you take that car out on to the road. If you cannot drive the car and do not know your own limitations, i.e. how well or how clumsily you are liable to handle the controls, you'll certainly be inexperienced and may well invite an accident. Shamanic journeying the Romani way is largely structured on the same principle and all about using simple common sense. So, if you were to ask an old Romani Gypsy exactly what 'shamanic journeying' is, he might well tell you it is all about knowing how to use your imagination!

Most of us are accustomed to what is called 'visualization' where using the imagination is concerned: thinking of certain positive images in order to induce a calm and positive state of mind. This is perhaps as close as many people get to understanding what the craft of shamanic journeying is all about, but it is nevertheless a good start.

Perhaps one of our greatest problems in modern times is in our not always acknowledging our imagination, for it is only through the imagination that we can journey at all. Having progressed through a religious and therefore more dogmatic age in the centuries behind us, and then into what we now call the scientific age, where all things were measured and weighed before being given approval, we have been influenced enormously in our psychological make-up and therefore face one of the most difficult challenges of our era in re-establishing a connection with our imagination. The imagination, as we see it, smacks so strongly of illusion that we feel we are in danger of becoming fanciful - not to mention losing our marbles - if we allow ourselves to believe in it for any length of time! But at the end of the day we are going to have to blow the dust away from our imagination so that we may perhaps start looking at it in a more scientific light, perhaps realizing that we are dealing with something that has 'substance' after all - even if we don't yet know exactly what that substance is.

The more we accept that the imagination has worth - purely because it has been around for far too long to be ignored - the more we'll start to believe that we should investigate and explore this great, ancient human enigma. We may then hopefully start to believe that what we are likely to see in our imagination may not be so 'whimsical' after all, if it is properly worked with and managed in a constructive way. Perhaps we will also then be able to practise journeying to the Otherworld as a more structured craft.

First, though, we perhaps need to take on board how very much we are inclined to use our imaginations throughout every minute of our day. For example, we *imagine* where we want to go before we ever physically go to that place, we *imagine* ourselves walking across a room before we actually do it, we *imagine* picking up a pen before we pick it up. If we didn't imagine ourselves doing these things prior to the physical act, we probably wouldn't act them out at all. Similarly, we can, if we use our imaginations skilfully enough, imagine flying over a mountain top like a great bird or gracefully diving into water like a dolphin. It is true that we human beings are not able to carry out these acts every day, but understanding that the imagination has a large part to play in deciding anything that we do can contribute towards the realization that we are in fact using the imagination not just some of the time but *all* of the time – and we can cross many great boundaries within ourselves with this simple realization.

So when we are talking about successful journeying, we are really talking about more conscious use of the imagination. When sitting down to journey for the first time, we are being invited to step through a precarious gateway, precarious simply because we are unaccustomed to using the imagination. It is a daunting prospect when we suddenly find ourselves being given permission to explore, to its fullest capacity, that secret place which has remained a secret for so long that it is liable to harbour many of our greatest pleasures but also our deepest, darkest fears; and to make matters worse these will all be in their more untamed form. Is it any wonder that in giving vent to what is in the imagination we also feel that we are giving vent to a rather primitive world?

But I believe there is a healing process going on when we learn how to use the imagination again, because we are effectively taking the stopper out of that primitive world and therefore releasing a part of ourselves which we have all been suppressing for far too long. The Romani shamanic journey helps us give vent to hidden worlds which we can express in a most enjoyable and manageable form. And it doesn't have to be all doom and gloom and fear and feelings that we cannot control. For the Romani Gypsy, the craft of shamanic journeying is a distinctly earthy and sometimes quite sensuous exercise in which we make use of our senses in a quite physical way, so that when we meet the Otherworld we actually begin 'seeing' it, 'hearing' it, 'tasting' it, 'smelling' it, 'touching' it and making full contact with it in every possible way. This allows us to cross hidden boundaries and to attach a reality to the imagination which we may not have been able to do in quite such a way before.

Above all, by journeying in the Romani Gypsy way we can become openly passionate and romantic about the Otherworld. To the old Romani, giving passionate, dramatic - and sometimes even boastful - accounts of the adventures which have taken place in the vibrant realms of the Otherworld has been part of the magic of journeying. The *paramooshengro*, or storyteller (this word literally means 'dream man', or 'dreaming thing'!), often captivated camp-fire audiences with long stories of Gypsy journeys undertaken in the harshest of conditions and starring some of the most popular journeying celebrities, such as Jack the Hero, giants, innocent damsels, numerous dragons and miscellaneous fairies.

In the eyes of the Romani Gypsy, the imagination, from so-called idle day-dreaming to the most magnificent epic folk tale, has been as real as anything you might encounter in the physical world - in fact many things were considered to be *more* real, because they were a lifeline to your personal world, which was always considered to be your truer existence.

Perhaps the biggest problem people face when journeying for the first time, though, is wondering what is real and what isn't! Many people have trouble in believing in what their own mind is telling them and I so often hear the words: 'I don't know if this is real or not, but during my journey I...'

This stumbling-block occurs in the beginning for *all* of us. I do not believe that it has always been this way, but that it is a result of our having ignored the natural process of imaging over many generations. The unhealthy state of the human imagination has occurred, I believe, because of a religious mental 'branding' that has gone on throughout recent centuries, when we were all taught to think in the same way. Fortunately, this did not happen in Romani Gypsy society and Romani Gypsy imaginations remained a reliable means of accessing the Otherworld for a very long time.

My advice to anyone who experiences problems with knowing what is real and what isn't during journeying, or who wants to know the difference between constructive thoughts and misleading time-wasting ones, is to try to remember that *all experiences are real*, no matter what they are, or where they happen to have occurred, because they are *your* experiences, part of your own personal inner world. Ask yourself: 'Did this imaginative experience happen to me?' If the answer is yes, and it can only ever be yes, then it is real. It is worth making a habit out of remembering to ask yourself this question. If you ask it enough times, you'll find that the misleading time-wasting thoughts will dissolve, because they will simply become superfluous under such constructive questioning.

There is of course one element that can help this problem and which separates Romani Gypsy shamanic journeying from other forms of journeying. It is also something that is usually very attractive to those with European blood: the Romani Gypsy's connection with the old fairy tales.

Romani Gypsy 'journeying' is so uniquely linked to the old fairy tale that it often comes quite naturally to many Europeans to embark upon Gypsy-flavoured journeys with great excitement. I have found that the fairy-tale element, which we all knew and loved in childhood, tends to rekindle the old imaginative flame more than anything else. It is as if the memory of the old fairy tale, as a learning tool, is still warm in European blood, still able to ignite the flame of the European soul into a personal search for knowledge and wisdom of the ancient world. It is worth mentioning that the Gypsies themselves were so very charmed by fairy-tale figures that some female Gypsies only in the last century still used the name Cinderella!

Such journeys can contain numerous encounters with sleeping princesses, brushes with dragons, swordfights with giants, meetings with wizards and, of course, with annoyingly witty fairy people who might just want to outwit you or to talk you to death! And it can all take place against the backdrop of the traditional enchanted castle concealed in the mists beyond the great forest.

At its deepest level, the fairy-tale form of journeying involves a return to our native European past when we took these images seriously. We may be influenced by Disney renditions of fairy tales today, but practising this form of journeying means that we are tapping into what I believe was once commonplace in the mind of every Euroasian individual a long time ago. These stories, I believe, were not just for children, but very much for adults as well, with their complex psychological twists, great riddles and wise messages.

Some have said that the fairy tale came into Europe from India, where it had its beginnings, via the Grimm Brothers, while others have said that the Gypsies themselves helped to popularize it in Europe after bringing it from India. Whatever the truth, I believe the foundations of this remarkable imaginative world stretch a long way back, to our Indo-European roots, and I believe the Romani Gypsies helped to keep such a flame burning, because they believed so implicitly in this hidden magical world. I also feel very strongly that the fairy-tale world and its regular use in journeying, as practised by Romani Gypsies, not only has the power to enrich our lives, but also the capacity to reunite us with our original Indo-European ancestry, and it will be instrumental in helping us feel that we finally, truly *belong*.

Some, when journeying Romani-style for the first time, are looking to experience the convincingly 'good' journey, because in more modern times we tend to believe that journeys containing positive imagery must inevitably be more credible. But this isn't necessarily so.

As a brief example, a 'good' journey might read something like this:

I WENT TO THE OTHERWORLD AND MET A BEAUTIFUL LADY GUARDIAN. SHE GAVE ME A ROSE AND I THEN GOT UP ON TO A BEAUTIFUL WHITE HORSE AND IT CARRIED ME AWAY INTO A WONDERFUL SUNSET.

In old Romani lore a 'good' image like this on its own is an empty image. After listening to an account of a journey of this kind, an old Gypsy might well be inclined to ask, 'So? What happened next?' Just as in a fairy tale, he would be eagerly waiting for the gripping scenes of confrontation, the back-stabbing, probably a few gory bits and the eventual dawning of justice, all of which naturally occur as a story progresses. Indeed, if we are told a story where nothing but 'good' prevails, it quickly becomes boring.

Similarly, a so-called 'bad' journey would be as empty as the 'good' journey, again because a 'bad' image has little purpose in being there on its own.

A 'bad' journey could, briefly, read thus:

I WENT TO THE OTHERWORLD AND MET AN UGLY EVIL OLD WOMAN. SHE

HIT ME OVER THE HEAD WITH A HARD
PIECE OF WOOD AND I THEN GOT UP
ONTO SOME KIND OF BLACK MONSTER
AND IT CARRIED ME AWAY INTO A
COLD THICK FOG.

At this, the old Gypsy might well frown once again, because such a journey, to him, would make no sense whatsoever. He would see that it is impossible to have good without bad, and vice versa. Yet totally 'good' journeys and totally 'bad' journeys are extremely common today, when many of us feel nervous of journeying, and this is entirely due to living - through no fault of our own - with a distorted view of the human imagination.

It is perhaps necessary to define how the old Romanies perceived 'good' and 'bad'. I have already mentioned that 'good' and 'bad' played an exceptionally small part in my family's spirituality when I was a child. It was more a case of being 'witty' and 'gullible'!

This view allowed for the challenge that life was. Living by your wits encouraged the development of courage and accustomed you to taking the occasional risk, which was usually a requirement during journeying - and at many other times during your life! Wits could be increased by qualities borrowed from wild animals. Romani Gypsies looked upon wild animals and birds as being witty - when not being gullible - and also extremely courageous, so they were often considered to be more advanced beings. According to my grandmother, Jack Lee is supposed to have said that animals and birds were more advanced *human* beings!

The qualities of animals and birds were also sought and highly prized during journeying, and the Gypsies saw that within nature there was a general rule, adhered to by all in the wild, that nothing ever stepped across the fine line which kept all authority and power in Grandmother Earth's hands. So, animals like the fox, the badger, the hare and the hedgehog and birds like the owl, the swallow, the hawk and the wagtail were all special influences, with unique powers. In earlier times the bear, the wild boar, the eagle and the wolf - who all graced our lands and skies in Britain before becoming rare or extinct - would also have been cherished. Together with the horse - always a sacred animal to the Gypsies - and the dog, these fellow creatures provided qualities which we human beings lacked.

I believe that it is always preferable to journey using the qualities of the animals and birds who are native to the area in which you may be living. Familiarity builds relationship. If you use the qualities of the bear, for instance, and are unaccustomed to spending time watching bears, how will you know what a bear is really like? It is far better to borrow the qualities of animals and birds that you are accustomed to, because you will have had time to observe them more and familiarize yourself with them. Much of the time, Gypsies interacted with the animals and birds that they saw regularly in the countryside. We are also talking here about relating to the Earth around us and not attempting to cut ourselves off from it by choosing animals to work with who are never seen on the land or in the air outside our homes.

If you don't know which animals and birds are in your area, it is probably time to go looking for them. Even if you live in a town you can do this by using the Gypsy art of *dikking* and *shooning*. You can then find out which animals and birds are naturally attracted to your path. But you can also accustom yourself to various birds and animals by watching wildlife programmes. This can be an excellent way of extending your knowledge and your 'watching and listening' skills if you cannot do it by any other means. It is not at all cheating. I believe that all those on the shamanic path should observe how birds and animals behave and relate to each other, so you can never spend too long observing them. And don't forget to ask to borrow their spirits if you wish to take them on your journeys!

As a method of healing, the Romani journey is also instrumental in helping an individual answer questions, decipher riddles and solve mysteries relevant to his or her life, whilst preserving links with the more important Otherworld at the same time. It was always common for the *Chovihano* to advise individuals in his clan to journey regularly, especially when personal problems arose. Being a frequent visitor to Otherworld landscapes himself, the *Chovihano* has always been able to assist in initiating smooth, trouble-free flights across what may sometimes be difficult terrain.

The Gypsy shaman will use rhythm in the form of a tambourine, which he will smack steadily and monotonously as a means of getting an individual 'airborne', or safely on the *drom* into the Otherworld. The sound induces a state of light trance, rather like the state between wakefulness and sleep, and the individual will then move out of his or her body and into the shifting planes of the mysterious Otherworld. The 'pupil' can sit or lie when experiencing the journey. There are no set rules regarding the position you wish to adopt. You only need to feel comfortable and to be able to relax.

Some people have problems with coping with noises when attempting to journey, particularly when they do it for the first time and when they attempt it without the presence of the *Chovihano*. Of course we live in a very noisy world and it is difficult to find absolute peace, but for some every little noise becomes a big noise and just about anything distracts them, making them fidget and sometimes even making them become very irritable. It is probably good to remember that if you wish to journey alone, being strict about creating the 'right and proper' conditions will not necessarily result in the 'right and proper' journey. You can help yourself by persevering and by trying not to take it all *too* seriously.

If you do have trouble journeying, try to see it all as an adventure that will enrich your life and above all try to see it, at least at first, as fun.

My case for promoting Romani shamanic journeying as a healing tool comes out of many years of working with people and studying their imaginations. Many will launch themselves into a complete fairy-tale journey almost instantly at my suggestion during the 20 or 25 minutes or so that my tambourine taps out its hypnotic Romani rhythm.

Those who are open to exploring their imagination are those who produce the most fascinating and enchanting journeys, and the human depth that has been present in many of these tells a story about the richness of our relationship with a Europe of long ago. Some relevant experiences of Romani-style journeys are given below.

I TRIED TO ENTER THE OLD CASTLE, BUT THERE WAS A GIANT THERE HOLDING A VERY LARGE SPEAR, WHICH HE WAS USING TO PROD ME EVERY TIME I CAME CLOSE TO THE GATES. I COULD REALLY SEE THE SPEAR'S TIP GLINTING IN THE LIGHT OF THE SUN. I TRIED MY BEST TO FIGHT HIM BUT HE CAUGHT MY SHOULDER WITH THE SPEAR AND IT WOUNDED ME ENOUGH TO BRING ME DOWN. I COULD FEEL THAT I WAS BLEEDING. BUT I LANDED IN THE PRINCE'S ARMS AND HE RUSHED ME INSIDE THE CASTLE AND LOOKED AFTER ME FOR A LONG TIME, NURSING ME BACK TO HEALTH. AND ONE DAY WE WENT TO SEE THE OLD WIZARD OF THE CASTLE, AND HE MADE A SPELL AND TURNED BOTH THE PRINCE AND ME INTO WHITE DOVES. WE WERE

THEN ABLE TO EXPERIENCE SUCH A LOT OF FREEDOM, FLYING UP INTO THE SKY AT GREAT SPEED, AND THEN DIVING DOWN AGAIN, NARROWLY MISSING THE CASTLE TURRETS, WHILE BELOW US, THE GIANT KNEW NO DIFFERENT. HE SAT SLEEPING IN THE COURTYARD, NEVER KNOWING THAT WE COULD BECOME SUCH BEAUTIFUL BIRDS, FOR WE COULD EVEN FLY AROUND HIS HEAD AND HE WOULD NEVER KNOW WHO WE REALLY WERE. HE JUST THOUGHT IT WAS THE WIND TICKLING HIS NOSE! BY THIS MEANS WE WERE ABLE TO MAKE OUR ESCAPE.

I ATE THE GOLDEN APPLE, TAKING THREE BITES OF THE DELICIOUS FRUIT SO THAT THE SPELL WOULD WORK. THE OLD WITCH STOOD BY, WAITING FOR HER VICTORY, WAITING FOR ME TO TURN INTO A FROG. BUT THIS DIDN'T HAPPEN, BECAUSE I HAD SEARCHED FOR THE APPLE IN THE RIGHT WAY, PICKED THE APPLE IN THE RIGHT WAY AND EATEN IT IN THE RIGHT WAY. AND THIS SERVED TO BREAK THE SPELL SHE HAD PUT ON ME. SHE WAS FRUSTRATED AND VERY ANGRY, DANCING UP AND DOWN AND COMPLAINING. AND I WAS ABLE TO RIDE AWAY THROUGH THE WOOD ON THE BEAUTIFUL WHITE HORSE THAT

THE KING AND QUEEN HAD GIVEN TO
ME. I KNEW I HAD PASSED MY TEST
AND THAT THE OLD WITCH WOULD
TROUBLE ME NO LONGER.

❧

I AM GIVEN A FLUTE BY THE *BITI FOKI*,
OR AT LEAST TWO THIRDS OF A FLUTE,
THE TOP PART AND THE BOTTOM PART!
THE TOP PART SEEMS TO BE THE WHIS-
TLE AND THE BOTTOM DOES HAVE
HOLES IN IT SO THAT YOU CAN PLAY IT,
BUT THE MIDDLE PART CONTAINS THE
MELODY, AND THAT IS THE PART THAT
IS MISSING, THE PART I HAVE TO EARN.
I KNOW THAT WHEN I HAVE FOUND
THE 'MELODY' PART, THE *BITI FOKI* WILL
SAY I HAVE PASSED MY TEST.

❧

I LOOK INTO THE WATER AND SEE THE
FACE OF A WIZENED OLD WITCH. SHE
IS HIDEOUS, BUT WHEN I PUT MY
HAND INTO THE WATER AND MAKE
RIPPLES AND THE RIPPLES SETTLE
AGAIN, I SEE THE FACE OF A
BEAUTIFUL YOUNG PRINCESS. I KNOW
THAT I CAN BE BOTH THESE THINGS,
AS WE CAN ALL BE BOTH THESE
THINGS: THE TRICKSTER AND THE
TRICKED. BUT WHICH ONE IS WHICH?

I take my lucky charm and put it on and I have two magic wands wrapped in red cloth tied on to my back like a quiver of arrows. I and my spirit guardian and a member of the *BITI FOKI* burn mugwort in our Otherworld bender for protection, for we know that there will be a bit of a fight ahead. We then make our way along a path through the wood towards the mountain and the guardian tells me we will meet Jack the Hero at a crossroads.

Jack is at the crossroads, a real swashbuckling type. We look up at the castle ahead, and there are dark clouds forming and claps of thunder and lightning all around it. Jack says there is a way into the castle through a window at the top, but that we must change our shape into buzzards to get in. I explain to Jack that I don't know how to be a buzzard. Jack tells me that I have to think myself a buzzard and he produces a buzzard's feather, which he sticks into my chest. I feel no pain, but I start to feel an awareness I've never felt before;

EVERY SENSE IS HONED AND VERY
ALERT. I REALIZE I HAVE GROWN
FEATHERS AND MY ARMS HAVE BECOME
WINGS, AND I *FEEL* LIKE A BUZZARD.
THE *BITI FOKI* MAN JUMPS ON TO MY
BACK, I FLAP MY WINGS AND WITHOUT
ANY EFFORT AT ALL FLY UP TOWARDS
THE CASTLE WITH EVERYONE ELSE ON
THE BREEZE.

BUT WHEN WE ARRIVE AND CHANGE
BACK INTO OURSELVES AGAIN, THINGS
SOON CHANGE. FOR THERE IS SUDDENLY
A FOUL STENCH. WE LOOK AROUND AND
THERE IS THE CASTLE'S GUARDIAN,
EYES GLARING LIKE RED FIRE, SKIN
SCALY BLACK WITH BRISTLES. I
REALIZE THAT HE IS THE GREED,
ANGER AND ARROGANCE OF OUR WORLD.
HE IS THE SHADOW SIDE OF LIFE THAT
WE ALSO HAVE WITHIN US. THIS
CREATURE MOVES IN A CIRCLE LIKE A
WHIRLWIND AROUND US ALL, UNTIL
JACK TAKES FROM HIS BELT A LARGE
LEATHER BAG OF SALT, WHICH WE
SPRINKLE OVER THE CREATURE. THE
CREATURE SCREAMS AND FALLS BACK,
SMOKE POURING OFF HIM AS THE SALT
BURNS INTO HIM. I THEN CALL ON *YAG*,
THE FIRE SPIRIT, TO HELP ME. I HOLD
OUT MY HAND, MY PALM UPPERMOST,
AND A FLAME APPEARS VERY QUICKLY
IN MY PALM, AND A VOICE INSIDE MY
HEAD TELLS ME TO BLOW THE FLAME

IMMEDIATELY TOWARDS THE MONSTER. THIS I DO AND THE FLAME SHOOTS OUT AS IF FROM A FLAME-THROWER. THE CREATURE IS THEN COMPLETELY COVERED IN FIRE, REELS BACK AND BLASTS THROUGH THE CASTLE WALL AND WE ARE ABLE TO RESCUE THE PRINCESS.

WHEN I FIND HER THOUGH SHE IS LIKE THE CORPSE OF AN ANCIENT OLD WOMAN, HER SKIN WRINKLED LIKE CRACKS IN ROCK. I BEND FORWARD AND KISS HER, THREE TIMES, AND AS SHE SMILES AND OPENS HER EYES SHE BECOMES A BEAUTIFUL YOUNG WOMAN. SOON THERE IS A RUMBLING SOUND, THE FLOOR STARTS TO SHAKE AND THE WALLS START TO CRUMBLE; THE WHOLE CASTLE IS THEN FALLING TO THE GROUND AND BEING SUCKED BACK INTO THE EARTH.

MY GUARDIAN THEN TELLS ME, 'SEE, YOU HAVE DONE IT. THINGS FOR YOU WILL NEVER BE THE SAME AGAIN. YOU HAVE MADE THE CHANGE NOW.'

THERE IS MUSIC AND CELEBRATION AFTER THAT, AND IT SUDDENLY POURS DOWN WITH RAIN, WHICH SEEMS TO CLEANSE EVERYTHING. BUT AS I AM MOVING AWAY I TURN TO LOOK BACK, WHICH IS WHEN I SEE THE BLACK

CLOUDS AND LIGHTNING STILL FAR
AWAY ON THE DISTANT HORIZON.
SO I AM REMINDED THAT THIS WILL
NOT BE THE LAST TIME I HAVE TO
FACE THE MONSTER.

These five examples are typically Romani Gypsy
and therefore very typically composed of fairy-tale
imagery, but they were experienced by people who
are not Romani Gypsies - as far they are aware -
though they all have European blood. Interestingly,
they are all tapping into the old European
Otherworld language of imagery long used by
Romani Gypsies in western Europe in the past, and
all of the people who experienced these journeys
were able to produce such imagery without very
much suggestion from me at all, perhaps by calling
upon their own inner reserves or their own ancient
European inner memory.

Such imagery is effective when used in journeying
because it helps us to see things as they are, even
though on the surface it appears that we are using a
more flimsy method for our explorations when calling upon fairy-tale figures.

Certain stereotype images and common magical antidotes are commonly used in Romani Gypsy journeying, as these are most powerful and can be relied
upon to help produce results, such as the appearance
of a wizard to help conjure a spell that will be effective in breaking another spell, or the empowering
image of Jack the Hero, who occurs in many fairy
stories and who is employed as a warrior kind of

figure in Romani mythology, for he will always be summoned to help Otherworld travellers fight through their obstacles and win the day. Jack the Hero is a commanding, youthful and sometimes humorous male spirit, an entity in his own right, and to have him on your side invariably helps you achieve success.

There is also the magical practice of doing something three times, such as kissing the princess three times or biting from the golden apple three times, which helps to seal something or free something from restriction. The golden apple occurs again and again in Romani Gypsy folk tales and symbolizes knowledge, wisdom, attractiveness, love and many positive attributes. Traditionally from the golden apple tree in the Otherworld, it also, however, tests us to the hilt - are we worthy enough to receive its gold, its sensual pleasures, its profound wisdom? I sometimes think that the apple in the Garden of Eden must be something of a test for Adam and Eve in this same way. If the romantic couple don't pick it and eat it at the right time, or perhaps if they don't bite from it three times, bad things will come, for they will not have satisfied this ancient law or passed their test!

Students of Romani shamanic journeying soon begin to experience the Otherworld as a reality, as it suddenly begins to talk to them through the many different characters who represent it and who travel with the journeyer through his or her imagination. The Otherworld also comes more alive to the senses the more the journeyer travels through it. For example, most get to feel the cold stone of a castle wall if they touch it, or the bark of a tree, or the soil of the Earth. When I take students on journeys, I constantly ask them to feel the soil of the Earth in the Otherworld, to dig their fingers into it and to allow it to run through their fingers, to smell the soil and even to taste it. This links a person with the Otherworld in a very real and profound way.

At a more basic level, the journeyer can use the journey as a relaxant. Participants are at first taken along a peaceful river into the Otherworld, where they can learn how to use their senses and where they can establish for themselves an 'Otherworld home', perhaps in the form of a bender or a traditional Romani wagon or a little old hut. At the beginning they need to feel secure in their new surroundings, and that they are supported, so they spend a lot of time relaxing and also exploring the Otherworld environment, while different Otherworld characters and situations are introduced. They are advised to stay in the Middleworld, so that they learn to feel their feet. Their challenges will come later.

The student of the more advanced Romani shamanic journey discovers just how involved Gypsy journeying can be, in the sense that it reflects just how involved one's journey through life can be. It is a more profound exercise in learning how to work through one's life problems with a view to finding a solution. Perhaps the ultimate challenge, though, is in learning how to manage the monsters, the ogres, the black shadows and all those things we find fearful and which usually represent ongoing problems that we have.

In the last journey of those given above, we have a very good example of someone who is learning to meet his own challenges and learning how to manage his own life's monsters. The phrase, 'So I am reminded that this will not be the last time I have to face the monster' can only come from a person who is learning how to look himself squarely in the eye, without excuses. The more advanced journey teaches us that we will never stop meeting difficulties in life, but, if we use our wits and common sense, it is possible to learn how to manage them. This approach can in itself serve to lessen some difficulties, for we also learn to see them coming, rather than invite them by falling back on behaviour patterns that are usually based on bad experiences in the past.

Another common theme in the advanced journey is the theme that occurs with the flute in the third journey given above. The middle section of the flute, the melody, is missing. This sums up the importance of having a beginning, a middle and an end in all journeys, so that we can learn the importance of beginnings, middles and endings in our lives, for whenever we begin a project of any kind, it usually presents us with a mystery we may be wishing to solve or a question we may wish to have answered. A challenge will then develop and we must seek the best solution to the mystery or question, thereby rounding off that miniature 'journey' we might have taken in our social, working or domestic lives.

Again, there is the importance of the number three, which will often repeat itself in so many situations, and completion of the 'three' means we are more easily able to move on to 'four', which gives us greater stability and material grounding.

So all Romani journeys are expected to be very similar to a folk tale, with a beginning, a middle and an ending. The 'melody' in the flute journey represents the lady's attempts to harmonize with the tune her soul needs to play. Her courage is shown in her decision to wait until she has earned the middle part of the flute. In other words, the middle part of a project she is attempting to play out in her life will come to her when she is ready for it. The irony and indeed the complexity of this kind of journey lie in the fact that the journey itself already contains a middle part, for the lady has really already met the challenge! Threes within threes can become common in Romani lore and are indeed quite common in our own everyday lives, for there are always projects within projects, challenges within challenges, stories within stories we are constantly trying to live out. These are present in a great many folk tales and are the magical concoctions which *Chovihanos*, as old wizards, would have attempted to work into their spells.

Without doubt, the more frequently you conduct shamanic journeying, the more skilled you will eventually become during the all-important middle section of a journey, which is undoubtedly the most difficult part for anyone to achieve. And if you employ spirits like Jack the Hero, you will be surprised at the depth these seemingly fragile fairy-tale characters can contain when their spirits are brought to life.

Journeying in a group is always a good idea, although you can also journey alone. In a group you are able to inspire each other and draw energy from each other and tell each other your journeying stories - especially if you are able to do so around a camp-fire. Always journey around a flame, even if it is just a candle, if you can, for the flame has always been the central part of any Gypsy shamanic exercise.

Occasionally, a person will say that he or she cannot imagine anything during a journey. A lady I worked with some years ago could not for the life of her imagine anything at all - or so she said. I do not believe that people cannot imagine anything at all, for, as mentioned earlier, it takes imagination even to be able to pick up a pen! In this case the lady told me she loved the sea and seashores, so we overcame the problem by my asking her to imagine *imagining* the sea and the seashore. She could do this and it helped her to overcome her gross inadequacy about 'competing' in the group situation. This problem can arise for some people who feel that everyone else's journey will inevitably be better than their own - which of course isn't true. The lady's journeys did steadily progress to experiences which gave her a little more freedom, once she got the hang of them. But this incident saddened me enormously when I realized that we had arrived at the stage where we now have to *pretend to pretend* in order to get results where our imagination is concerned!

It takes time, patience, courage and indeed a sense of humour to be able to journey well. Those who will have success are those who experience the journey as a riddle and as an exciting adventure, but who do not expect every obstacle of the journey to be resolved at the snap of their fingers.

Because I encourage people to 'believe' in the imagination, some misinterpret this and think that to be very accepting of all the imagery one discovers on a journey is the best approach to the craft, but that is not the Gypsy way. What happens to you is real, but it doesn't necessarily have to be acceptable, and we must all ask our own questions and make our own decisions about what we accept and what we do not accept. The Gypsy is a natural questioner and is not afraid to challenge. Also, always with the 'wild self' at heart and always ready to make the best use of his or her wits, the Gypsy *expects* the confidence trick - and usually from *all* the spirits and characters that are encountered on the journey. But that is the nature of the challenge.

The modern use of imagery, often consigned to television commercials, computer imagery and computer-assisted movies, certainly seems to have replaced the old European shamanic journey. But once we regularly and adventurously entered uncharted terrain and courageously wrestled with and outwitted darker forces in the many Otherworld realms. And we nearly always became heroes and heroines at the end of the stories, modelling ourselves on those of ancient legend, just as we may model ourselves on movie stars and pop stars today. But we did all this then as a fundamental part of everyday life, not just as a pastime. So the imagery would doubtless have been a good deal more vivid in our minds.

It is true that if we journey in a group regularly the imagery does become extremely clear. We are able to see and sense things more clearly than usual. The experience can be quite remarkable and I sometimes think that compared with our ancient cousins, who would have journeyed as regularly as we might go shopping, our imaginations today must be very tame and colourless indeed.

I, like my great-grandfather, have journeyed on many occasions for a week or more, living for the whole of that time in the Otherworld while my body remained in this world. I was younger at the time and desperate to learn about the vastness of such a magical place, and I would emerge from somewhere outside, where I might have been sitting with the trees, to have my dinner or a snack, or to sleep, and then I would return my body to its state of light trance and carry on with my journey.

Developing this unique art was very similar to developing my general powers of vision, for just as I was left in a darkened room to allow this to happen, so I was left alone during these important times too. My elders understood what was going on, and my mother prepared my meals and made me cups of tea here and there, but otherwise didn't disturb me. I was able to slip in and out of the trance state and indeed the Otherworld, with great ease, and within my own time, which meant that I could continue the journey exactly where it had left off, rather like a soap opera. Afterwards I was able to recall the entire journey as if it were one continuous story - which of course completely defies our physical sense of time.

This gave me a new concept of time as we know it today.

In later years I have been on journeys that have lasted for months at a time, but this works by allowing the inner part of yourself to journey while the rest of you remains in the physical world, which again alters the concept of our physical understanding of time. This kind of journeying is a difficult art when practised in this way and takes many years to develop. Care has to be taken when learning how to practise it, for it would be all too easy to lose that sense of constructive grounding and to slip off into a more illusory dream-state. But it can all be achieved if one works hard enough at it. In fact, the general rule for all journeying techniques is: the more work you put into it, the more results you will achieve.

Jack Lee travelled regularly, widely and indeed 'lightly', so he said, as that was by far 'the best way to be dressed for such occasions'. What he meant by this was that if you travelled with a light heart, you would be enriched beyond your dreams, but if you travelled with your overcoat on, journeying would indeed become a chore, even a bit of a nightmare on certain occasions, and you would end up returning from the Otherworld probably as puzzled and confused as when you first entered it. I have found this to be true and always advise those who are very serious about life to perhaps try lightening up a little, suggesting that if they have problems they might like to try mentally removing their overcoats! It often works. Journeying is a craft which should be enriching and educational, but it should also be lots of fun.

But if there is one influence which helped me understand journeying in all its forms, it was undoubtedly my great-grandfather's capacity to believe. He instilled this in me from an early age and I soon discovered that it was the best tool to carry with me when journeying into the Otherworld, for my experiences were then valued and cherished beyond words, and they were *always* considered to be real, no matter what form they took. The fairy-tale castles were real, the dragons and witches living in the great Otherworld forests were real, the golden apple tree was real, the *Biti Foki* were real, and Otherworld giants and princes and princesses and kings and queens were real. That was the wonderfully magical world I was introduced to as a child and which I still live in much of the time today.

But on the other side of the coin I was also always encouraged to be always ready to face a challenge, for your journeys will constantly challenge you and your own ideas. In more modern times I always tell my students to be always ready to ask questions and to study the imagination, and to believe what one sees within the imagination. To challenge and to believe: these are perhaps two assets which you are wise to take with you on your journeys.

During journeying programmes I have met many people who believe that because the Otherworld is unrestricted by time and space, and because spirit travelling is a somewhat free exercise, they can go wherever they like and do whatever they please during journeying exercises. This is of course possible, for the Otherworld is a place with absolutely no limits. But the limitlessness is itself a test. If you discovered a table 1,000 miles long laden from end to end with food, would you eat all the food in one sitting? If you did, you might well die! The absence of limits in the Otherworld is itself a great testing ground and is something that should never be overlooked or misjudged. The journeying process, like nature herself, is always ready to teach us as valuable a lesson by what it doesn't show us as by what it does!

When I began to learn about the journeying craft from my elders, I was taught that there were in fact many strict rules and more than anything else, we needed to keep the same reverence for the Otherworld as we keep - or should keep - for this physical world, for all worlds are only ever borrowed. It is the biggest mistake to assume that the Otherworld, and indeed the journeying process itself, is always there for the taking, but still many people fall into this trap.

When visiting the Otherworld, try if you can to remain cautious and respectful always, because the Otherworld is full of different (witty and gullible) spirits - or influences - and all these are there to test you as well as to bring you comfort.

My Romani Ancestor once told me, when I was questioning travel, that we always assume that we are the ones doing the travelling, when in fact it may be the reverse and some things may well be travelling to us! We were speaking of space flight at the time and the Ancestor said, 'What makes you think you travel to the moon in your rockets? Perhaps the moon is travelling to you!' It was a comment which made me question travel even more. It led me to realize that the universe is not a playground for the traveller alone. Many other forces and spirits and beings are at work, and this fact should always be respected.

I believe that travel was originally linked to communication in our deeper past when we didn't rely solely upon verbal language to converse with each other, especially as in earlier times we were not only conversing with human beings but with a multitude of other creatures and things as well.

If elements within nature - such as the moon - are travelling to us, then they are doing so not just because they are travelling, but because they are communicating. I believe that an inner language, a sacred language, exists in this way and has always had the power to transport us to other realms. I also believe that in our distant past, journeying as we know it today would have been our main form of travel upon Grandmother Earth, simply because we didn't know what it was to travel geographically without also travelling personally. Your personal, borrowed life, always came first. This is a language that would have been spoken by all *Chovihanos*, a language composed of sounds, gestures, interaction with various elements within nature, reading the omens resulting from this, telepathy and anything that was an expression of personal life. It is a language I still use today.

'If there were no written word, the ignorant would rule the world.' I once saw this quote, written by an eighteenth-century Georgian poet, pinned on a notice-board in the house of a man I was visiting and I thought at the time that it quite seemed to sum up how we see language and the imagination in our 'civilized' world. As a writer, I love the written word, but this quote saddened me, because it assumed that there was not, and perhaps had never been, a sacred language of imagery and symbolism that could well have been the principal form of communication in many ancient and tribal cultures all over the world.

It saddens me to think just how *much* we have pushed the fairy-tale world underground, this beautiful magical world which once fashioned everyday life and the initiations of our deeper past in Europe. But a student of mine once said to me, 'These Romani teachings of yours reawaken the Sleeping Beauty within me.' This comment could simply sound like romantic fantasy, but it touches the very heart of the Romani shamanic journey. The lady who spoke these words was French, but this phrase also says a good deal about the spirit of the imagination which once thrived in western Europe and which is now very much like a great and beautiful princess, sleeping within us, and also beneath us within the Earth.

Long ago, Sleeping Beauty, a spirit recognizable to all of us who have European roots, came under the spell of a wickedly clever fairy, whose spirit worked through many gullible sorcerers. These sorcerers threatened to kill the beautiful princess – or to take the beauty of the imagination away. The princess would prick her finger when she was 18 – civilized life would be a test for this natural spirit, nine being a crucial number for testing the soul, even the soul of a great princess - and she and all her people would fall into a deep sleep in which they would know nothing of their older life, until a handsome prince found his way to the castle, kissed the princess and woke her. Then they would all live happily ever after - or reunite with their imaginative lives again. I believe we are still in that deep hypnotic slumber in our physical world, together with the beautiful Earth spirit, or princess, of our land, and I believe that this seemingly eternal sleep affects us when we journey.

*The Sleeping Beauty* was thus a sad tale expressing the story of the *Bari Weshen Dai*, 'the Great Forest Mother', who was a beautiful feminine spirit residing in the forests of Europe. Her fate was sealed when the spell was cast. And she still now sleeps, entombed beneath the Earth, and also within us, waiting to be kissed and brought back to life again by her dashing prince - whose brave spirit is also within us. Interestingly, in the French language *The Sleeping Beauty* is called *La belle au bois dormant*, 'The Beauty of the Sleeping Wood'!

I often tell students who come to learn the craft of Romani journeying how we can all take on the role of the handsome prince who kisses this beautiful lady. For a greater part of us is sleeping along with her, as we are all entranced by the spell. But when she wakes, in the future, we will wake too, and she *will* wake, because that is her fate also. No bad spell can last forever. The 'good' image must inevitably follow the 'bad' one! And we will eventually outwit the one who created this powerful soul-numbing slumber. Who knows what will happen when the Sleeping Beauty finally wakes!

The journey I conduct with students around the theme of waking the Sleeping Beauty is always one of the most important journeys, for it serves to re-kindle the student's relationship with Puv, the Earth Spirit, via the *Bari Weshen Dai*. It can help to develop essential assertiveness and also direction.

The journey involves trying to get into a castle to retrieve something that must be released, but at the same time you are restricted by the protector of that castle, who will challenge you when you arrive at the castle gates.

The protector can take many forms. He is invariably a male, whom some will see as a large man, perhaps a giant, or else as some kind of dragon or monster. Some have been so afraid of being challenged by this being that they have turned and have taken flight, never to return, while others have drifted off into a journey of a completely different kind in order to avoid the situation completely.

It is not the object of the exercise to get into the castle in any specific way, for you can only ever do things in your *own* way. But it is necessary to find out how you will tackle certain rigorous tests which may occur and to learn what spirits may be best for you to borrow in order to achieve your own results. It is up to you to find out just how you can win by over-powering this protector. Your wits and courage can come into play, and also your senses. But it is also important to realize that we all meet this protector, who is really our own shadow, in many different forms during many situations in everyday life, and we may not even be required to approach him in the same way twice. I have therefore asked some of my students to carry out this journey more than once, for the results are often quite different the second time.

Any approach we use in journeying may symbolize much that is going on within our physical lives, but it can also often be the reverse within Romani Gypsy lore: much of what we do in our ordinary lives can symbolize what is going on in our Otherworld lives! This would seem to be a somewhat topsy-turvy way of looking at the craft of journeying, but shamanic journeying within the Romani culture is seen to be as real an act as that of walking along the street! It is not a therapy, although it can be considered to be therapeutic, and it is never the *Chovihano's* task to psychoanalyse each and every individual experience, because many individual journeying experiences will contain elements of what is going on in the many different worlds we all reside in.

It is the *Chovihano's* role, however, to help the individual understand how both the inner/imaginative life and the physical life are liable to function, and how very intertwined they may be. Therefore, he may explain some of the symbolism and may offer advice on the spirits who may have been attracted to interact with an individual and the spirits who may be called in to help in the future.

A journey containing more obvious elements of what is going on in both worlds might read something like this:

I WENT TO THE OTHERWORLD AND MET A BEAUTIFUL LADY GUARDIAN. SHE HIT ME OVER THE HEAD WITH A HARD PIECE OF WOOD AND I WONDERED WHAT ON EARTH SHE WAS DOING. I THEN REALIZED THAT SHE WAS REALLY AN UGLY EVIL OLD WOMAN IN DISGUISE, SOMEONE WHO LOOKED LIKE A WOMAN I KNEW IN MY PHYSICAL LIFE BUT WHO HAD BEEN TRYING TO OUTWIT ME ALL THIS TIME, WITHOUT MY KNOWING.

I DIDN'T WANT TO BE TAKEN FOR A RIDE, SO I PRETENDED THAT I WAS STILL GULLIBLE AND WENT ALONG WITH HER. SHE HIT ME OVER THE HEAD SEVERAL TIMES MORE. BUT THEN I CALLED JACK THE HERO TO MY AID AND THE HARE WHO IS MY FRIEND. THEIR SPIRITS GAVE ME COURAGE. JACK, BECAUSE HE IS BRAVE, TOLD ME TO CALL THE OLD WOMAN TO ME, WHICH I DID, THOUGH I WAS TREMBLING WITH FRIGHT. SHE CAME, HOLDING THE CLUB OF WOOD OVER MY HEAD, ABOUT TO STRIKE ME AGAIN. THEN, AS IF BY MAGIC, MY FRIEND THE HARE ALSO CAME TO MY AID. 'RUN!' HE YELLED SUDDENLY, SEEING WHAT THE

OLD WOMAN WAS ABOUT TO DO. THE
HARE HAD JUMPED TOWARDS ME AND
INTO ME, AND THEN I RAN, WITH HIS
LEGS, LEAPING OVER MANY OBSTACLES,
RUNNING AND RUNNING FOR ALL I
WAS WORTH, CRASHING INTO MANY
THINGS AS I WENT, BUT THAT WAS
BECAUSE I WAS NOT USED TO BEING
A HARE AND HADN'T LEARNED HOW
TO USE HIS LEGS.

I STOPPED AT A HEDGE AND CHANGED
BACK INTO MYSELF AGAIN, AND JACK
WAS THERE. 'NOT BAD!' HE SAID,
CHUCKLING, AMUSED. 'COULD BE
BETTER. YOU MIGHT NOT HAVE GOT
RID OF THAT OLD WOMAN, BUT YOU
CAN GIVE HER A GOOD RUN FOR HER
MONEY NOW!'

Not only does this journey contain the vital beginning, middle and ending, or the mystery, the challenge and the solution, but also the good and bad
imagery, the use of wits and senses, and a somewhat
roguish Gypsy approach! We may also see that the
person is about to learn how to run like a hare in
both worlds, the ordinary physical life and the inner
life, *both* of which are useful exercises.

We are perhaps so accustomed to the psychological
approach to things in our lives - the inner symbolizing
the physical - that we find it hard to believe that
what we experience in our journeys can be a *real inner
experience* for its own sake, i.e. whether the evil

woman hits the student on the head in the physical life or in the Otherworldly life, the student has met a challenge in how to deal with this kind of spirit in all worlds. Yet we may eventually understand that we don't just have a representative of the woman in the Otherworld, but the woman herself, or the spirit of the woman itself. So when the student meets the spirit of this kind of influence next time, wherever he may be, he knows exactly how to deal with her and this will be instrumental in altering his attitude for the good in the future.

This is, of course, a journey in a more advanced stage, and most people might feel obliged to find a more decisive and positive ending, but the whole essence of journeying in the Romani way is to discover how to walk your path successfully, wherever you happen to be walking it, and ordinarily we are all walking paths in two worlds. Most importantly, we are learning how to manage what we discover upon our paths, rather than living for what we may find at our path's end. There perhaps is no end, no real horizon, no goal where we sit down and say, 'Well, that's that.' Otherworld journeying can always assist you in learning what you need to learn at the time you need to learn it. That is why it is an ongoing adventure and that is why you will never travel your last journey. It is an eternal exercise, like life itself.

Moving back into the imaginative life will teach us all how we may once again believe in these Otherworld experiences which we believed in for so many thousands of years. And once we give our souls over to the Otherworld, we will find an existence that is more in keeping with the existence our ancestors once had, and that will reawaken the Sleeping Beauty indeed.

'BELIEVE?' I SAID TO MYSELF, AS I WALKED ON TOWARDS THE CASTLE, TOYING WITH THE WORD. I HAD TO RETRIEVE SOMETHING WHICH WAS CONTAINED WITHIN THIS PLACE AND DIDN'T KNOW WHO OR WHAT THAT SOMETHING WOULD BE. BUT ABOVE ALL I KNEW I HAD TO BELIEVE.

I FINGERED THE MAGIC BUTTON WHICH WAS STILL ATTACHED TO MY COAT AS I APPROACHED THE CASTLE GATES. I KNEW I WOULD MEET THE CASTLE GUARDIAN THERE, HE WHO HAD A REPUTATION FOR TERRIFYING THE MOST COURAGEOUS OF PEOPLE. I HADN'T A CLUE WHAT FORM HE WOULD TAKE THIS TIME.

BUT WHEN I GOT THERE I SAW HIM: A SMALL MAN, ABOUT TWO FEET HIGH, SITTING ON A TINY CHAIR. JUST LIKE THE GIANT I HAD LEFT IN THE WOOD, THIS LITTLE MAN WAS SLEEPING, A STRANGE HIGH-PITCHED GASPING SOUND ESCAPING FROM HIS TINY MOUTH AS HE ATTEMPTED TO SNORE.

I DECIDED THE BEST THING TO DO WAS TO CREEP PAST HIM, WHICH TOOK ME A

VERY LONG TIME. HE ROUSED HIMSELF
ONCE, BUT SOON RETURNED TO HIS
DREAMS AGAIN. BUT THEN JUST AS I
WAS ALMOST PAST HIM HE OPENED HIS
EYES WIDE, AS IF HE KNEW I HAD
BEEN THERE ALL THE TIME.

SHOULD I RUN? I THOUGHT. BUT
WHICH WAY SHOULD I RUN - FURTHER
ON INTO THE CASTLE OR BACK TO THE
RIVER, WHERE THE GIANT MIGHT BE
WAITING FOR ME? THE WIZARD HAD
ASKED ME TO RETRIEVE SOMETHING
CONTAINED WITHIN THE CASTLE AND
IF I RETURNED WITHOUT IT I
PROBABLY WOULDN'T PASS MY TEST.

I LOOKED UP AT THE CENTRAL TOWER,
WHICH WAS DIRECTLY IN FRONT OF
ME, STRETCHING UP INTO INFINITY. I
COULDN'T SEE THE TOP OF IT, AS IT
ENDED IN THE SKY. IF I RAN FURTHER
INTO THE CASTLE NOW I WOULD
CERTAINLY NEED TO CLIMB THIS TOWER
IN ORDER TO COMPLETE MY TASK.

BRAVELY, I STOOD MY GROUND AS THE
LITTLE FAIRY MAN CAME TOWARDS ME
WITH A CRUEL SMILE TWISTING HIS
SMALL FACE. HE HAD A SWORD AND I
KNEW THAT HE WAS ABOUT TO CUT OFF
MY ARMS AND LEGS. EVEN WORSE, I KNEW
HE HAD NOTICED THE MAGIC BUTTON AND
WANTED TO STEAL IT FOR HIMSELF.

HE HAD MAGIC POWERS AND LIKE LIGHTNING HE CUT DOWN SOME OF THE VINE WHICH WAS WINDING ITS WAY UP THE TOWER WALL, WAVING HIS FINGERS AT IT, CHARMING IT, AND HE THEN STOOD THERE LAUGHING AS THE VINE BEGAN WRAPPING ITSELF AROUND MY LEGS AND ARMS AND BODY, SECURELY, SQUEEZING THEM TIGHT. I WAS POWERLESS TO MOVE AND SLOWLY HE CAME TOWARDS ME, PREPARING TO PLUCK THE MAGIC BUTTON FROM MY COAT, AS FRANTICALLY I TRIED TO RELEASE MY ARMS.

I LOOKED UP INTO THE SKY AND REMEMBERED WHAT THE WIZARD HAD SAID. 'BELIEVE!' I COULD HARDLY BELIEVE WHILE IN THIS SITUATION, COULD I? THE VINE WAS SQUEEZING MY BODY TIGHT, LIKE A GREAT SNAKE CURLING AROUND IT. AND THE LITTLE FAIRY MAN WAS LAUGHING HIS HEAD OFF, THINKING THAT HE HAD WON THE DAY.

'YOU WILL REMAIN SO UNTIL NIGHTFALL,' HE SAID, GOING BACK TO HIS TINY CHAIR TO RESUME HIS DREAMS, 'THEN I WILL TAKE THE MAGIC BUTTON AND CUT OFF YOUR ARMS AND LEGS.'

I remained there struggling in the vine's grasp with this little man tormenting me with his snores until dusk began to fall. I knew I had to do something before he woke. So I looked up at the darkening sky and called out to my friend Owl. Owl would be waking up now to do his hunting and he might just hear my cries. I disguised his name by pretending that I was in pain and calling out, 'Owl! Owl!'

To my surprise Owl soon started circling overhead. As soon as he was within range, I called, 'Pluck the magic button from my coat, Owl! Pluck it and keep it safe in your beak! Take it up to the top of the tower for me. It will give you entrance to the tower and to retrieve what must be retrieved. We mustn't disappoint the wizard. Go now, Owl. Go!'

Owl swooped down and plucked the button, just as the little fairy man was waking. But he managed to fly away with it in time.

'You cannot get the magic button now!' I cried. 'Owl will keep it safe. Believe me, you can cut off

MY ARMS AND LEGS AND DO WHATEVER YOU PLEASE, BUT IT DOESN'T MATTER, BECAUSE IT -'

BEFORE I COULD GO FURTHER OWL HAD SWOOPED DOWN AND FROM OUT OF THE SKY HE DROPPED A LARGE SWORD WHICH, AS IT FELL, SLICED THROUGH THE VINE THAT WAS BINDING MY LIMBS. AND SUDDENLY I KNEW THAT THE MAGIC BUTTON HAD BECOME THE SWORD, BECAUSE I HAD UTTERED THE WORD 'BELIEVE'! I WAS FREE, AND I WATCHED IN AMAZEMENT THEN AS THE LITTLE FAIRY MAN SUDDENLY CHANGED HIMSELF INTO THE GIANT AND THEN WAS AMAZED FURTHER AS THE GIANT CHANGED HIMSELF INTO THE WIZARD, WHO STOOD THERE, SMILING AT ME, HIS EYES MOVING UP TO THE TOP OF THE TOWER.

I KNEW THEN WHAT I HAD TO DO AS THE MAGIC BUTTON FELL FROM OWL'S BEAK INTO MY HANDS. I BLEW ON IT THREE TIMES, SAID THE MAGIC WORD AND THEN I THREW IT, AND BEFORE MY EYES A GOLDEN LADDER APPEARED, STRETCHING UP INTO THE SKY. I CLIMBED IT AND WAS SOON AT THE TOP OF THE TOWER, CLIMBING IN THROUGH THE WINDOW THERE AND SEEING IN FRONT OF ME THE MOST BEAUTIFUL PRINCESS I HAD EVER SEEN, COVERED

COMPLETELY IN GREAT COBWEBS AND
SLEEPING SOUNDLY.

I BENT OVER AND KISSED HER SOFT
CHEEK AND SHE BLINKED AS SHE
OPENED HER EYES.

'I'VE BEEN WAITING FOR YOU,' SHE
SAID, WITH A TEAR ON HER CHEEK.
'I'VE BEEN WAITING SO LONG, JACK,
FOR YOU TO BELIEVE.'

# 8

---

# THE HIDDEN AND THE
# MYSTERIOUS WORLDS WITHIN

S omeone, some years ago, said to me,
'Whereabouts is the Otherworld located?'

I had to think about this for some time. I had never been asked such a question before, but understood it nevertheless. Since everything about the material world had 'place', and everything 'belonged' somewhere, the Otherworld should surely have a 'place' and 'belong' too?

The only answer I could find to give to this man was, 'Whereabouts do you find your imagination? Whereabouts do you find a dream?' I was repeating something I had heard my Ancestor say, that the imagination and dreams and the Otherworld were all seemingly intangible things, but were really the most enduring and well-established of all, but they did not exactly *reside in a place*. In all Otherworldly matters, 'how' and 'why' were always more important than 'where'. This significant factor has always been at the very heart of all issues concerning the Otherworld - questions about which I knew I would be required to answer on many future occasions.

For the *Chovihano*, perhaps one of the hardest tasks is to describe the Otherworld and yet this is very much a part of his job. In times past, it was the *Chovihano's* task to keep members of the Gypsy tribe not only linked to the Otherworld but also educated in its workings. He could be consulted on all matters in which the Otherworld played an active part and he knew a good many of the answers, being a traveller to its many realms on his many different journeys and initiations.

As already mentioned, the Romani Otherworld is composed of three separate worlds. These are the dramatic and sometimes ecstatic Upperworld, the often more dependable Middleworld and the distinctly formidable Lowerworld, all of which can overlap or blend into one another, much as the colours of a rainbow can overlap and blend and have no distinct dividing lines separating one colour from the next. Each 'world' also has three realms, totalling nine realms in all, and the realms themselves act in an upper, middle and lower capacity in whichever world they happen to be. For instance, in the physical world we are considered to be in the middle realm of the Middleworld's three realms. This would seem to suggest that the physical realm is indeed a place where balance is found, because we are slap bang in the middle of all the worlds. This is almost like being in the middle of a see-saw. This is how the Middleworld was perceived by Romani Gypsies in earlier times.

Within the Otherworld the *devlesko* spirits relate to the sky, or what is above the Earth – which could be considered to be Heaven – while the *bengesko* spirits relate to the Earth and what is below the Earth – which could be considered to be Hell. But these upper and lower regions are not as straightforward as the Heaven and Hell we have been accustomed to in more religious times. These two 'levels' seem so remote to the vast majority of us, they tend to mean more to us in name than anything else. We cannot visit either of them until death occurs, then we will have permission to remove ourselves to just one of them and are usually obliged to remain in that place forever more. This, for the old Gypsies, never allowed enough space for freedom and personal development in an afterlife, or even in the physical life, throughout which journeying to the Otherworld took place.

Some students I have worked with find it extremely difficult to find the Otherworld and also to relate to it; others can find it and relate to it very easily. The shamanic journey will give us methods and techniques for reaching the Otherworld, but the

Otherworld itself provides us with the necessary backdrop against which we can experiment and play.

When first visiting the Otherworld, a student is taken on a relaxing journey, because it is important to lessen or shut down, if possible, those parts of our brains that we tend to use in everyday physical life in favour of using those other 'hidden' parts.

I ask students to visualize a river within a peaceful natural setting and this gives them an opportunity to leave one world and to access another, via the imagination, which they can apply during the guided journey. They visualize a small boat and are asked to step into it and to allow it to carry them down the river, at a slow pace, during which time they are asked to use their senses to make contact with the Otherworld, to look at, listen to, touch, taste and smell all that is going on around them. They can drape a hand in the water if they wish as the boat moves along, drink some of the water if they wish, reach out and touch the reeds on the bank perhaps, listen to any birdsong, sniff the air and generally stretch their minds to accommodate such a scene in a more physical kind of fashion - except this is not the physical body doing all these things. And yet a reality prevails and will begin to colour these journeys as they experiment with such imagery.

I remember an interesting experience with water in the Otherworld when I went on a journey some years ago. I put my hand in a pool in the lower realm of the Middleworld and when I pulled it out again it dried instantly, as if it hadn't become wet at all. This naturally caused me to dip my hand in several times more in order to test out this strange effect, and each time my hand dried as soon as I had removed it from the pool. Successive dippings revealed that it never became wet at all.

Becoming complacent with this idea, I decided to throw my whole body into the pool, only to find that I was suddenly being sucked under by what appeared to be mud. It was like quicksand, pulling me under with some force, until I got up to my hips. The pool then chose to release me.

In realms of the Middleworld points are made very concisely. The Otherworld is not a predictable place; its landscapes can change, just as a human being's moods can change. The Otherworld moves, breathes, lives. It is a 'being'. And it will usually react in a way you won't expect.

This was a valuable lesson that I have never forgotten.

By the time students get out of their boats on their journeys down the river to the Otherworld, they are slowly being absorbed by another realm of the Middleworld. At this point it is not necessary for them to know which realm this is. If we pigeonhole everything and enforce too many rules about where we should be going, we can put up barriers, so it is best to allow everyone to find the place they need be, within the basic guidelines of the journey, as eventually they will make their own adjustments quite naturally. In any case we can encourage alterations when there is sufficient confidence in journeying.

By the time they have reached the new bank, some are itching to explore, feeling quite at home straight-away, while others will wish they were suddenly busy doing something else because of mounting inner fears over the unexpected discovery of some new and strange dark inner forces. Whether you are long-ing to look around or longing to rush back to the physical world, there is every reason to work at things slowly.

You are at that precarious gateway, the rabbit-hole which Alice fell down, the looking-glass she stepped through, the wardrobe that the children went through when they found the lion and the witch. It is that mysterious indescribable doorway to another dimen-sion, which can take many forms.

In the case of the river journey, we are not jumping through anything or passing dramatically from one place to another. At this point in our training we are slowly, comfortably, being eased in to the *idea* of another world, because the Otherworld is extremely subtle and many of us in the physical world are scep-tics, so we need to be taken into the Otherworld in a very well-managed and what I would call a more lucid fashion.

Because it is not easy for any of us to acclimatize to the Otherworld as a *real* place, I find it necessary to strengthen the picture by asking people to build a home in the place they have found, generally giving them time and space to feel safe and secure about doing this. Building such a home is an important step for any student who is learning about the Romani

Otherworld, for as we make many return journeys to the Otherworld, in whatever shape or form we may find it, we need to feel safe and secure, and if we become accustomed to a home of our own being there, the place itself can start to take on more distinct features and we can use these as an anchor in times of stress. We have then established a means of being able to *live* in the Otherworld in a way that we can identify with, which gives the Otherworld a whole new but acceptable meaning.

Until we have learned constructive methods for dealing with the nature of the Otherworld - which is a large part of shamanic training - the Otherworld home must become not only our refuge but our bridge, a kind of half-way house between the two worlds. It is, after all, better to run back to our Otherworld home rather than abandon the Otherworld altogether, purely because we met something we didn't like.

This first 'home' is always built in the Middleworld - although we can eventually build homes in other worlds too - because in the Middleworld our home will be less subject to unsettling changes - rather like choosing to build your own home in the physical world away from war zones and earthquake regions and the hazardous perimeters of volcanoes.

Many of these ideas were inspired by my training with Jack Lee. He often talked of his 'homes' in the Otherworld - he probably had many of them - and I have found the building of the Middleworld home a most useful means of helping people establish a bond not only with the Otherworld, but ultimately with themselves, which leads to more confidence, an increase in trust and a sense of adventure, all of which are needed before true exploration can begin.

Once we have built our Otherworld homes it is then safe to travel further afield. If students feel comfortable and strong enough to cope with Upper and Lowerworld activity and the adventures and challenges which can await them there, they are encouraged to move on. Here is where they learn about their own personal contribution in Otherworld travel, i.e. what is given of the self constitutes a magic key which can open up numerous doors to Otherworld landscapes. Invariably, although we don't know it, it is often we ourselves who end up forming the barrier which prevents a relationship with the Otherworld from developing. What we have in our psychological make-up often constitutes something of a currency for entrance into the Otherworld, and where there is restriction, unless we are prepared to make changes within ourselves we can sometimes find the road to the Otherworld a much longer one than it needs to be.

This is very different from travelling across the landscape here in this world. Any of us can walk along a beautiful country lane idly throwing litter around and committing any number of crimes to the countryside without any reprimand from nature at all. But in the Otherworld, the laws are vastly different. We cannot access those *real* places without a *real* contribution from who we are, like keying in the real password on your computer or using a particular key for a particular door. Where the Otherworld is concerned, only that which is required brings the results. It is as simple as that. There are no compromises, but neither is there any holding back on nature's part if you have given of your best. This will be the best time for both you and the Otherworld to be honest with each other where intentions are concerned. This very fact proves to me that the Otherworld is far more real than we suppose it to be, simply because if we do not make that real contribution, we just do not get the results. Should we try to cheat on it, the real Otherworld will continue to bask in obscurity and will even remain non-existent.

So, when students travel along the river in their boat for the very first time to the Otherworld, they are also travelling along a road in their inner world to meet themselves. If they are enthusiastic, open-minded, honest and courageous enough, they will meet any obstacles which serve to keep them from themselves – and the Otherworld – by calling upon the spirits and fairy-tale figures who will help them make the changes they need to make in order to use that all-important currency.

When they take up residence in their Otherworld home, they begin to find a whole new world of things, both beautiful and ugly, within the new landscape, just as we may find things we like or dislike in our neighbourhood in the physical world, except these things will be more pronounced and will have more of a personal flavour for each individual. There may be beautiful rockpools and sunbeams in the trees in a restful wood, or a dramatic windy seashore, but there might also be enormous potholes, dark recesses or concealed caves which trouble the students. What is happening is that our students are finally meeting those parts of themselves that have been obscured over a long period of time and which have transposed themselves into their Otherworld landscape. Some of the things the students meet will inevitably present challenges for them, as there will be obstacles to overcome, past memories to let go of and parts of themselves to look at which might never have been looked at before.

Examples of a first ever journey and a more experienced journey, undertaken by the same person, are given below.

I GOT INTO THE BOAT AND IT WAS LIKE A CANOE. BUT IT KEPT CHANGING AND WAS SOMETIMES A CORACLE OR A ROWING-BOAT. THE WATER HAD RAPIDS. IT WAS NOT A QUIET STREAM AT ALL AND IT RUSHED AT ME IN PARTS, MAKING MY BOAT MOVE UP AND DOWN QUITE VIOLENTLY AND AT ONE POINT CAUSING IT TO NEARLY SMASH INTO THE ROCKS THAT WERE ON THE BANK.

EVENTUALLY THE WATER CALMED AND I WAS ABLE TO GLIDE ALONG, BUT ON THE WAY THERE WAS A DISTINCT SENSE OF FOREBODING WHICH I DIDN'T LIKE, AS IF SOMETHING WERE ABOUT TO ATTACK ME. THERE SEEMED TO BE A JUNGLE ON EITHER SIDE OF THE

RIVER, WITH ALL MANNER OF DARK AND CREEPY THINGS LURKING THERE. BUT I HELD ON TO THE SIDES OF THE CANOE FOR ALL I WAS WORTH AND ALLOWED IT TO CARRY ME ON. I THINK MY HEART WAS BEATING SO FAST WHEN I EVENTUALLY REACHED THE BANK, I THOUGHT I MIGHT JUST NOT MAKE IT.

I REALLY DIDN'T WANT TO STAY TOO LONG IN THAT PLACE. IT WAS NOT VERY PLEASANT AT ALL MOVING AROUND AND IT IS SOMEHOW DIFFICULT TO DESCRIBE. THERE WAS QUITE A THICK FOG ENCIRCLING EVERYTHING AND WITHIN THE FOG THE FOREBODING I'D FELT EARLIER. SO I PADDLED VERY FAST ON MY WAY BACK, NOT STOPPING TO LOOK BACK. IT HAD BEEN SO HORRIBLE, I WAS REALLY GLAD TO GET BACK AND OUT OF THAT BOAT.

I GOT INTO MY USUAL CANOE. IT WAS PAINTED BEAUTIFUL COLOURS AND I PADDLED FOR A WHILE DOWNSTREAM UNTIL I DECIDED TO LIE BACK AND LET IT CARRY ME, AS IT HAS BEEN DOING RECENTLY. I FELT QUITE SAFE AND SECURE AS USUAL, AND LAY ON MY BACK LOOKING UP AT THE CLEAR blue sky. A smell of blossom was in the air, and was extremely strong, so I knew it must be spring.

I was alert when I reached the bank and leapt out, eager for my adventure to begin, bending down to finger the soil there, which felt so clean and good. I found my Otherworld home, my bender, which is always waiting for me, and stepped inside it. There I found hanging all the lucky charms I'd gathered over the recent months and I sat there for a while, feeling good about myself and good about this homely place. The birds were all busy singing outside and all was right with the world.

Then I went outside and gathered some of the beautiful branches of blossom which I'd smelt earlier to put inside my bender - after asking the tree's permission, of course.

The feeling of spring was very strong within myself and I thought I could have stayed in that bender with all that beautiful blossom forever.

The two journeys are distinctly different, but the first is typical in illustrating how vulnerable we can *all* feel at times when we first turn ourselves over to the Otherworld. Between the two journeys there will have been all kinds of soul-searching within the student, realizations that unless the self is looked at with a view to more understanding, the Otherworld may remain unreachable, even perhaps a treacherous and dark place.

But remember that you can always work your way around your difficulties and obstacles if you approach them by using your wits in the Gypsy fashion, so there is no need to think that anything is a real obstacle at all.

As an example of this I worked with a lady some years ago who wanted to journey with me down the river, but who hated water. Her fear was so enormous that it posed the greatest threat, until she used her wits to challenge the situation and ended up putting a life-jacket on, which meant that she went gliding down the river to the Otherworld in relative safety. Some might say that she shouldn't have needed to worry about the water harming her, as this experience was only contained in her imagination. But this is where we learn that what we call the imagination can be real enough to bring people's fears to the fore - and they are *very* real for the person concerned - but it is possible to work out constructive ways of dealing with them.

The constructive use of wits was also used by the student in the second journey given above, and there is a skill and ease in that journey which wasn't there at all in the first journey. A landscape that held her deepest darkest fears eventually became a landscape she loved to spend her time in, which also means that she originally wasn't very fond of herself, but with a little work learned to love herself. I always tell students that the place which holds your greatest fears can often be the very place where you will find your greatest dreams! And Otherworld travels can usually help to reunite you with those.

So, whenever you do encounter problems, always make a rule to be patient with yourself. I have seen too many students with potential fall by the wayside because they believed that their Otherworld would only ever be a container for their fears, when all it would take would be a little work and some courage on their part to alter things. Determination pays off. Remember also that you are not the only one experiencing difficulties. We have all experienced difficulties at one time or another.

The lady whose journeys were given in the examples above went on to make many fascinating pilgrimages into her Otherworld and she is still exploring it today.

Once students step out of their boats and familiarize themselves with the land in the Otherworld, I have them make as much contact with it as they can, getting to know all the trees, rocks, cliffs, pools, lakes, mountains and rivers there, inside out if necessary! I encourage them to walk about as much as they possibly can, fingering leaves and touching soil, familiarizing themselves with their new neighbourhood in every possible way. They are taken back to their Otherworld home intermittently from wherever they are, so that they do not lose contact with it, and gradually the radius around their home widens and there are soon no dark corners that haven't been looked at or shadows lurking that haven't been questioned. Then, if darkness and shadows should arise, they are not a problem any more and can be dealt with constructively and usually quite swiftly.

It is important to establish this kind of contact and this kind of knowledge about your Otherworld. Then it is safe to visit the upper and lower regions with confidence.

Below is an example of a first visit to the Upperworld and a first visit to the Lowerworld. These accounts are by two different people, but they are fairly typical illustrations of what usually happens to people who visit upper and lower worlds for the very first time after a good Romani-style grounding in a middle realm of the Middleworld.

I CLIMBED THE VINE THAT HAD APPEARED AND WAS CAREFUL TO KEEP MY WITS AND SENSES ABOUT ME AS I WENT. THE VINE SEEMED TO HANG FROM NOWHERE IN THE FOREST AND I WAS INTRIGUED TO SEE WHERE IT ENDED - OR WHERE IT BEGAN! I CLIMBED IN A STEADY RHYTHMICAL MOTION, MOVING MY ARMS AND THEN MY LEGS, FEELING LIKE A CATERPILLAR MOVING SLOWLY ALONG A LEAF. BUT I

HAD MY MAGIC CHARMS WITH ME AND
ALL MY EXPERIENCE FROM MY PREVIOUS
LESSONS IN THE MIDDLEWORLD, SO I
WAS ABLE TO ASCEND WITH CONFIDENCE.

I SOON BEGAN TO FEEL LIGHT-HEADED
AS I ROSE FIRST ABOVE THE TREE-TOPS
AND THEN ABOVE THE CLOUDS.
BECAUSE I'D LEARNED TO USE MY
SENSES SO MUCH, I FELT THE
ACUTENESS OF THE COLD UP ABOVE,
BUT THEN AS I CLIMBED, THE COLD
LESSENED AND A WARMTH SEEMED TO
STEAL OVER ME. I KNEW THEN THAT
I WAS REACHING THE UPPERWORLD.

A SILVERY KIND OF LIGHT WASHED
ACROSS MY EYES, AS IF THE SUN WERE
SHINING BRIGHTLY IN THEM, AND I
WAS SOON STANDING ON FIRM GROUND,
WONDERING VAGUELY HOW I WAS ABLE
TO DO THIS, HAVING CLIMBED SO HIGH
INTO THE SKY. I THEN REACHED OUT
AND TOUCHED SOMETHING SOFT. IT WAS
SOFT LIKE WOOL OR COTTON, AND I
PULLED ON IT AND HEARD A THUNDER-
OUS NOISE FROM ABOVE ME. BUT WHEN
I REALLY FOCUSED ON MY HAND, I
REALIZED I WAS HOLDING A HANDFUL
OF WHAT APPEARED TO BE SOME KIND
OF CLOTHING. THE THUNDEROUS NOISE
RATTLED ABOVE ME AGAIN AND I KNEW
THEN THAT IT WAS THE NOISE OF A
GREAT MAN LAUGHING.

THIS MUST BE A GIANT, I THOUGHT, AND LOOKING AT MY HAND AGAIN, I REALIZED THAT I ACTUALLY HAD A HANDFUL OF THE GIANT'S STOCKING ROUNDABOUT WHERE HIS KNEE-CAP WAS AND I SEEMED TO BE STANDING ON HIS KNEE! HIS FACE WAS ABOVE ME, LOOKING DOWN AT ME AS HE LAUGHED. FORTUNATELY FOR ME, HE WAS A VERY FRIENDLY GIANT AND I WAS ABLE TO ASK HIM ALL ABOUT HIS WORLD.

I WENT DOWN INTO THE HOLE UNDER THE TREE ROOTS. IT WAS DARK AND DISMAL AND I COULDN'T SEE ANYTHING AT ALL. AT FIRST I WAS CRAWLING, BUT THEN I FELL AND ACTUALLY FELT AS IF I WERE FLYING, FULLY EXPECTING TO HIT SOMETHING *EN ROUTE*, BUT THE TUNNEL SEEMED TO BE NEVER-ENDING. I SAW BELOW ME A ROUND POOL OF WATER, WHICH I WAS FAST HEADING TOWARDS. THIS THEN SEEMED TO BE A LARGE WELL I HAD FALLEN DOWN INTO. I HELD ON TO MY MAGIC CHARM, SPOKE SOME OF MY OWN MAGIC WORDS TO MYSELF AND JUST LET MYSELF GO.

SPLOSH! I HIT THE WATER WITH A FORCE AND SANK DOWN AND DOWN

AND DOWN TO THE BOTTOM. I
THOUGHT TO MYSELF, I COULD NEVER
HAVE DONE THIS BEFORE I'D GOT USED
TO THE MIDDLEWORLD. I WOULD
HAVE BEEN VERY AFRAID. BUT NOW
I COULD ALLOW MYSELF TO SINK. I
WASN'T AFRAID OF SINKING OR OF
WHAT I MIGHT FIND.

SOON THEN A DRAGON APPEARED, WHO
LIVED IN THE WATER IN A GREAT CAVE
THERE, AND HE TOOK ME ON A SPECIAL
JOURNEY IN ALL THE UNDERWATER
CAVES, PROUDLY SHOWING ME VARIOUS
PLACES WHICH I DIDN'T ACTUALLY
THINK I LIKED VERY MUCH. HE
SEEMED TO BE VERY PROUD, SO MUCH
SO THAT I THOUGHT HE MUST SURELY
BE MY FRIEND, AS HE SEEMED TO HAVE
MY INTERESTS AT HEART. BUT THEN HE
TRICKED ME AND SHUT ME IN ONE
OF THE CAVES, AND I HAD TO SPEND
THREE WHOLE DAYS AND NIGHTS
THERE, ALONE. AND WHEN THE
DRAGON RETURNED, HE SAID HE WAS
GOING TO EAT ME, SO I TOLD HIM I
NEEDED FATTENING UP BEFORE THAT AS
I WAS REALLY QUITE A SKINNY PERSON.
HE BELIEVED ME AND STARTED
BRINGING ME FOOD, BUT I DIDN'T
REALLY GET ANY FATTER AND I
NEEDED SO MUCH FOOD TO MAKE ME
WORTH EATING THAT HE FOUND IT
ALL DIFFICULT TO CARRY, SO I

VOLUNTEERED TO HELP HIM WHEN HE
NEXT WENT UP TO THE SURFACE AND
THE MIDDLEWORLD.

THAT WAS HOW I TRICKED HIM AND
MADE MY ESCAPE. I TRICKED THE DRAGON
WHO ALMOST SUCCEEDED IN TRICKING ME.
I RUSHED BACK TO MY OTHERWORLD
HOME IN THE MIDDLEWORLD WHERE I
FELT SAFE AGAIN.

The two students are able to enter their worlds with such confidence and enthusiasm because they have had their thorough grounding in the Middleworld - which the second student acknowledges.

The giant in the first journey is strikingly real for the fact that the student finds himself standing on the giant's knee - a most imaginatively vivid experience which somehow serves to strengthen the unique aspects of it. In this journey the giant is friendly; he might well not have been, as the student points out, so it is all the more important to have a good grounding and training in the Middleworld as preparation for the unexpected. The senses are extremely acute in the student's experience of the hot and cold air that he encounters as he ascends the vine. This is, of course, very reminiscent of *Jack and the Beanstalk*. Jack also ascended into Upperworld heights where challenges awaited him with a giant native to that world.

In the second journey, the relaxation experienced by the student whilst falling down the hole comes out of her skill in being able to let go, something she has learned in her Middleworld explorations. Her wits are used to free her from her dragon's prison, and there is a skill and courage in the way she handles the whole experience.

One of the many rewards of these Upper and Lowerworld journeys is that before long the skills a student uses within them unavoidably filter through to many different situations in life, so Otherworld exploration is always a useful tool for strengthening inner reserves and gaining inner confidence.

The landscapes in both Upper and Lower worlds are always vastly different from the landscapes in the more balanced and sedate Middleworld. It is a differ- ence one could equate with the fast and slow lanes of a major highway. In the slow lane - or the Middleworld - you must proceed at a modest pace, whilst in the fast lane - or the Upper and Lower worlds - a different set of rules apply and you must move at a more brisk pace in order to move with the flow. The sedate slow lane may not give you the feeling of speed, but it is neces- sary for each individual to start off there.

The Upper and Lower worlds are so dramatic in their characters, we could look upon them as giant beings. To look upon these worlds as beings rather than places may sound strange, but it is in fact a more fitting description. The Otherworld landscapes may be described as dramatic, powerful, fierce, intense, bold, graceful and exquisite - and these descriptions are apt, for the fact that the emotional content does in fact comprise the landscape itself!

In old Romani lore 'soul' is as much in the landscape as it is in human beings and animals. In the light of this we could say that all the upper, lower and middle worlds might really all be living individuals in their own right, perhaps giant super-beings! Although this is very much a Romani Gypsy understanding of the Otherworld, I believe it can probably answer a great many questions for us.

For instance, if we think about this idea long enough we might well come up with the religious concept of 'God', for if Otherworld realms have a sensitivity and life of their own, they could, collectively, constitute an extremely all-powerful being, a super-giant of some kind whose head was in the Upperworld - or sky - and whose bowels were in the Lowerworld - or earth. This is my own theory, but I have sometimes thought that it could have relevance when looking at the development of the idea of God, and how the ancient Otherworld might have changed as we became more 'civilized' human beings. The Otherworld has certainly been pulled completely out of shape in the developing modern world, compared with the way it used to be.

The Lowerworld could very likely be where we acquired the picture we have of Hell, the place where everything - senses, feelings and experiences - can rage so violently that no one really wants to go there. An apt place to send people who need to be punished perhaps! The Lowerworld has undergone many a transformation. Previously it was perceived by the old Romani Gypsies as a place of great learning and then in more religious times it was outlawed because it was a place to be avoided (unless you were an experienced shaman, in which case you were brave enough to tackle it). Lately, it has been a 'trendy' place where many modern and inexperienced spirit travellers feel they must go as soon as they begin their training in order to become initiated into shamanism.

This way of viewing the Otherworld is not only inaccurate but also extremely disrespectful. You are far better exploring the Middleworld until you know deep in your soul that the Lowerworld isn't the kind of place you go to do your shopping! Not everything in the Otherworld is good and not everything in the Otherworld is pleasant, and far too many people are chasing mere shadows in their attempts to travel to the Lowerworld and causing themselves a great muddle. The Otherworld has a very negative side as well as a very positive side. This is a fact which we need to take on board, especially as it has become a feature of shamanic exploration here in the West to believe that the Otherworld is only ever 'good'. We have sadly forgotten the realities in our modern times - or perhaps we have chosen to ignore them!

I have visited the Lowerworld when I have needed to, as it is the *Chovihano's* task to familiarize himself with all realms in the Otherworld, and the intensity there is really no picnic. It can be unbearably strong, as anyone who has ever really been there will testify. One does not return to such a place without good reason.

Jack Lee told me never to take the Lowerworld lightly, as he said it can be your very worst nightmare and the very seat of your greatest fears. Everything you've ever really feared can lurk in the deepest darkest recesses of the lower realm of the Lowerworld and it is a fight, even for the hardiest of shamans, to come and go from it with ease. Jack Lee told me that everything in the Lowerworld can be so razor sharp - feelings, thoughts, senses, literally everything - that you can be cut to pieces by a single thought. It is a place in which my great-grandfather said you could easily 'burn up' if you stayed for any length of time! Hell indeed!

Probably the closest we can ever come to describing the experience of the Otherworld is to describe the dream state. Time and space have a completely different set of rules when we are sleeping and in a dream we don't question where we are or how we got there - until we are awake.

I once dreamed that I was eating a large slab of cake, which seemed to be a chocolate cake, but it was also a piece of fruit cake and a piece of bread pudding as well! All these flavours were somehow intertwined, and within the dream, eating this quite strange combination was completely normal. Only when I woke did I wonder what kind of cake it was really supposed to be.

The dream and all its symbolism contains the reality whilst we are sleeping, just as the Otherworld and its lessons contains the reality whilst we are journeying. If in a dream we are in our sitting-rooms at home one minute and then in a foreign country the next, we do not, ordinarily, question how we got from one place to the other, but simply seem to accept it. A part of Otherworld travel that is very close to this is shamanic flying.

Much of the time in Otherworld explorations I have people *walk* about in their Middleworlds before they learn how to fly. Learning to have our feet on the ground is good, as it contributes very much to learning how to lift our feet off the ground when we need to! We cannot do one without having learned to do the other first. After all, birds don't.

I have mentioned that I have people make contact with the ground in the initial stages of Otherworld exploration - fingering the soil etcetera - as this initially enhances an understanding of 'grounding' as a fundamental part of shamanic training. So, when people fly about their Otherworld landscapes, particularly at the beginning, I encourage them to make perhaps more contact with the ground than usual, as they may often have a tendency to use flying as a means of escaping the pressures of having to look at themselves, and the object of the whole exercise is to bring the life back into the self, and ultimately the ground, so that the spirit within the self is reunited with the spirit of the ground. Getting people not only to finger the soil, but to roll in it, bury themselves in it if they wish and to spend as much time with it as they can inevitably helps them not to be *afraid* to ground themselves.

Almost as soon as life comes back into the soil, then - or as soon as the individual gives respect back to the

Earth - the person is freed in very many ways, able to identify with him/herself at last, and able to identify with the Otherworld in a way probably never experienced before. Shamanic flying will then be a more enjoyable and balanced exercise, and will be looked upon in a very different way.

For my great-grandfather, the art of shamanic flying was most aptly demonstrated by birds when taking flight. He considered that birds would know how to leave and enter various worlds because they kept their respect for *Bavol*, the Air Spirit, and for *Ravnos*, the Spirit of the Sky. Birds were therefore important and it was advantageous to observe and copy them.

When birds deliver their bodies to the air they are giving their all, for they are sacrificing themselves to the strength of their wings and need to respect the laws of the sky if they want the sky to keep them safe. This is something we human beings never experience in a physical capacity, simply because we are not naturally fitted with wings, so it takes us longer to learn such a thing. But we can nevertheless learn that much of flying is all about respecting other birds' space. For instance, how many times do birds crash into each other? Rarely, if at all. In large flocks they perform the most brilliant and perfect aerial displays, creating the most intricate patterns in the sky. I don't believe that birds fly simply because they have wings; I believe they are able to fly because they hold *Ravnos*, the sky, in great esteem. Their wings developed as a *result* of this respect.

I have flown many times to the Otherworld and around the Otherworld. It can be an exhilarating experience flying low over the landscape, close to the tops of trees and down into the Earth and up again, through numerous realms where both giants and *Biti Foki* dwell. I wasn't able to do this without undergoing a good deal of training with Jack Lee and my Ancestor, and of course, with birds. But my ability to fly only resulted from my abilities to relate to myself and the Otherworld landscape.

The Otherworld has always been so important to the Romani *Chovihano*, it was not uncommon for Gypsy healers in past times to offer much of their souls and bodies in order to learn what it was all about. This is doubtless the meaning behind sacrifice, which I will go into in more detail in the next chapter. But it was normal in many folk tales for the hero to slice flesh from his body to offer to the Earth and her spirits in return for gaining access to the Otherworld. The *Chovihano* may not always have sliced up his own body to give to the Otherworld - although who can tell to what lengths devout Gypsy shamans would have stretched to in past times - but the giving of one's blood as fair exchange for knowledge would have been more usual.

Without doubt, the Romani way of identifying with the Otherworld as a world with a more 'earthy' flavour can prove helpful in times when belief in the imagination has almost disappeared altogether. A Romani story, which I often use to remind myself and others of the way we can so easily diminish Otherworld power, perhaps best explains the relationship between the Romanies and their very *real* Otherworld.

The story is called *The Sevenfold Liar* and, briefly, it is about a traveller who meets a deaf and dumb man on the road and asks him how far it is to the next village. The deaf and dumb man replies, 'Quite a way. Perhaps three to four miles.' The traveller moves on, next meeting a blind man and asking him what the time is. The blind man looks at his watch and says, 'Ten to three.' The traveller moves on again, next meeting a naked man, whom he asks for a smoke. The naked man obliges by producing from his pocket a pouch of tobacco. The traveller moves on again, and next meets a man with no arms wheeling a sack of potatoes along, whilst being chased by a man with no legs who is crying, 'Stop, thief, stop!' The traveller soon arrives at the village where he meets a man who is over 100 years old. The old man is sobbing. 'I was living with my grandfather,' he weeps, 'and he has just thrown me out because he's getting married again and doesn't want me around.' The traveller finally reaches the centre of the village and as he passes the church a coffin moves past, and the lid of the coffin is lifted and a face looks out and recognizes the traveller. 'Would you like a pint of beer?' the body in the coffin asks. The story ends with the storyteller saying, 'That is the truth. No truer words have ever been spoken!'

And so they haven't! The whole story, so typically full of Romani humour, seems to make a mockery of the so-called truth of physical law as we have developed it today. *The Sevenfold Liar* is all about telling the truth - but perhaps the truth according to the Otherworld! In the story daily life as we know it is turned completely upside down - perhaps a message that our truth is linked with the Otherworld, where our wholeness and freedom can always be returned to us.

Again, the magical effects of numbers appear within the story, such as number three, suggesting that by the time the traveller reaches the village, *three* miles will have been covered - or a valuable lesson would have been learned, a lesson in how *not* to believe that the physical world is the only world, perhaps. The presence of the number seven is also significant, seven being the magical number often associated with clever lies or tricks which can aid in bringing luck, as in the *Bari Hukni*, when the Gypsies professed to be wandering Europe as Christian penitents for seven years! As mentioned before, the number seven would be more important than the fact that the story-teller is considered to be a liar, for if he achieves something seven times over, he has truly mastered the art of luck!

Where the Otherworld is concerned, I believe that in modern times we have become so accustomed to the 'imaginary' being 'unreal' that we have lost the ability to tell the difference between the justifiably real and more incomprehensible illusion, and have therefore become so muddled that we have created realms of existence where perhaps such realms didn't exist before. I believe that we are faced with numerous shadow worlds, modelled on upper, middle and lower existences of the past, which we have created and superimposed over the Otherworld in order to suit our current needs.

These shadow worlds, I believe, are often what we refer to as astral worlds, or astral planes, but in reality they are more like 'mental projections'. In the last few hundred years many people have 'lived' in these places, or had an awareness of them, with the result that the shadows have grown exceptionally long there.

In earlier years I became quite involved in these shadow existences myself, when I used my shamanic skills to contact the spirits of the dead on behalf of others who were still in this physical world. There were advantages and disadvantages to these experiments. On the good side I was able to re-educate people on Otherworld matters: how we could live with the landscape, what we could do to further a relationship with the landscape; on the bad side I was taken on an extremely lengthy journey through numerous shadow worlds where I got caught up in their very sticky webs. But the experience nevertheless taught me exactly what the shadow worlds are all about and how to deal with them in a practical way.

A good many people who experience the death of a loved one so desperately wish to communicate with that person that they will do anything to receive vital evidence that the individual still exists. They will turn to those who are called 'mediums' in Spiritualism for such reassurance. When many people got to know that I was capable of providing such a facility, they naturally turned to me and my ancient shamanic skills for the same purpose.

Spiritualism has been closely linked with Romani Gypsy shamanism and I believe that in the past many facets of it have been borrowed from Romani shamanic practice, particularly where communications with the dead are concerned. But there are special rules to take on board when you are reproducing or remodelling such practices and if these rules are not observed, problems can arise.

Certain aspects of my people's culture would have been modified or even excluded to suit more modern social needs, especially when Spiritualism gained popularity during the two world wars, when so many people were dying. The ancient Romani Gypsy belief that a soul must have a clear space and an allotted degree of time in which to journey to the ancestral world was not observed by Spiritualists in earlier parts of this century. Answers were desperately needed and losses compensated for, especially when so few knew little or nothing at all about the afterlife. An afterlife, therefore, needed to be created, an afterlife which could help soothe the pain of the bereaved, but which could also guarantee that those who had died so young and in such tragic circumstances would still contain life on the 'other side'. Many people began not only communicating with the dead on the 'other side' during these difficult times but were also loath to let the dead go.

It is of course possible to prove life after death, but at what cost to the soul? This may be far better off being released. Are we not, after all, once our grieving time has passed, merely holding on to someone for our *own* benefit? That is how my people would see it and that is how the *Chovihano* sees it.

One lady I got to know had lost a daughter through suicide. The girl had been just 20 years old and the mother felt sure that she was not at rest because she had died in such terrible circumstances. I contacted the girl, who was indeed travelling about in the shadow realms, including this physical one, and who badly needed to have her soul rescued. She spoke to her mother many times through me whilst I was in trance and the best I could do for both of them, according to old Romani lore, was to try to exorcize the girl's spirit so that she could travel on into ancestral worlds and live her Otherworld life in peace, away from the physical world, until she could become a true ancestor. This was traditional in my culture. But it was difficult for the mother to accept, because she was uneducated in these matters and was upset by the thought of her daughter shifting into another reality and being lost to her altogether.

I had many conversations with the daughter in the 'astral' shadow worlds and many conversations with the mother in this world, and it was a very long time before we all came to an agreement and conducted a necessary exorcism – or soul-retrieval ceremony – and the daughter could finally move on to 'rest in peace'.

I believe it is wrong to 'call back' the dead, even though I have become involved with promoting that myself on many occasions. I have had contact with many dead persons in the past, and many famous dead persons during a particular phase of my life, particularly after developing the gift of being able to communicate with deceased souls merely by feeding their names into a specific part of my mind. Some of these would respond when they knew I could contact them, visiting me on a regular basis; others would close themselves off completely, because they didn't want me interfering with their souls. I would receive a kind of 'character print-out' from these people: what their inner worlds were like, what their emotional lives were like, what they might be involved with at the time of communication, what they had done in their past and what they were about to do in their future. But this skill turned into a bit of a game, with endless lists of names being given to me to 'feed into the computer' - as we all jokingly referred to this ability at that time. It was all very fascinating, and indeed skilful on my part, but I soon realized that it was endangering souls by keeping them out of the ancestral worlds and locking them into shadow worlds, and that wasn't what life was about, according to the old ways. At the end of the day we were all merely inventing shadow worlds and stepping away from the real Otherworld. It was certainly something my great-grandfather would have disapproved of!

I do still use this ability occasionally in my work today, as it is part of the *Chovihano's* healing craft to be able to communicate telepathically with people in all worlds, but it is strictly controlled. Also, I use the skill now to pull people out of their shadow worlds rather than cast them into them.

Exploring the Otherworld and its many realms can be educational for any of us who wish to initiate healing in the soul. It cannot be recommended too highly. There are, after all, so many vast landscapes of indescribable beauty and unbelievable distances to explore once you have learned the rules. There are great ancient forests to walk through or fly over, where spirits may act as friendly guides or outwit you in their attempts to teach you a lesson, and where in little leafy glades the *Biti Foki* may preside in great majesty over their magnificent fairy kingdoms. We can find great forests stretching for miles behind our eyes, the sound of great rushing waterfalls living between our ears, and great lakes and whole mountain ranges resonating within our hearts. This is because the personal Otherworld map, unlike the physical geographical map, is immeasurable, which makes us all immeasurable on the inside, because every human being has the potential to touch the sky and to wallow in the deepest bowels of the Earth.

Throughout all of this, we are constantly putting the life back into nature, back into earth and sky, so that we understand that we human beings are not the only beings in this universe who are alive! We and the Earth are both alive, at the very same time. And we and the Earth can only ever borrow each other, if we are to return to a more harmonious relationship.

For the old Romani Gypsy nomads, living *with* the Earth, as opposed to living *upon* the Earth, was perhaps most important - becoming familiar with each tree, each branch, each leaf, and hearing the leaves growing in spring and falling from the trees in autumn. We can still do all that today if we try. If we live with and borrow the Earth, in our own personal way, as far as we are able, we are not so distracted by those things that rob us of energy in our modern world and we can focus our attention entirely on the *power* of nature, which is one of the greatest healers.

To access the Otherworld the old Gypsies often travelled 'to the edge of the Earth', as in many of their folk tales. This, for me, suggests that there was a time when the Romanies perceived the world as being 'flat', something which has long caused me to ask what I consider to be an important question: did our ancient cousins believe the Earth was flat because they were simply ignorant or did this belief help them gain access to the Otherworld? This is indeed an interesting question and one we should all perhaps be asking. For when the land was perceived as 'flat', people were probably still doing most of their travelling in the Otherworld, as it still contained their reality on personal and social levels. The vastness, the distances, the depth and breadth, the beauty and the absolute freedom that existed in the dramatic and powerful Otherworld landscapes were still part of everyday life. Today, for me, it is exactly the same.

I predict that we will soon be entering a new era where we will be unafraid to explore the Otherworld, recognizing that we are all wanting to come home to those ancient lands again, after perhaps thousands of years of going astray.

I do not ask people to believe what I say of the Otherworld; I only ask them to question and to explore for themselves, to persist and keep persisting, until they find their own answers. That is how we find the Otherworld, and indeed ourselves, and without doubt, we are all now in greater need of rediscovering our own roots than ever before.

If we can simply find the courage and enthusiasm to search for ourselves, we will almost certainly stumble across the ancient Otherworld, as if by accident. We may just come across an old giant slumbering in a realm of the Upperworld, waiting just for us to appear, or a member of a *Biti Foki* clan sitting on a tree root at the edge of the Lowerworld, appearing to be minding his own business but in fact waiting to test our dedication and resolve in those darker lower realms.

Test us many Otherworld beings will, for the secrets of the Otherworld will never be revealed to us lightly.

And that's as it should be.

## THE GYPSY SHAMAN'S PATH
# THE ARDUOUS ROAD OF THE ROMANI *Chovihano*

Shadows play behind your eyes and small fears leap up from the depths of your being, stabbing unmercifully at your attempts to calm yourself. But still you carry on, in search of that special something, that antidote that will let you know that everything is all right. You reach out for things to cling on to, to steady yourself, but you can find nothing and no one to help you feel secure, and you are scared, so scared of what will

await you on the other side of yourself.
Should you go on? You could of course
turn back. But something in you tells you
that you cannot turn back and you move
on, trembling, with a 'now or never'
attitude. You know that all this means
that you are ready to take that fateful
step beyond your own boundary, where
you have never been before.

~

I don't know of any serious student of the Romani
*drom*, or any other shamanic path, who hasn't experienced what I have attempted to describe here: taking
oneself beyond one's own boundaries.

This can be quite an arduous business. Yet it is what
the Romani *Chovihano's* life is mostly about. He is
obliged, perhaps more than any other in his clan, to
cross any boundaries which may serve to keep him
separated from himself. He knows the kind of
ordeals that can await him and the overall messages
contained within ordeals. It has, after all, always been
his role to set an example to those who come after
him, both his apprentices and the people who live
around him.

Many in our times believe that the shamanic path is
a glamorous one - but then, perhaps people always
did! Today many dream of the enviable position of
the shaman without really knowing exactly what such

a position entails. In the Romani community, the *Chovihano* was certainly envied and revered, and sometimes even feared, but it was also understood that a Gypsy healer's mysterious path was ultimately bound up with gruelling challenges, particularly of a spiritual and emotional nature, which non-shamans were invariably loath to handle.

The psychology of the Gypsy *Chovihano* may be difficult for people to comprehend, unless they have studied tribal culture in depth and are attempting to understand the role shamans are likely to play within their own societies. Some of the ingredients that make up the *Chovihano's* personality could well be considered to be egocentric in our times, but we have to remember that in earlier Gypsy clans that which we may today refer to as 'ego' would have had an entirely different meaning. In my great-grandfather's day and before, it was expected of a *Chovihano* to be at least a little bit 'showy' or extrovert in his personality; after all, he had to demonstrate a good helping of confidence in what he was doing, as so many people were depending upon him. Yet he was also an extremely modest person and rarely talked openly about his healing abilities, preferring simply to perform any healing and then get out of the way.

The *Chovihano* or shaman may often be revered and feared and his powers may be considered to be well beyond the reach of the average person, but he is neither a god nor a deity, neither a prophet nor a guru - although I believe, without doubt, that gods, deities, prophets and gurus have all retained, in some shape or form, elements of what the old shamans and their spiritual and magical worlds were all about: devotion, supernatural power, wisdom, mystery and spiritual distinction. We must always remember that tribal shamans or medicine men and women pre-date prophets and gurus by thousands of years. As mentioned before, even our Christian God, as another more recent 'invention', could be seen to be imbued with Otherworldly powers which were once in the hands of nature's shamans.

*Chovihanos* have been placed high on the social ladder in their own societies because they would usually take full responsibility for, and indeed bear the full brunt of, any magical harm that might ever be directed at the tribe. The *Chovihano* was clever at devising *huknies* and spells, doing absolutely anything to protect his own people. Even in Jack Lee's day a story was told of a *Chovihano* who cast a spell to help his clan become invisible so that they would all avoid being pursued by the law!

But probably one of the greatest difficulties in our times is that we have to look at the *Chovihano* through Western eyes. We busily link shamanism with modern therapies and modern religious and social disciplines, and where we actually use these together with shamanism, we do not question whether this practice may in fact serve to weaken the craft. In the West today, we have a need to cultivate the 'modern' shaman, to update the ancient figure and adapt it to our own times. To my mind this 'modernization' is as controversial an issue as the raising of genetically modified crops! Can we really successfully change, or perfect, what shamans are and have been over thousands of years, with a guarantee that they will *still* retain their original power? And should we even be *attempting* to change, or indeed experiment with, a craft that is as old as the Earth and which we still know so very little about?

We may concede that a shaman can start 'living with the times' by updating or modifying the techniques, perhaps creating new ones befitting the twenty-first century. We may feel that in order to communicate more effectively with people shamans need to update their clothes, their lifestyle and their personalities, and they may also need to earn their 'bread and butter' at the shamanic healing craft. But what of their relationship with the Otherworld? Can this be updated too?

We live in a world now where 'adaptations' and 'reproducing' what has gone before are the norm, from rebuilding houses to restructuring ideas. And we have learned to adapt and readapt at a very fast rate. But we must take care that where shamanism is concerned, we don't move too far away from the original rhythms that once bound Earth and shaman together and which were, for thousands of years, a feature of this ancient figure's existence.

It is also wise to remember that times may change, but our souls do not, for they undergo exactly the same educational process on an inner level as they would have done back in prehistoric times, just as a tree growing today will have grown in much the same fashion long ago.

Can it not in reality only ever be our *problems* that are modern? The natural education of our souls, the workings of the Otherworld and the cycles of the Earth, these all constitute tried and tested methods within nature's law - tried and tested over many thousands of years - and surely anything surplus to that must inevitably be a product of the times in which we live? Perhaps, therefore, some of these 'modernizing' methods are simply superfluous to shamanism?

I am probably more aware of this issue because I come from an indigenous line of *Chovihanos*, or perhaps it is because I remember too well Jack Lee, who made it his business to resist, as far as possible, the many changes threatening the survival of the old *Chovihano* in the *gaujo* world.

Some believe that shamanism should be taken out into the world, while others, particularly tribespeople themselves, believe that shamanism should be left in the hands of the indigenous medicine men and women. I believe that we need to do a bit of both: take the *Chovihano* out into the world, but at the same time ensure that he practises and educates people in the original way, so that anyone who trains with him, be they Gypsy or *gaujo*, will be working solely with natural law and thus practising as the old ones would have practised many hundreds of years ago.

Is there not something magic in this, in knowing we are all practising as the old ones used to do? To my mind there is nothing more exciting. And there is no reason why non-Gypsies with a flair for shamanic development should not experience this as well. The craft, after all, can no longer be left to the pure-blooded Romani Gypsies, because there are so few left. In our times, it is crucial that we preserve the craft of shamanism and the Earth, but it is also crucial that we band together to do this. I feel a great deal for those who would be gifted shamans if only they had a culture of their own to nurture their skills. That is why I like to train those whom my own elders might consider to be *gaujos* - and therefore perhaps unsuitable to train. There are times when I have known the passion of the Romani spirit to live and dance in the blood of a *gaujo* as much as it would dance in the blood of my elders.

For anyone wishing to undergo training as a *Chovihano*, it is certainly wise to contemplate such issues as the modernization of shamanism, for I believe that we have arrived at a point in time where those of us who are practising the craft will need to see exactly what is happening, particularly here in the West, where we are especially vulnerable to 'adaptations', and especially if we are serious about helping the craft survive.

In the future I believe that the mechanics - or the science of the craft - will be just as important as its meaning, and discussing such questions as how exactly a shaman flies, or how exactly a shaman enters the Otherworld, or moves out of his or her body, will constitute important stepping-stones in any conservation plans we might design. But such an approach will also help to give the shaman a new standing in society, for like it or not, we are going to have to take shamanism into the scientific age if we want it to be taken seriously and talking more about the mechanics of the craft will inevitably help.

We must move forward, but we must also now think about moving inward. We have crossed the bridges of religion, science, psychology, sociology and anthropology in recent centuries, and these all served to dissect us and take us closer to ourselves, but now it is time to cross the bridge that leads to more specific inner discovery. This shamanic bridge will take us to new frontiers of self-awareness and the dawning of a different age.

When first undergoing training, many students are attracted to Gypsy shamanism by the more immediate tools of the trade, such as the tambourine, the *ran*, the strings of red wool that may be wound around the limbs for protection, the inside-out clothes, the *diklo* and waistcoat for the man, the earrings and headscarf for the woman, and the various sacred lucky charms the shaman may carry. But that inner tool - or the magic key I spoke of earlier - which commits you to self-discovery, and which undoubtedly makes the *Chovihano's* path an arduous road, is probably the most important tool you can ever carry with you. Each apprentice also needs to remember that where non-shamans will always be able to choose whether or not to discover themselves, the Gypsy shaman has no choice!

I believe all shamanic teachers are obliged to understand the deeper psychological and sociological complexities of self-discovery, the process students will undergo, from start to finish, in their training, so that teachers know where they are taking students, and indeed themselves, when they start out on such a journey.

When I am working with students I am often able to spot those with potential, for they draw strength to make changes in their lives without necessarily drawing attention to themselves. Failure is neither frowned upon nor feared, and is seen not as the end of the world but as a necessary stepping-stone along life's path. Perhaps learning how to fall down and get up again is one of the marks of the true Gypsy *Chovihano*. He will never mind falling down and looking the fool! Of course it hurts and he is as hurt as anybody else. But he also learns to take all problems seriously without holding them sacred.

Here we come back to the real meaning of sacrifice, or the art of letting go, for few of us are prepared to sacrifice the many ideas, thoughts and beliefs we have about ourselves and the rest of the world. The true *Chovihano* learns to understand the need to accept that one is hurt, but also the need to let go of what we don't need.

But one of the biggest shocks on the shamanic path seems to come when a student believes that he or she is eligible to begin shamanic healing work long before he or she is ready. Some who set themselves up as shamans in order to train others may not always have taken enough time to study the craft in any detail and may therefore begin healing or advising others a little too soon in their education.

When I lived in Germany, I began training a group of people, many of whom had excellent psychic potential. Running this group proved to be an interesting exercise in itself, as most of the members were German and Dutch and could not speak English, so the odd evening would arise when we only had one Englishwoman attending who was able to interpret what was going on! When I returned to England I had to leave the group behind. The members decided to carry on alone and although I gave them guidelines on how to journey and work with their ancestors and spirit guardians themselves, one English lady in the group believed she was now ready to take over as their adviser, as she had already been practising shamanic healing, and over several days just after my leaving, she made predictions that during their next meeting the telephone would ring at 8 o'clock and it would be a message for them all from someone very special - me!

Of course this did not happen. The meeting began and the group sat watching the telephone. First 8 o'clock came, then 9 o'clock, and there was no telephone call from that person whose message they were all waiting so eagerly to hear.

Because this young lady felt so foolish about her prediction not coming to pass, she chose never to speak to me again and whenever I saw her in London afterwards, she turned her nose in the air and began visiting many healers for help on the grounds that a

Gypsy had misled her and had introduced her to the 'black' side of his craft and she now had many health problems as a result.

This is one of the first, and often most painful, lessons for would-be seers, healers and *Chovihanos*: confidently voicing a prediction which doesn't come true! When we first go on to the shamanic path we are full of excitement and are often boosted with a new confidence to succeed, and this can make everything seem all too rosy when we are learning about our own visionary and healing abilities. We have a need to produce something astonishing, to impress people, especially our teachers, and to be loved. The pain that results from this very necessary kind of experience is rarely seen as part of the apprenticeship itself and instead becomes a clear sign to the apprentice that the shamanic path is not to be trusted – and the shamanic teacher is, in fact, to be trusted even less. The whole experience can become an embarrassing memory which the apprentice would rather forget.

Needless to add, it is the person who asks questions, who studies the imagination as a science and who uses that tool of self-discovery who achieves success. The ego takes a hard battering at a time like this and that is why it is always important to have a good teacher, one who will not only encourage the learning of the mechanics of shamanism but who will also support the apprentice all the way through the experience. Often, the person who overcomes a hurdle of this kind can become an excellent seer, with a good deal more balance and insight.

A sacrifice of pride is certainly one of the most fundamental lessons for us all in any situation like this. As good Gypsy healers, we must learn how to sacrifice some of our habits, some of our beliefs and some of our expectations. It is useful to think about the true meaning of sacrifice, on its many levels, for you will be bound to come across it in your life at some time or another.

Not everyone, of course, has an experience like mine with the young lady. Apprentices move along their paths in many different ways and our lessons come in many forms. But nowadays it can, unfortunately, be common to accuse a Gypsy of being a bad influence. In earlier days it was very much the reverse; it was considered lucky to meet a Gypsy along the road, but it was even luckier if a *Chovihano* crossed your path, whether you were Gypsy or *gaujo*. You might benefit by spitting three times on your hand to seal the luck as you passed this revered medicine man!

The Gypsies' associations with the 'black arts', as we might understand them today, are still quite new to me. I usually find myself having to confess to pupils that I don't actually have the foggiest idea what 'black magic' is! This is because, for my own people, the elements of 'black' and 'white', in magic, were unknown. Gypsies have, of course, long been labelled as sorcerers and *Chovihanos* have often described themselves as such. To the Romanies there are good and bad sorcerers in the sense that there are experienced and inexperienced practitioners of the craft. But in our modern times this word seems to have been greatly misinterpreted.

Sorcery always played a large part in Romani Gypsy shamanism and the word itself conjures up images of primitive or power-crazed magicians who by wicked means or trickery seek to impose misfortune upon others. We practised the art of sorcery in my family, but never did I associate it with anything evil.

Similarly, the idea of the Gypsy curse can bring mixed reactions - not to mention shivers down the spine - to people today. Some are sceptical and laugh at the curse, believing it has no power whatsoever, while others still fear it quite strongly. In either case, the power of the curse is something they feel they don't understand. But if I describe the act of cursing as a healthy means of saying no, many people see it in a surprising new light.

I have laid curses in my adult life and as a child I watched Jack Lee laying curses. When growing up it was normal for me to think of returning malevolent forces to their original homes - it was normal to say no to them! But I cannot say that anyone of my family ever used the craft simply to impose their own will upon another person or to create negativity simply for the sake of it. A people who live by borrowing all things on Earth are hardly likely to make an exception to this very sacred rule.

The mechanics of the curse are therefore important for the apprentice to understand. When broken down, the curse is actually instrumental in helping to lift us out of the numbing inertia we may have fallen into in our personal lives. Here we are vulnerable and in danger of becoming the victim in somebody else's game, and we cannot always summon the energy to use our wits and senses to help ourselves. So we will need the help of the *Chovihano* to put things right for us.

When a curse is being laid we are being given permission to reject certain things if we wish to and to make our own choices. On a lighter note we might say that today the curse would meet with approval from agony aunts and psychologists alike who are constantly telling us that it can be, after all, appropriate to say no!

Of course, when laying a curse, many are concerned for the aggressor. Does a curse mean that that person will be damned forever more? And if so, isn't this somewhat unkind? Two wrongs might not necessarily make a right. These questions are asked frequently.

First, there is no way that a curse can damn someone forever. The Romani *Chovihano* will need to listen to the story the victim has to tell, with discernment, in order to judge whether he thinks a curse will ultimately help the aggressor to understand the crime he or she has committed. When we are cursing we are not simply talking about 'tit for tat', which is probably how the majority of people view this ancient practice. For the *Chovihano*, the curse is introducing karmic retribution at an extremely high level, which means that it will cause events to turn into a learning/healing process for the aggressor, inviting challenges to enter his or her life which will cause him or her to 'think again'. The master *Chovihano* is something of a spiritual interior designer, if he works at this healing process in the highest way. For at that more detailed level he is designing life experience for those who need to understand what living on Grandmother Earth is all about. And at the end of it all the aggressor is likely to become the victim *only* if the experience has not succeeded in altering his or her path.

So 'cursing' and 'sorcery', both grossly misunderstood aspects of the *Chovihano's* craft, are, in their original forms, exalted practices and something the Romani shamanic traveller will inevitably encounter along the more advanced *drom*. There is no doubt that we are witnessing a significant method of healing being unfairly 'Satanized'.

It is important to learn to tell the difference between a good sorcerer and a bad sorcerer, of course, and if one hasn't learned the basics of Romani sorcery from an accomplished teacher, then it would be my advice to leave well alone, for some who dabble in this art can become power-crazed and extremely manipulative.

I have laid curses in more recent times and all of these have had productive results in terms of both victims and aggressors changing and beginning to work their lives out. Restoring this old craft in a big way has certainly contributed to lifting our family curse from my own shoulders. Perhaps I too have been able to change and to begin walking my own *drom* with a greater purpose.

But an important question can arise for many on the Romani shamanic path: when is an unpleasant experience the result of shamanic testing and when is it 'curse material'? For we may feel obliged to endure the first, but repel the second!

In Romani Gypsy tribes this was where the *Chovihano* was of service, for he would use his divining skills to explain to the individual whether he or she was being tested by good spirits or was in fact being led up the garden path!

This is another reason why the *Chovihano* must be very skilled at his craft and must understand the mechanics of it. There are many responsibilities and he is obliged to develop great insight, so that he sees things as accurately as possible. So he will need to be tested more than the average person, usually by a great many spirits. Some will deliberately mislead him to see whether they can catch him out, while others will be more direct with their lessons. But all of the nature spirits have the *Chovihano's* interests at heart. Only if he strays from his path or starts to expect too much too soon will he be tested in perhaps a more firm fashion, because then it will be justified.

The Water Spirit, *Pani*, and the Air Spirit, *Bavol*, are two very strong spirits in Romani lore and they can be both supportive and devious with those they choose to put on trial. The Fire and Earth Spirits also test us, but these are more often than not direct with their lessons and are therefore somewhat easier to work with. All Gypsies in earlier times went in fear of *Pani* and *Bavol*, and often gave offerings to them to appease them.

*Bavol* reigns over matters of communication and how we choose to fight the personal battles we have, whilst *Pani* reigns over our emotions and how we choose to express ourselves. These two great spirits govern major events in our lives today where battles are likely to occur and where our feelings are likely to be stirred or hurt. My own relationship with these two spirits has been a challenge indeed, but as a *Chovihano* I have worked very hard on developing a rapport with them and they have graciously shown me many of their ways - which are often very devious indeed, but nevertheless teach us never to repeat the same mistakes twice!

When I first left home and began practising my shamanic work out in the world, my biggest tests came courtesy of *Pani* and *Bavol*, who made sure I started walking a path where I was deprived of friends and money. These tests have recurred at various intervals throughout my life, bringing me to the edge of poverty on more than one occasion, and starving me of the affection of family and close friends. I experienced homelessness and also the death of a close friend of mine, at a time when there was very little support from my family. These were very difficult experiences to live through and tested my limits to the extreme.

In my earlier days there were many occasions when I slept rough and wondered what would become of me. I remember lying on Brighton beach on a summer evening, watching the stars and feeling very alone, wondering why I didn't just walk into the sea and get it all over with. I saw no purpose in being taught the ways of the *Chovihano*, because I saw no use for it in the world. My culture and traditions were, after all, completely out of time with the modern world. It sometimes felt as if I had stepped from AD 1000 into the late twentieth century, in one giant leap! But although it was hard making social adjustments, because of being separated from *gaujo* society as a child, my earlier training had also equipped me to become a survivor in a *gaujo* world, and the more time passed, the more I was able to realize that I was in fact surviving amazingly well, which I think, in retrospect, is because I had not learned to take *gaujo* rules to heart. I didn't *believe* in the world that was going on around me day and night. It seemed somehow fictitious – or perhaps I was fictitious! Deep down, I was still with my people, still living in a place which nobody really talked about in *gaujo* society, a world that didn't seem to exist for anyone else, somehow wedged between this physical world and the Otherworld. Wherever or whatever it was, it certainly kept me alive during that very difficult period in my life.

*Bavol* and *Pani*, I knew, were behind these lonely times, testing me and reassuring me, sometimes over and over again to the point where I thought I could take no more. I suffered a breakdown and with no one to look after me I had to pull myself out of my desperate situation alone.

I remember lying on a park bench, shaking, calling out to my long-dead *boro dad* to help me. Tears were rolling down my face and I felt that this was the end. There was no more I could do to put things right in my life and there was certainly no more that I could take. I thought at the time that I would just lie on that park bench and keep lying there until I died. Who would care anyway? They would just pick up this useless body and carry it away, and there would be an end of it all.

I lay there curled up in a tight ball on the bench for what seemed like an age. I was cold and tired, but managed to slip off into a strange sleep, in which I was walking through the nearby wood, crying, 'Help me! Please help me!' But as soon as these words had been spoken, everything around me seemed to change.

As I stood in the wood a wind blew across my face, tousling my hair and stirring the tree-tops above, a strange, briefly forceful wind that seemed to come out of nowhere. I knew it was *Bavol*, the Air Spirit, and therefore also the Spirit of the Wind, and that he had a message for me. I stood still and soon an eerie stillness had come over the wood. Then a man appeared, walking towards me. Although I wasn't within range to hear what he was saying, I could hear the words that he was speaking, as he said, with an equal amount of affection and impatience, 'We thought you'd never bloody say those words! We've been waiting for you to ask for our help for so long. Why did you believe that you could get better all by yourself? Don't you realize that it is sometimes as noble to ask for help as it is to help others?'

*Bavol* was speaking all the time as he walked towards me, coming closer and closer, until I was able to see him more clearly. It was then that I realized it was, in fact, Jack Lee coming towards me. *Bavol* had spoken through him. I had called for my great-grandfather and he had come, bringing the Wind Spirit with him. As he came closer I saw that he was carrying daffodils. 'When the daffodils come,' he said, simply, 'you will be better.'

As he reached me, I threw my arms about him and we hugged for a brief moment. Then he put the daffodils in my hand, squeezed my hand with his affectionately and turned and walked away. As he neared the edge of the wood, the wind blew up keen again, blowing more strongly this time so that it seemed to sting my face. That was when I woke up, still lying on the bench, with the wind and rain hitting my face.

I had that dream, or vision, in October and I carried those daffodils with me throughout that following winter, never letting them go, never failing to ask for help again and never leaving the greater Spirits of Air, Water, Fire and Earth out of my prayers. By April, I was indeed making a full recovery and beginning to work at my shamanic craft more purposefully again.

It is true that many of us do not ask for help when we need it and instead feel obliged to show a brave face, but what is important to remember is that there is always a way out of every dark corner, no matter what your problem is. I found my own way out that day in that wood. I was tested by *Bavol* and rewarded by *Bavol*. He helped me find a new way to borrow his spirit and communicate in a more effective way.

*Bavol* has often made an appearance in my life in order to bring me a message and now he sometimes communicates through me, too, just as he did through Jack Lee. He can 'waft' into your life with the greatest of ease with his tests and challenges. And *Pani* will 'seep' into your life in much the same way. Many who start out on the Romani shamanic path will be tested by *Bavol* and *Pani* a number of times and my advice is to befriend these two very strong spirits from the beginning. Talk to them, give them offerings and they will always become your allies rather than your invisible enemies. When I look back I can see that I had to go through these difficult times with *Bavol* because he knew that the Romani Gypsy spirit, being untainted and undiluted, needed to feel that she was in safe hands if she was entrusted to me. I fell down, but I also got up again, and *Bavol* needed to see that I could do both those things.

Perhaps if I were to sum up what it is to be on the Romani Gypsy shamanic path, I would describe it as learning to understand and talk openly with each small part of the jigsaw puzzle of life in all its variations.

The Romani shaman is witty, astute, childlike and indeed passionate and romantic. It may be strange to some to associate romance with a shamanic path, but that is also very much a part of the old Romani Gypsy way. When saving the damsel from the castle in the forest, the prince must be a romantic to be able to rescue her! But this also links us with another important feature of Romani shamanism as we find ourselves criss-crossing the boundaries of gender within ourselves.

Traditionally, the *Chovihano* can swap gender, or 'shapeshift' into what is considered to be his 'other half'. This 'gender-swapping' has never by any means been common, but shapeshifting in general has been, having been widely practised by *Chovihanos* for many hundreds of years.

Swapping gender roles can be beneficial for the *Chovihano* in certain instances - as it would also be for the *Chovihani*. Jack Lee believed he could more easily identify with 'feminine' spirits if he communicated with them using the feminine half of himself. So if I want to shapeshift into a doe, for instance, it helps if I first shapeshift into my 'other half', the woman in me, because she will more easily identify with a doe.

It may sound like quite a long-winded process, but it works, because all the spirits are being respected and are thus keen to oblige. That is why when I was young my own hormone imbalance was seen as something quite normal for one in my position, because it would aid me in future gender-swapping in my work. I have found it necessary for people who want to complete shamanic training to have a thorough understanding of their own 'other half', which lies concealed within.

Jack Lee often said that *Kam*, the sun, and *Shon*, the moon, being male and female in Romani lore, could shapeshift into male and female humans, and could easily find their way into our spirits and into our blood. That was why we were so affected by the sun and the moon. Because these two great spirits were also the Gypsies' father and mother, they could affect Romani Gypsies quite easily.

We are all made of Air and Fire, considered to be masculine, and Earth and Water, considered to be feminine - at least according to Jack Lee. So we carried the likeness of all these masculine and feminine spirits within us every day of our lives. Some of my elders believed that it would be impossible and quite ridiculous to suppose that we were influenced by the one gender alone in our lives.

When I first saw a picture of one of the androgynous Hindu deities, Ardhanari, I could identify with this being instantly. He/she has four arms; Siva and his wife also hold the four suit signs of the playing cards, or tarot cards, in his/her four hands, representing for me the fact that the human being is composed not only of the two genders but also of the four elements, as Jack Lee had always suggested. So there was much in this picture that was very much in keeping with our own beliefs.

I have sometimes toyed with visualizing this ancient deity being in the mind of an ancestor in early India, travelling within the memory down through generations of Romani Gypsies as they crossed the enormous deserts of Asia and the developing lands of Europe, to finally rest in me, here today in modern Britain!

The Romani Gypsy spirit has a tremendous capacity for deep reflective emotion, particularly the Lee clan, courtesy of *Pani*. Jack Lee had seemingly infinite depths. Sitting with him was like sitting beside a great well whose bottom you could sense but never see. And you were always wanting to be down there playing within those depths, because for a child it was the most comforting thing. He was, like all true Romani *Chovihanos*, able to give all things around him spirit and life, and this inevitably made you feel special, because you knew that you too had spirit and life, and you fancied also that you had those same far-reaching depths within you.

I believe that the development of emotional depth is as necessary as learning about the mechanics of shamanism when learning the craft of the Romani healer, for we cannot hope to help others if we don't understand this very delicate balance.

Probably the deeper emotions, the passion, romance, the active imagination and the awareness of the mechanics of the shamanic craft sounds a complex mix, but I believe that these things are naturally, and uniquely, present in varying degrees in all of us who are of European extraction. We are intrinsically bound together with this mix and by this mix. I have seen it in so many of those whom I have worked with.

I also believe that the roots of this mix lie in the deeper past, with those earlier Indo-European people I often talk about. To my way of thinking, we must all still carry their blood and their spirit, because we have all been born from their bones and we certainly still carry traces of their old language. The name of Ana, the beautiful Romani fairy-tale princess of the mountains, is a Sanskrit word that can be linked with Dana, the Celtic goddess, for instance. We carry the ghosts of these invisible ancient people in many ways.

If we feel lost and that we do not quite 'belong', we might do well to look across our shoulders now and again at those now shadowy figures of our deeper past in order to remind ourselves that they are still as much our ancestors today as they ever were. This won't change.

I believe that the wild romantic passion of the Romani Gypsy spirit, heart and mind comes closest to our original ancestral roots and the reason I believe this is because the Gypsies managed to preserve so much of a uniquely ancient spirit, which seems to contain many of the qualities, customs, beliefs and traditions that are found in both India and Europe. I am fortunate to have the blood of three separate Romani families intermingling in my veins and so there is much of the old Gypsy spirit that was bound to be preserved.

But on a deeper level, preservation is perhaps more about what the Romani Gypsies are than about what they do, and that makes them a remarkable feature of the human race. At the end of the day, traditions can only truly run skin deep and can only become, collectively, a vehicle for the spirits, an accompaniment to the way we choose to move along our paths. They are mere pointers.

Perhaps it is more important that an ancient 'character' has been preserved in the Romani Gypsy. We may just be glimpsing a characteristic of the deeper past, as it might once have been, when we look at a Gypsy. I certainly feel this is true today when I look back on the memories I have of my great-grandfather, who at times had nothing short of what we might term a 'primitive' mind.

But what of the *Chovihano* and his path? Where is he going? What is his future? I have already talked a little of that already, but I believe also that the *Chovihano* will only truly survive where ancestors are surviving with him. Jack Lee talked a good deal about ancestors and was always deeply respectful of them, for many of them had died along the treacherous *drom* over the centuries on their way from India to Britain. He also talked of our greater ancestral family, *Kam* and *Shon*, the mother and father of the Romani Gypsy race, encouraging me whenever I looked along my own *drom* to see all our ancestors still contained at the 'edge of the Earth', in the places which we called 'the points of mystery'. This was where all ancestors were found, he said.

There is a dip in the hills near my present home where, on a clear day, a single farther hill is visible. And I call this place 'the point of mystery', because it reminds me of what I learned from Jack Lee: that wherever there is mystery, there will be the ancestors, the people you know but yet will never know, the people who guide you and watch over you, even though you will never discover who they are. So although we are attempting to look at the mechanics of shamanism and to see the imagination as a science, we must also allow room for the element of mystery as a pointer, a beckoner, something which spurs us on to each new horizon.

I believe the path ahead of us, as well as the path behind us, contains many points of mystery. We can never quite see what is ahead nor what is behind. But perhaps we are not always meant to. The dawning of science made us believe that it was right to explain the unexplainable, but perhaps we once believed that whatever lay beyond each hill should remain just out of reach, and perhaps there is an element of science within that. We certainly pay the biggest price for arrogantly believing that it is possible to know absolutely everything. We have paid with the loss of our ancestors and our old shamanic ways and, in many cases, our very souls.

I see Jack Lee standing, walking, talking, sitting beside his flame during a ritual, laughing, crying, drinking beer, cracking jokes, swinging me up over his shoulder as a young child and presenting me with a bunch of bright yellow daffodils - and hope - as a young disillusioned adult. It is all so very simple.

But I also see him spurring me on to ask questions, to take up all my challenges and to always look that arduous road in the eye. He is perhaps doing all these things at the edge of the Earth, within the point of mystery, but he is still breaking boundaries - and still teaching me to break them today.

# 10

## MEETINGS WITH ANCESTORS
# REVIVING THE ROMANI GYPSY ANCESTRAL WORLD

Ancestors have always been extremely important for the Romani Gypsy. There are ancestors in the trees, ancestors in the stars, ancestors in birds and in stones, and even ancestors in the fairy-tale figures who journey with you and who reside in the Otherworld; and there are also, of course, human ancestors. As important to the Romani as food and air, an ancestor has the power to transcend all worlds.

Earth and sky, *Puv* and *Ravnos*, are the oldest ancestors of all. These are considered to be our grandparents and to have lived long before humans existed. *Kam* and *Shon*, as mother and father of the Romani Gypsy race, are also very old, and human ancestors - some of them thousands of years old - all dwell in the ancestral realms.

Today, we do not honour ancestors. We take flowers to the graveside and keep photographs of those we have loved in our time, but those generations who are farther back in the past and who have never been personally known to us are very rarely thought about. We sometimes act as though we had no ancestors at all. It is perhaps understandable that our mixed roots here in the West are a source of confusion to us, but our roots also run deep. And if it were not for those who came before us, we would simply not exist today! Our ancestors were real people, just as we are real people, and even though we don't know who they were, they are all still our mothers and fathers.

Reviving the Romani Gypsy ancestral world has become one my greatest challenges, because I see the loneliness that exists in people through not having ancestors in their lives. It was such a normal part of Gypsy life to honour ancestors, as it was normal for all of us in earlier times, I do not believe we will be fully healed until we properly reunite with our ancestors again.

According to Romani lore, knowing or remembering the names of ancestors who are in the deeper past, what they did and where they lived whilst on Earth is not really necessary. Labelling ancestors may focus too much attention on the departed soul and it is important that the soul is given every opportunity to move on to live a new life in a free way.

But just by thinking about our ancestors we are reconnecting with the souls of our people, and we are, in the inner life, linking up with all the human families we ever had. We are also, unconsciously, putting ourselves in touch with *Puv*, the Spirit of the Earth, who is considered to be a member of the greater ancestral Gypsy family; the Romanies believed that Puv was grandmother to all human beings everywhere. It is perhaps not so difficult to imagine this as we are all built of a similar substance when we are taken apart and analysed scientifically.

My Ancestor, *Puro* or 'Ancient One', usually takes a human form, but occasionally he takes others, trees and animals and birds, appearing to me in dreams and also in daily life. This is all quite normal. A human ancestor will borrow the spirits of other life-forms – or shapeshift into them – in order to send messages to those in the physical realm.

As an example of this 'shapeshifting' technique, I was once going through a bad patch in my life when everything negative was seemingly being directed at me. One night I had a dream in which a large black bird, a little like a crow, came into my house, flew into each room and then flew out again through the bathroom window. Having learned the symbolic meaning of black birds and just how much human ancestors can enter dreams, I was able to put the two things together to provide myself with an interpretation. A black bird or a crow has many meanings in Gypsy lore, particularly concerning trials and tests, and of course negativity, possibly because a crow is black. But at this particular time in my life, *Puro* was instructing me in something important that I was having to learn and I was not always giving him my undivided attention. I knew that he had shapeshifted into the crow and flown around my home in the dream in order to collect up all my negativity - much of which was at the time self-imposed - and carry it all away. After this dream, I could think more clearly and, feeling a good deal better, was able to resume my instruction with *Puro* in his human form again. So we could say that the spirit of the crow provided *Puro* with a more efficient means of ridding me of my dark mood, perhaps in a way he could never do in his human form.

So, how do we know when an ancestor may be shapeshifting into other life-forms to help us?

First, there is no doubt that your ancestors will help you on a much more detailed level if you are aware of them. If you regularly honour them by giving them offerings, you can usually procure their help. You can take offerings out to the woodlands or onto the hills or to a stream, to special natural places which may mean a lot to you, for they are likely to reach your earlier ancestors there, those who prized these places and lived within them much more than we do today. You can also give offerings to ancestors at specific times, such as Hallowe'en, as the veil between this world and the Otherworld traditionally thins at this time. It is a good idea to offer something you enjoy. Food and alcohol are traditional within the Romani culture. When you set down the offerings, see whether a bird or an animal comes to take them. You may then see your ancestors shapeshifting into these specially selected creatures and accepting your gifts!

When we spend more time thinking about ancestors we start to ask many questions, i.e. how do we find our ancestors if we don't know who we're actually looking for? And what are we basing our investigations on when looking for them in this more Otherworldly way? It isn't, after all, like looking up our family members' names in parish records and getting all the factual details! It seems that in order to find our *real* ancestors in the Otherworld, we are obliged to - *imagine* them?

This seems to make no sense at all. Yet reality and fantasy cross paths again! We soon find ourselves standing on a bridge with the world of the imagination on one side and the world of fact on the other, and both are tugging hard. It is a very shaky bridge, but it is one the Romani Gypsies have been able to stand on quite easily for many hundreds of years. Needless to add, we may need to be here more often if we are to begin to understand the imagination and the Romani Gypsy mind.

Something, however, we would do well to remember is that we only find such questions difficult to answer in these times *because* we are living in these times. This may be some consolation!

As already mentioned, before the dawning of the scientific age, in the last few centuries, and when it was not so important to think quite so geographically, the imagination was not considered to be such a confusing issue, but it has now been suppressed for so very long, we have completely forgotten its capabilities; our relationship with our imagination has changed because our relationship with ourselves has changed. We therefore really have no option but to study the imagination - with a view to understanding the Otherworld - with our present understanding of science. And the Romani shamanic way can provide us with a few clever guidelines for tackling this seemingly strange idea.

First, it is advantageous to remember that the Gypsies made facts out of their legends, while today we prefer to make legends out of facts! If we can begin to look at this objectively, with a view to understanding how fact versus fantasy are constantly splitting us down the middle, we might then be able to see what we have all been composed of for an extraordinarily long time: the factual *and* the imaginative.

We are all affected by the creative imagination, no matter how logical we might consider ourselves to be, no matter how imaginative we might consider ourselves to be. The imagination exists, just as a fact exists. We use it unconsciously throughout much of the day. The only difference between fact and the imagination is that we do not have to *prove* that the imagination exists. It is actually something we *can't* prove and yet we can all agree that we can all choose to use it, for good or ill.

So we start with that one 'fact', the imagination exists, and it gives us a foundation upon which to work, even if it seems at the moment to be a rather precarious one. We are looking for our ancestors. Where are they? We might well close our eyes and start to imagine a picture of a man or a woman, attired in clothes of a previous era, someone who answers the description of an ancestor. And then we might immediately think that we created that picture, that isn't really real and, feeling we are getting carried away somewhat, we instantly erase or dismiss it with our minds. At this point we are likely to blame our own imagination for creating someone whom we think is in all probability fictitious. But at the same time have we ever stopped to think that we use the same imaginative technique for erasing or dismissing a picture in our minds? And never do we say that the erasing or dismissing process is unreal! This proves that in our times we will often only use that part of our imagination which we feel it is legitimate to use: the mental erasure!

We need now to be thinking of the health of our imagination. It is such a strong part of us that where it lies dormant we are in danger of losing much of our self-confidence and our self-belief. And that is most uncomfortable to live with.

Experimentation is the key, something else the Romani Gypsies were good at doing on an imaginative level. It is best to set aside some time during the day when we can allow our imaginations to flow free, perhaps just five or ten minutes at first. If we can create someone befitting an ancestor, we might like to try giving that 'figure' permission to exist in our minds on and off just for those few minutes during that special time of the day. Create the figure and just set him or her aside for a while, without making a judgement as to whether he or she may be legitimate or not. By doing this you will allow the figure time to mature and grow and develop of its own accord, without your control, and just watch and see what happens.

This is the first stage of the Otherworldly process of finding an ancestor and it is all about transferring your energy over to your imagination for a while. Your 'inner tool' will assist you: asking yourself questions, being objective about yourself, opening yourself up to new challenges regarding your own opinions and beliefs - without necessarily chastising yourself - and experimenting with all those things which make up the fabric of your inner world with a view to making necessary changes if you need to make them.

If you can manage to start doing this, then the next stage of the process will begin and an Otherworldly figure will soon be stepping into the shoes of the one you have imagined, with his or her own unique individuality. Then will you see an ancestor with his or her own character beginning to live and you will have earned access to the ancestral realms.

All of this will take time and perseverance. It is not an easy process and no one should start looking for their ancestors with a complacent attitude, as it takes a lot of continuous hard work and only works if the inner tool is used properly, with the greatest respect. But yet another of the golden rules is to remember to keep a sense of adventure and even a sense of humour about it all - give yourself permission to play and to recognize what is being communicated to you. Then, over a period of time, you will be using the right kind of management skills for perfecting this ancient craft.

Generally, we need to begin questioning ourselves rather more frankly where the imagination is concerned and we certainly need to start opening our minds to the possibility of seeing the imagination as a field in its own right, worthy of considerable exploration. The imagination must no longer be thought of as ineffectual, artificial or unreal. All of the greatest scientific inventions we have in our world today began with the imagination, as did all the greatest works of art and everything we use. Even the chair you are sitting in began in someone's mind before it was brought to the drawing-board!

We need radical changes for any revolution to take place and for some there is no doubt that the imagination will prove to be a very scary, unpredictable world at first. But we must always remember that it hasn't been used properly for such an extraordinarily long time that it will have to be oiled again, its creative process trusted and its existence seen as something sacred, rather than something that is just a nuisance. Without doubt, consideration of the imagination as a healing tool must feature somehow on the next rung of the ladder of human development.

For me, without question, *Puro*, my Ancestor, is always my guardian, my mentor, my brother, my father and my friend, and he is *real*. He is a normal healthy human spirit, with his own thoughts, feelings, insights and his own personal ways. When I was very young, he was almost a part of the furniture to me. Then, when I first began journeying with him, it was put over to me that he was a member of the family in more ways than one. I was given various warnings that learning from him would be tough sometimes, because he was such a thorough teacher.

'Take care,' the *Puri Dai* said. 'The Ancestor not only rose to position of Master *Chovihano* whilst on Earth, but he has also now had time to learn the devious ways of all the spirits in the upper and lower worlds.' She was very serious when she spoke these words.

Jack Lee was more blunt. 'Watch that old bastard,' he said, 'for he'll trick you as soon as shake your hand.'

This was typical Gypsy elder advice. Ancestors are revered, but their ways are not always tolerated, or even understood! I myself have often said that it is probably best to treat ancestors as you would treat wild animals! This must obviously be explained.

I have sometimes thought that we would understand our ancestors, and indeed the workings of the Otherworld, a good deal more if we all still had something of the wild left in us. Once there was a time when we copied animals, learning what their body language meant for hunting and ritual purposes: we knew what a toss of the head meant, a licking of the lips, a stamp of the foot. All this was very simple to us and all carried a powerful meaning. Now it is the reverse. I stood in a shopping precinct not so long ago and saw a mural there, intended for children, depicting various wild animals - rabbits, badgers, squirrels and hedgehogs - all having a picnic on a beach. The cloth was laid before them and food was spewing forth from a hamper, and they were all dressed in human clothes, some up on their hind legs, walking as humans walk, and others using their front legs as arms, as humans do.

Understanding and communicating with our ancestors is very similar to approaching wild animals. They will come so far to meet us, but we are obliged to learn how to meet them half-way, on their terms, and to communicate with them as human beings used to do. This will all take time for us to learn, but if we work at it steadfastly and with a view to seeing the process as a constructive exercise, we will achieve success.

Personally, I conduct much of my healing work regarding ancestors in a place I call my 'healing wood', which is in the Otherworld. I usually get there via a wood near my home. This is part of a most beautiful ancient forest, extremely magical, teeming with spirits, quite perfect for ancestral journeying and shamanic healing. Here I will walk or sit while I talk to the spirits of the trees and the *Biti Foki* and I will spend some time thinking of all those who lived on Earth before me.

I find *Puro* very easily in this place and if I ever take offerings to him I always place them here, as the connection with the Otherworld is strong. I sit somewhere comfortable, where there is not too much activity from other human beings, picture the woodland around me in my mind and take it into my soul. There, the seed of the picture will germinate and a picture of the woodland in the Otherworld will soon start to form. Then I can work more purposefully on transporting myself there, perhaps journeying along my river so that I feel I am travelling there, perhaps riding a white horse, or running to the edge of the Earth and jumping into the picture, or sometimes even simply walking into the Otherworld wood. Then I simply sit and watch the activity that takes place, until it is time to return, usually by the same process.

The Ancestor will usually appear, perhaps as a young man, perhaps as an old man, and he will sometimes link me with the spirits of those on Earth who are receiving healing from me. I see the spirits of these people in various ways, doing various things in the woodland of the Otherworld, perhaps standing or sitting or laughing or crying, dancing or even restlessly pacing about. At times I am able to talk to their spirits far more easily than I could in the everyday world, for spirits are honest, rather like animals and babies; the natural instincts are still strong when we are properly linking with the Otherworld. Perhaps this means that our problem isn't that we are unable to find the Otherworld so much as simply always being separated from it!

*Puro* is often very mischievous when he comes to me as a young man in the Otherworld. His swarthy skin and dark eyes contrast strikingly with his white teeth whenever he grins. He is probably about 35 years old as the younger man and perhaps about 70 years old as the older man. But when he is the 'young handsome one' - as he often jokingly refers to himself - as opposed to the 'old delicate one', he dresses himself very finely, wearing breeches and a loose-fitting green tail-coat which make him look as if he has just stepped out of the eighteenth century. But he also wears a top hat and boots, both of which seem to belong to another, somewhat later era. The hat is usually decorated with ribbons, streamers, feathers and gold and silver coins, all of which bear significance, and his dark hair curls down from beneath his hat to his collar. All his clothes sit casually, almost clumsily on his slender body. If I ever had to sum up his appearance, I would probably say he looked something like an old-fashioned over-dressed Morris dancer! As an older man he is usually wrapped in a coloured blanket, which was how many of the old Gypsies used to dress. He is heavily bearded and often bare-footed, and has the darkest eyes which will look deep into you.

Why do I see him in these particular guises? This has to do with what I am learning about at the time, whether I would benefit from an older or a younger teacher and the fact that by using these guises the Ancestor is able to express himself more effectively.

'*Sarshin*,' I will usually say, in the traditional Romani Gypsy manner, whenever I greet him, and he will usually wish me *kushto bok* in return.

I have not always met the Ancestor in the Otherworld. Quite a lot of the time he comes to me in my own physical world and will often speak through me in the trance state. True to his character, these times are not solemn, but always enlightening and full of fun. In the past, when the Ancestor spoke through Jack Lee, true to the Gypsy way, the conversations were conducted in a very casual manner, with Jack Lee lying on the floor or sitting cross-legged in the way Gypsy males do when gathered together socially around the camp-fire, and my grandmother sitting on the floor also, hardly looking up from her crochet work. Often, singing or tambourining, or some other rhythmical activity which serves to lighten the atmosphere and make everyone happy would take place prior to a trance session. Then the Ancestor, via Jack Lee in the trance state, and my grandmother would often engage in 'Otherworld gossip', talking of spirits and shadows quite as one might speak of annoying neighbours! A typical conversation might go something like this:

ANCESTOR: There are a lot of shadows around today.
PURI DAI: *(laughing)* Well, we don't bloody want them, do we? Take them back to your own world! *(After a pause)* Here, they're not mine, are they? I had to sweet-talk a horrible man today. He gave me a headache, he did. I bet they're his shadows really and they're all stuck to me, aren't they?
ANCESTOR: No, they're not yours or his.
PURI DAI: Whose are they, then? And what can I do to help get rid of them?

Ancestor: *(laughing)* You could give me some beer! *[This is a reference to beer given in the wood-lands as an offering to ancestors.]*

PURI DAI: Haven't we given you enough bloody beer?

*(The Ancestor grimaces at the shadows. He and Jack Lee then invite the shadow to speak and a husky, feminine, somewhat seductive voice comes through JL.)*

Shadow: I'm looking for a voice. I badly need a voice.

PURI DAI: *(putting down her crochet work and giving the Ancestor her full attention)* I know who you are. You're the shadow who's been trying to take Marie's voice away, aren't you? She's losing it because she's got a cold coming on and it's you who's stealing it, isn't it?

Shadow: *(still seductively)* No, it isn't me.

PURI DAI: *(firmly)* Yes, it is.

Shadow: *(even more seductive)* No, it's not.

*(The Ancestor and JL, together, wrestle for a short while with this shadow and eventually send it back into the Otherworld.)*

PURI DAI: Is it gone now? You take your own shadows back to your own world. We don't want them here. Has it gone?

Ancestor: Yes, she's gone.

PURI DAI: *(relieved, returning to her crochet work)* Good. You can relax now, then.

The Ancestor: *(humorously)* Yes, but some more beer would be nice!

The above conversation is loosely based on a trance conversation which actually took place between the

Ancestor and my grandmother. There is never any strain or formality between those who are talking together during a trance session - in either world - and because of this, stimulating discussions can often develop, enabling members of the group to learn in a very simple way.

Many spirits can communicate through the *Chovihano* during trance sessions, in my own case as many as 19 in one evening, but the *Chovihano* who is skilled at his craft always maintains control. These spirits will be a selection of nature spirits, *Biti Foki*, shadows, human spirits, animal spirits, ancestors and all manner of life around us. A skilled *Chovihano* is invariably revitalized at the end of such a trance session - even though some may think he may need to lie down!

There have been times when the Ancestor has been with me in this world for hours at a time in the trance state and there have also been times when I have been with him in his world for hours at a time in my journeys.

As the 'old delicate one', the Ancestor is a lot less troubling: that is, because he has mellowed, he is not so full of tricks. He is perhaps more inclined to spend time reflecting. When I was first thinking about writing this book and becoming more open about my culture, I visited the healing wood, largely to think about it all and to decide whether it was the right thing to do, and the old Ancestor was there, sitting in the middle of the wood. He had made a fire and was poking it with a stick. It was as if he knew what I had come for and was waiting for me.

'*Puro*,' I said, walking up to him. When he is in this older guise it always seems more appropriate to address him as 'Ancient One'. In contrast the younger one is not unlike an annoying elder brother!

On this occasion the old man was beckoning me to sit beside him, which I did.

'So many questions, *Prala*, so many questions,' he said, obviously reading my mind and sighing with exasperation on my behalf.

'What should I do, *Puro*?' I asked. 'You've always helped our family and you more than anyone knows what is best. Will talking about the Romani culture and the *Chovihano* help or hinder the Gypsy spirit? And will it help or hinder my world?'

He looked into the fire for a moment, in that wise and reflective way that he has. He often takes a long time to answer questions. Jack Lee had been known to say that you could go fishing between the time you asked *Puro* a question and got your answer! Now I watched the Ancestor. It was dusk and flashes of pale firelight were licking his kind dark face. 'Which world?' he asked, tossing a small piece of wood on to the fire. I frowned. 'You asked me if it would help or hinder your world,' he added, 'and I am asking you which world you are talking about.'

Of course, as a *Chovihano*, I lived in a multitude of worlds and *Puro* had to remind me often about the many realms within all the worlds, and real worlds and their shadow worlds all overlapping each other.

313

He had encouraged me to refer to this physical world
as 'the middle realm of the Middleworld' so that we
both knew which world I was talking about, and it
was helpful to learn to think like this.

'Let us see what is in the flames,' he said now, tossing
onto the fire a handful of herbs, which made the
flames crackle as they gave off the most wonderful
aroma. The old Gypsies would throw sacred herbs
such as mugwort and rosemary onto their fires and
then stare into the flames until the flames had
turned themselves into shapes and people, which
would provide the answers to questions.

On this occasion I concentrated and looked deep into
Yag's spirit and he drew me into his flames and I
danced with him for a while. Then I went up into the
smoke which came from the fire and was able to
look all around me and far into the future. I saw
many fires and many people dancing around the
fires, laughing, enjoying themselves in their dance
with the Romani Gypsy spirit. I knew then that talking about my culture could only benefit people, for
there were those who were waiting to learn from it
and who were naturally identifying with it.

But then I also saw, very distantly, something sticking up out of the soil. I stretched out a hand so that I
could brush the soil away from whatever it was. As
I did this, the ground began rumbling and moving
beneath me, as if some kind of earth tremor were
taking place. Listening to this rumbling was like listening to the grumblings of distant thunder when
a storm is in the air. It was both exhilarating and

disturbing. Then I became aware of a great vortex of energy which was attempting to spiral its way up to the surface.

I soon realized, to my astonishment, that this was a giant lady's face emerging from the Earth. I brushed this great face gently and made her clean, and she rose and sat up, large against me, for I was still contained in the smoke of the fire and wasn't human at all. I curled around her and she coughed whenever I attempted to brush or kiss her cheek, for my smoke blew over her face. She was very big, bigger than any giant I had ever seen. The trees and hills near her were so minute, she might have been a normal-sized woman sitting in a bonsai garden!

'Bari Weshen Dai!' I muttered, and I was suddenly sitting beside the fire, back in my human form again, and the great lady was gone. I knew I would see her again; I had to see her again, for she was our hope for the future and for the future of our Otherworld.

'I believe that is my answer, *Puro*. I only need to think of the *Bari Weshen Dai*, the old forest mother, our important woodland ancestor. She is the Sleeping Beauty who now needs to wake and the Romani Gypsy spirit will help us to bring her back to life again.'

I turned with excitement to look at the Ancestor, but he had gone. Perhaps he was still contained in the flames or perhaps he was somewhere else. I sat beside his fire for a long time, until it became dark, then I returned to my own world - or perhaps I should say 'the middle realm of the Middleworld'. And that particular ancestral journey goes on, for its theme continues in every ancient woodland I ever visit.

Restoration of woodland areas is, I believe, one of the most important conservation tasks we human beings have. This also extends to restoration of the spiritual life of woodland areas and that is why I encourage people I work with to conduct journeys around the rescuing of the *Bari Weshen Dai*. Our old fairy-tale world lies sleeping within these enchanting places and it is, without doubt, the true essence of what the real old Romani Gypsy world is all about.

I now have a special *ran* in my keeping, which was given to me by the ancient woodland near to my home. This *ran* conceals a sword, which was given to me by the woodland on a journey and which symbolizes my fight to restore the *Bari Weshen Dai* and her woodland and fairy-tale spirits. They are all still there in that wood: the *Bari Weshen Dai*, Jack the Hero, the princes and the princesses, the giants at the end of the vines which stretch down from the upper world in the sky, the *Biti Foki* and the dragons, who are down in their holes beneath the Earth. They are all still alive; they are all still waiting to join us in the great journey through life again.

And these are our ancestors, too. They will always be a part of an indescribably beautiful and complex world which existed for thousands of years as an integral part of our European landscape and an important part of our education in life. And I, as a

*Chovihano*, as a guardian of it all, will make it my task to revive and preserve this ancient world, as many Gypsy *Chovihanos* have done before me.

At times like this, I find myself thinking of one of my most important ancestors, my great-grandfather, who taught me so much of what I know. Without his dedication and determination, I know I would not be able to talk about my culture in the way I do today. But somehow, because I am able to, I know that the old curse on our family is lifting now and I want to say to him, 'See, Jack, it has turned out right, hasn't it? Our Romani Gypsy spirit lives on.'

I toast that greater ancestral place where he is now and where I know I will one day also live, the place where all the fairy-tale spirits reside, where the imagination is respected, where there is no prejudice, no ownership, no geography and no time.

# GLOSSARY

—❦—

| | |
|---|---|
| *Ana* | female Spirit of the Mountains |
| *bakterismasko ran* | magic wand |
| *Bari Hukni* | the Great Lie or Trick |
| *Bari Weshen Dai* | the Great Forest Mother |
| *Bavol* | Spirit of the Air, or the Wind |
| *bengesko* | spirits of the Lowerworld |
| *bengesko yak* | evil eye |
| *biti Chovihanos* | insects or small clever animals |
| *Biti Foki* | the fairy people |
| *boro dad* | great-grandfather |
| *boro prala* | big brother |
| | |
| *chavvies* | children |
| *chore* | to steal (or borrow) |
| *Chovihano/i* | Gypsy shaman, healer, sorcerer, witch, wizard |
| | |
| *devlesko* | spirits of the Upperworld |
| *devlesko dikkiben* | sacred vision |
| *diddikai* | one-quarter Gypsy |
| *dik ta shoon* | watch and listen |
| *diklo* | neckerchief |
| *dordi, dordi* | oh dear! |

| | |
|---|---|
| *dosh* | money |
| *Drabengro* | doctor or man of poison |
| *drom* | road, path or way |
| *drukerimaskro* | soothsayer or minister |
| | |
| *gaujo* | non-Gypsy |
| *grai* | horse |
| | |
| *hotchiwitchi* | hedgehog |
| *hufa* | cap or bonnet |
| *huknies* | tricks or lies |
| | |
| *jal* | to go, walk, travel |
| | |
| *kalo rat* | black blood |
| *Kam* | the sun |
| *Kashali* | fairy people or *Biti Foki* |
| *kushto bok* | good luck |
| | |
| *meriben* | life, death, existence, soul |
| *mokado* | magically unclean |
| *mokado poktan* | magically impure smock (worn during menstruation) |
| *mortsi* | skin |
| *mulesko doods* | death lights |
| *mulo* | spirit |
| | |
| *pal of the bor* | brother of the hedge (hedgehog) |
| *Pani* | the Spirit of Water |
| *paramoosh* | dream |
| *paramooshengro* | dream-man or storyteller |
| *Patrinyengri* | female Romani herbalist |
| *pen* | sister |
| *poachy* | pocket |

| | |
|---|---|
| *posh rat* | half-breed |
| *prala* | brother |
| *Puri Dai* | grandmother, lit. 'old mother' |
| *Puro* | the Ancestor, teacher and guardian to PJL |
| *puro moosh* | old man |
| *Purrum* | the Lee tribe |
| *puvengro* | mole or potato |
| *Puvus* or *Puv* | the spirit of the Earth |
| | |
| *rakerimasko bara* | talking stones (ancient standing stones) |
| *ran* | magic wand or shaman's staff |
| *Ravnos* | the Spirit of the Sky |
| *rukengro* | squirrel |
| | |
| *sarshin* | how are you? |
| *sherrengro* | chief |
| *Shon* | the moon |
| | |
| *tacho paramoosh* | true dream |
| *tacho Romano drom* | true Romani road |
| | |
| *urchos* | early name for hedgehog |
| | |
| *vardo* | wagon or caravan |
| *vastengri* | tambourine |
| | |
| *wafdo bok* | bad luck |
| | |
| *Yag* | the Spirit of Fire |